The Poker Face of
WALL STREET

The Poker Face of WALL STREET

Aaron Brown

WILEY

John Wiley & Sons, Inc.

Published by John Wiley & Sons, Inc., Hoboken, New Jersey
Published simultaneously in Canada

For general information on our other products and services or for technical support, please contact our Customer Care Department within the United States at (800) 762-2974, outside the United States at (317) 572-3993 or fax (317) 572-4002.

Wiley also publishes its books in a variety of electronic formats. Some content that appears in print may not be available in electronic books. For more information about Wiley products, visit our web site at www.wiley.com.

Library of Congress Cataloging-in-Publication Data

Brown, Aaron, 1956-
   The poker face of Wall Street / Aaron Brown.
       p. cm.
   Includes bibliographical references.
   ISBN-13: 978-0-471-77057-2 (cloth)
   ISBN-10: 0-471-77057-4 (cloth)
   1. Stocks. 2. Finance. 3. Risk. 4. Poker. I. Title.
   HG4661.B766 2006
   332.63'22—dc22

                                                                   2005031902

Printed in the United States of America

10 9 8 7 6 5 4 3 2 1

Contents

Foreword

Nassim Nicholas Taleb[1]

I

One would tend to think that gambling is a sterile activity that is meant to occupy those who have not much else to do and others when they have not much else to do. You would also think that there is a distinction between "economic risk taking" and "gambling," one of them invested with respectability, the other treated as a vice and a product of a parasitic activity.

This book shows that the distinction between what is called purely gambling and "productive economic activity" is one of those socially constructed ones that remain sticky in our minds. While many may disagree with the point (our economics culture is vitiated by these mental boundaries between activities), it remains that gambling injects currency into economic life in the form of the expectation of future cash transfers and *that*, and not just narrowly defined "productive" activities, may make the world advance. We may not accept it because economics is a narrative discipline and this appears to be the wrong narrative. It is not that gambling imitates economic life, but that economic life is largely modeled after gambling. That was the idea of the original thinker John Law, made infamous with his bankruptcy; Aaron Brown, another original thinker, revives it and takes it further.

1. Author, *Fooled by Randomness: The Hidden Role of Chance in Life and Markets.*

II

Until the day when I opened the manuscript for this book, I was not interested in gambling, any form of gambling. I had taken the aggressive view that, contrary to what we were taught in all these probability volumes, and in the misguided books on the history of probability and "risk," gambling could not offer us lessons about real randomness, nor that it could be a laboratory where you could get actual training for the messy, *aPlatonic* real life. Just as we tend to underestimate the role of chance in life in general, we tend to *overestimate* it in these games, by the mechanism of the availability heuristic that makes things the more salient when they easily come to mind.

Indeed, I found it infuriating to listen to people who, upon being informed that I specialize in problems of Chance, immediately jump to references to dice. Two illustrators for a paperback edition of one of my books spontaneously and independently added dice on the cover (the cover illustrator) and below every chapter (by the typesetter), putting me in a state of rage. The editor warned them to "avoid the ludic fallacy" as if it were a well-known intellectual violation—amusingly, they both reacted with "ah, sorry, we didn't know." What I call ludic fallacy (after the Latin *ludus*, play) is the misuse of games as the wrong epistemological ground.

How does randomness end up disappearing in these games? Just consider that you know the probability, and that the payoff does not change throughout. The casino never surprises you by announcing that it will be paying you 100 times more, or a tenth of your take. Furthermore, the dice average out so quickly that I can say with certainty that the casino will beat me in the very near long run at, say, roulette, as the noise will cancel out, though not the skills (here, the casino's advantage). The more you extend the period (or reduce the size of the bets), the more randomness, by virtue of averaging, drops out of these gambling constructs.

The ludic fallacy is present in the following chance setups: random walk, dice throwing, coin tosses, the infamous digital "heads or tails" expressed into 0 or 1, the "Brownian motion" corresponding to the movement of pollen particles in water, and similar examples.

These generate a quality of randomness that cannot be even qualified as *randomness*—protorandomness, or Mandelbrot's "mild randomness" is a more appropriate designation. At the core, all these theories ignore a layer of uncertainty. Worse, they do not know it!

The revelation was that poker differs greatly from the random walk—hence, one could learn from it; furthermore, it may be the sole venue for us to learn about randomness. How? Simply, it has other hidden higher layers of uncertainty—many of them. It has suckers, people who invite you to take advantage of them. It also has people for whom you are the sucker (of course, without your being aware of it). You are not flipping a coin and moving left or right. You are not betting against a large machine like a roulette wheel. You are not engaging in a blind draw. You are playing against *other* humans. You cannot easily control their maximum bet. Your betting policy matters far more than the probability of getting a given card. You can bluff your way, confuse other players, win in spite of a bad hand, or lose in spite of an unlikely good one. Not least, bets can escalate.

In short, there is *autistic probability* and *social probability*, one that is made complicated (and interesting) thanks to the messes and convolutions of human relations. Poker and this book bring us to the latter.

So poker resembles real life, owing to uncertainty about the cards, uncertainty about others' betting policy, and uncertainty about the perception by others of your own betting policy. But it is even more similar to real life, as we saw, in quite unsuspected ways.

III

In spite of having known Aaron B. for several years, mostly as an empirical-minded intellectual of probability, I did not really know what he was about until I read this book. I knew that he has the unusual and valuable background of someone who engaged in the intellectual activity of risk management, but had experience in trading and gambling, therefore got to know uncertainty with more depth and an open mind—which is what uncertainty requires. In other words, a finance professor practitioners could talk to without getting angry.

But here is a person with a single, but large, idea, and who spent his life exploring it vertically and horizontally, maturing it, getting into its interesting wrinkles. This is far rarer than the already rare category of open-minded probability intellectuals. Pokernomics or just generalized gambling is what Aaron B. is about. He views the world from a prism, that of play.

In opposition to the ludic fallacy, there is the ludic virtue, the model of man as an agent of play, presented by Jan Huizinga's *Homo Ludens*, generalized by Roger Caillois's *Les Jeux et les Hommes* (Man, Play and Games), or, more recently, in Mihai Spariosu's *Dyonisus Reborn*[2]—though it remained difficult to make the leap between these literary and philosophical ideas and a modern explanation of economic life. What makes this a landmark book is that it does not just mix *Homo economicus* with *Homo ludens*. It tells us, quite convincingly, that *Homo economicus* is *Homo ludens*. Economic life is gambling.

I hope the reader will start viewing the world in a different manner, as I did.

2. Johan Huizinga, *Homo Ludens: A Study of the Play Element in Culture*. New York: Roy Publishers, 1950; Roger Caillois, *Le Jeu et les Hommes* (Paris: Gallimard, 1958); Mihai Spariosu, *Dionysus Reborn: Play and the Aesthetic Dimension in Modern Philosophical and Scientific Discourse* (Cornell University Press: Ithaca, NY, 1989). See also Spariosu's *God of Many Names: Play, Poetry, and Power in Hellenic Thought from Homer to Aristotle* (Duke University Press: Durham, NC, 1991).

Preface

One January night in New York City, I was playing Texas Hold 'Em with some financial people who were attending the Global Association of Risk Professionals annual conference. I had spent the day teaching a course called "Using Credit Derivatives," then rounded up some new and old friends for a poker game. One of them happened to be Bill Falloon, senior editor for finance and investment at John Wiley & Sons. Before long, we got to talking about some of the poker articles I had written. It took a few months, but Bill came up with a contract to write *The Poker Face of Wall Street*. Bill, his assistant Laura Walsh, marketing managers Kim Craven and Nancy Rothschild, and everyone else at Wiley have been incredibly helpful and supportive.

The best part about writing this book is the extraordinary amount of help volunteered by friends and strangers. Everyone loved the topic and dropped important work to explain things to me, give helpful advice, and introduce me to others. Rather than put in a long list here, I've mentioned them at the appropriate points in the text, to encourage them to read the book. A few people did not make it into the text, but their ideas did, and they were extremely generous and encouraging: poker guy-of-all-trades, player, writer, and pundit Dave Scharf; superstar financial risk journalist Rachael Horsewood and her equally talented colleague Nina Mehta, who specializes in quantitative finance writing; and noted poker columnist Amy Calistri. David Parlett, the world's expert on indoor games, provided helpful answers. Tom MacFarland, a physicist turned hedge fund guy at Parallax Fund, provided helpful information and referrals, although he confessed to avoiding the high-stakes games encouraged by fund manager Roger Low. Michael Heneberry got tired of making suggestions and just rewrote, and vastly improved, three of the most important paragraphs in the book. In the process, he gave me the nine-word tagline that crystallized my thinking. I received more essential support from people posting in the online forums at www.Wilmott.com, the best site for quantitative finance, and www.twoplustwo.com, the best site for poker. I'd thank the people who run these sites here, but they're mentioned in the text.

I've had some wonderful teachers in finance and related fields. I learned a lot from social network theorist Harrison White (my advisor at Harvard); accountant Katherine Shipper; statisticians Fredrick Mosteller, Craig Ainsley, Miriam Green, Harry Roberts, Robert Engle, John Tukey, Arnold Zellner, Charles Stein, and his student Ed George (my advisor at Chicago); economists Kenneth Arrow, Graciela Chichilnisky, George Stigler, Gary Becker, and Milton Friedman; finance professors Eugene Fama, Jon Ingersoll, Merton Miller, Robert Jarrow, and Fischer Black (who was particularly inspirational for this book, although he strongly disagreed with about a third of the core idea). In more than one case, I returned the favor with some lessons at the poker table. If someone ever offers an award for lifetime net poker winnings from Nobel Prize winners, I would immodestly place my own name in nomination (I have no way of knowing whether I would win). I learned as much from my fellow students and students I taught as a professor, some of whom appear in this book. I met Marco Avellaneda, Peter Carr, and Emanuel Derman after my course-taking days were over, but I benefited enormously from the wonderful mathematical finance seminars they run in New York.

Some of the poker players whose talents are indirectly reflected in this book are John Aglialoro, Mike Caro, Bob Feduniak, and David Hayano; I list only the famous ones and omit many of comparable abilities who play mainly private games and might not thank me for the exposure. Stan Jonas and Mike Lipkin took the time to give me long interviews—Stan had some great stories and Mike some great theories, all of which ended up on the cutting-room floor. I apologize, but I don't throw writing away; I'll use the material in articles. I never met James McManus, the author of the incomparable nonfiction poker novel *Positively Fifth Street,* but he provided some answers and encouragement for the book, as well as access to some of his unpublished poker writing. Not least, I thank him for a wonderful line I stole for a subchapter heading, which would have made a good title for this book.

Muhammad Cohen, the founder of Writing Camp, provided editing above and beyond the call of duty, taking random fragments of thought from me and returning what you will see in the following pages, putting in enough hours and changing enough words to almost justify a coauthorship. Inspired by Graham Greene novels to join and then smart-aleck his way out of the Foreign Service, this product of Yale and Stanford hides out from husbands of ex-girlfriends, Christmas music, people who wear suits—or file them—and government gunmen, in a part of Hong Kong that appears on no maps. If you find him, you'd better bring cards, chips, and Krugerrands. Copy editor Ginny Carroll improved the text immensely, one letter or punctuation mark at a time.

Writing a book is stealing from your family. Time, energy, attention, patience, and civilized behavior you owe them get shoveled down the black hole of the book. It doesn't seem right to thank people for stealing from them. Fortunately, I can thank my wife, Deborah, as a partner. She took time away from her own work as a portfolio manager to track down interviewees (some of whom tried hard not to be found), research facts, and talk people into giving me quotes. I made a deal with my children, Jacob and Aviva, which they both kept better than most grown-ups I know. Now that I'm finished with the book, I can keep my end.

Aaron Brown
August 24, 2005

CHAPTER 1

The Art of
Uncalculated Risk

This book is about how to gamble and win.

Gambling lies at the heart of economic ideas and institutions, no matter how uncomfortable many people in the financial industry are with that idea. Not surprisingly, the game most like the financial markets—poker—is hugely popular with financial professionals. Poker has valuable lessons for winning in the markets, and markets have equally valuable lessons for winning at poker.

This book will give you insight into both kinds of gambling. We'll begin with basic information about poker and finance, then delve into the psychology of finance and the economics of poker. We'll review elementary and advanced tactics for winning. Along the way, we'll see how America's passion for gambling at poker and in the markets has shaped the country's economic success and national character, and spilled over to make the globalized world we live in today. I've stuck bits of my autobiography in the Flashback sections to make the points personal. Finally, we'll look at some of the cutting-edge work being done in these fields and some of the dangerous nonsense to avoid.

RISK

My first point is obvious but often overlooked. In order to win, you must take risk. Therefore, to someone who wants to win, risk is good. However, I have great respect for risk. It is real. Trying to make a living at poker or trading, or anything else that involves risk, means you might fail. You might end up broke or friendless and miserable or dead. Or worse. If you don't really believe that, if you think that God or the universe or a Hollywood scriptwriter guarantees a happy ending for a shrewd, good-hearted adventurer—or that nothing really bad ever happens to people like you—this book will do you more harm than good. Of course, since God's looking out for you, you don't have to worry about that.

It's easy to say that there's no alternative to gambling, that you take risk by getting out of bed in the morning or crossing a street. That's true enough, but you *can* try to avoid unnecessary risk. More important, you can avoid uncalculated risks; you can always look before you leap. It's hard to win much that way, though. Other people snap up the riskless profits pretty fast and bid the price of calculable risk opportunities to near their fair values. Things get a lot less crowded if you go for the incalculable risks, leaps of faith that cannot be inspected carefully before takeoff. So that is where you find extraordinary opportunities.

If you can tolerate what life offers in low- and calculable-risk opportunities, you should take it. That is the defining strategy of the middle class, but it can be adopted by anyone, rich or poor. Choose a career in a low-risk field, and get plenty of good training. Be nice to everyone. Select sound investments; make conventional choices; pay your taxes; obey the law. Do a little better every year than the year before, and raise children who will do a little better than you. For many people, this is the American Dream. For others, it's the only sensible choice, the only kind of life that allows happiness without achieving it at the expense of someone else.

This book is for the rest of us, the ones who cannot imagine living that way. For some of us, conformity is the problem. We are sexual, political, or religious deviants, or uncategorizable eccentrics who just cannot fit into polite society. For others, born in war zones or under horrific governments, or abused as a result of caste or genetic aberration or other prejudice, the rewards of the limited safe choices on offer are too meager to merit consideration. Still others among us are just bored: Conventional comfort is too dull. But the most common reason for embracing risk among people I know is pure egotism. We believe we have some talent that must be nurtured and allowed to flower. We must write or act or research or explore or teach or create art or just be ourselves as an end in itself. This obsession puts us above the rules and justifies any risk or action. I've never met a successful poker player or trader who didn't believe he or she was better than everyone else. Some make it obvious, but for most it is a quiet article of unexamined faith. If you have it, it's impossible to settle for what everyone else gets, however comfortable that is in absolute terms.

To me, that's the real American Dream. For most of history, there wasn't a big middle class. There were rich and poor, life was risky for both, and everyone gambled. The growth of the middle class began in seventeenth-century Holland. Europeans who achieved middle-class security generally stopped gambling and soon afterward tried to get everyone else to stop. But in the United States, the middle class grew so large by the nineteenth century that a sizeable population began to try to escape it. Europeans were shocked to see the western frontier populated not only by drifters and refugees, but also by prosperous eastern farmers who wanted more land, who risked ruin and death for the chance to get rich. Other successful people moved west to escape conformity—social, religious, or otherwise. Traditionally in world history, mines were worked by slaves or oppressed peasants. In the United States, college graduates, clerks, and men with property flocked to mining camps all over North America (to dig and play poker). Even more surprising, these same kinds of people often volunteered to serve as foot soldiers in wars (to fight and play poker). All of them threw away middle-class security to bet their lives and fortunes for wealth or freedom, and many of them found both. This unprecedented combination of opportunity and anarchy produced both poker and modern finance.

That some risks cannot be calculated does not justify ignoring careful strategies or acting on blind hunches. In the last 15 years, the field of risk management in finance has developed sophisticated mathematics to transmute chaotic profits of traders into valuable revenue streams. For the first time, there is a legitimate science of uncalculated risk. The key is not minimizing risk, but managing it. A trading desk with good risk management can take on risks that would blow up an unmanaged desk. The same techniques can be used in poker and other risky endeavors. Poker players who understand risk management principles can play more aggressively in larger-stakes games with smaller bankrolls and have a better chance of succeeding.

RISK RULES

Here are four rules for taking incalculable risks. They apply to poker and trading, to getting married, to hitchhiking to New York to become an actress, and to devoting your life to developing a new theory of physics that everyone thinks is crazy.

1. *Do your homework.* Think like a middle-class person. Is there a safe way to get the same result? Can any of the risks be calculated? You don't stop figuring just because there's one aspect about which there is no useful information. Can you learn anything from people who have tried this before? Caution follows from my respect for risk. You must avoid unnecessary risks and, just as important, avoid taking risks blindly when they can be calculated. In traders' terms, you must take risk only when you're getting paid enough for it. In poker terms, you must extract all the value you can as a cardplayer before you start relying on your poker skills.

2. *Strike for success.* As Dickson Watts wrote in his nineteenth-century classic *Speculation as a Fine Art,* risk taking requires "Prudence and Courage; Prudence in contemplation, Courage in execution." If you do decide to act, act quickly and decisively. Go for maximum success, not minimum risk. Remember Macbeth's resolution after he decides to attack Macduff's castle: "From this moment, the very firstlings of my heart shall be the firstlings of my hand." If you want to learn to ride a bicycle, you have to get on and pedal. You might crash, but you might learn

how to ride. If the risk is too great, don't get on the bike. Going slow guarantees both not learning and taking a fall.

3. *Make the tough fold.* A popular method for losing at poker is to become "pot committed." After deciding to put a large bet in the pot, a player refuses to give up, even when subsequent events make it wiser to fold the hand. To be even an average poker player, you must often throw away good cards, regardless of how much you have bet on them, even when there is a good chance that you could have won the pot if you kept betting. And you must learn to fold as early in the hand as possible. Traders know well: "Your first loss is your least loss." As you attack incalculable risks, you learn things that help you calculate. If the result of that calculation suggests that you are not getting sufficient odds to justify further investment, give up just as quickly and decisively as you began. By the way, being willing to fold too soon rather than too late is one reason poker players sometimes make bad leaders. There are situations in which the leader should strive until all hope is gone, even dying on the battlefield or going down with the ship. That can be good for the cause, but it's bad poker and deadly sin for traders.

It should be obvious that application of rules 2 and 3, even moderated by 1, will leave you in a lot of tight spots. Rule 2 tells you not to hold anything back as you strive for success, and 3 tells you to give up often. If you keep anything in reserve, if you bet only what you can afford to lose, if you insist on a good plan of retreat, you should stick to risks you can calculate. But if you do choose to embrace incalculable risks, there is a safety net of sorts:

4. *Plan B is You.* The only assets you can count on after a loss are the ones inside *You:* your character, your talents, and your will. You don't have to relish the idea of being friendless and broke in a strange place, but the thought of it cannot fill you with despair. It's not quite this bleak: There are some social structures and economic institutions that can often soften your

landing a little. You can form networks among like-minded adventurers or join an organization that truly supports risk taking. But the networks are not always reliable, and the organizations are rare and selective. However big the loss, the true gambler will survive. As the saying goes, no one commits suicide at the racetrack. They might miss the next race.

Let me emphasize that these four rules are not a recipe for success. I don't have one of those. At best, if you master all four of these points, you are not certain to fail. If your goals are modest and you have adequate resources, you are likely to succeed. I can't quantify that, of course, because we're talking about incalculable risks, by definition. If your goals are wildly ambitious relative to your resources, you're likely to fail. But you might succeed. If having a real chance of succeeding—and a real chance of failing—is more attractive to you than what life offers in low-risk and calculable options, this book can guide you along the treacherous path you've chosen.

FINANCE AND GAMBLING

Finance can only be understood as a gambling game, and gambling games can only be understood as a form of finance. Many people have no trouble accepting the first part: They believe Wall Street is a big casino. When New York introduced offtrack betting (OTB) in 1971, it chose the slogan "If you're in the stock market, you might find this a better bet." Bernard Lasker, the chairman of the New York Stock Exchange at that time, sent a telegram protesting the comparison of horse race betting to stocks. New York City OTB president Howard Samuels replied, "I am sure that some of the 48,972 horses that raced in this country in 1970 feel they are a better investment than some of the dogs on the New York Stock Exchange." He may have been right: That month, April 1971, the Dow Jones Industrial Average closed at 941.75. That was the peak value in inflation-adjusted terms for the next 21 years. But even people who side with Lasker admit that many market participants are gambling.

However, I mean something different from the superficial comparison that you can make or lose money in Las Vegas or on the New York Stock Exchange. I mean that financial products have additional risk embedded in them, the same negative-sum, pure-random risk that underlies roulette and craps. It's true that a long-term buy-and-hold investor of a diversified portfolio of stocks is taking real economic risk, but that's a tiny fraction of what goes on in the stock market. No one gets paid a lot of money to sit around worrying about what the average return on equity will be over the next 20 years; no one screams and shouts about it. People do get paid a lot of money, and scream and shout, to trade one stock versus another or buy a stock and sell it five seconds later. The average investor in the stock market gets the average return; everything else is just gambling. Anything you win comes from someone else who loses, all relative to the average return. The bets are negative sum because there are taxes and transaction costs from the exchanges, just like the house edge in a casino. And at least in the stock market there is some underlying economic risk; it's not all one person winning from another. All other markets except commodity markets are zero sum. Every loan or bond has a borrower and a lender; every foreign currency transaction has a buyer and a seller; every derivative contract has one party paying another. For anyone actually working in the markets, all the excitement and opportunity come from these kinds of bets.

Economists sometimes argue that these transactions contribute to capital allocation and provide important price discovery. But most capital allocation takes place outside the trading markets and, anyway, is far too indirect to justify the amount of trading that takes place. While there's no doubt that the price discovery function is useful, no corporate manager needs to know a different stock price every second or the prices of dozens of different securities that all add up to one economically unitary firm. There are far more important social questions whose answers can be provided with amazing accuracy by auction markets, yet these remain a hobby of academics rather than a major economic institution.

I think that risk is added to financial products for four reasons, in increasing order of importance:

1. *Risk makes products more attractive to investors.* People like to gamble, so financial institutions add risk the way a fast-food company sneaks extra fat, sugar, and salt into its offerings. This is the first reason that occurs to most people, and it's true, but it's the least of the reasons.
2. *Risk is essential for capital formation.* People have to be persuaded to take assets that could be used for consumption and think of them as sources of future income. You need risk for this the way you need heat for cooking.
3. *Risk creates winners and losers, and a dynamic economy needs both.* Everyone is born with a lot of options in life, and volatility increases the value of options. The concentrated capital of winners is a force for change, and losses have freed many a loser to exploit the value of options a comfortable person would ignore.
4. *Risk attracts traders.* Traders are not passive order takers, but a hugely important dynamic force in the economy. There is a reason the successful ones make so much money. Without enough risk, the right kind of people don't show up.

The reason I think these things are true is that they explain lots of details about how financial markets are organized that conventional accounts do not. They explain what things are traded and how markets are organized. They explain the level of volatility, the margin requirements, and the profit distribution among traders.

I hope I don't come across as a crank with a theory of economics that no one has thought of before. There are many different ways to view financial markets, and each of them can have some truth. I don't claim that every other explanation of financial institutions is wrong; I claim only that it can be enlightening to traders and gamblers to consider their institutions from the other's perspective. Even if the analogy is not exact, it is illuminating and can serve as an antidote to the narrow thinking and blindness that can lead to disaster.

Modern finance is not an ancient or natural economic system, nor is it only what can be bottled in the form of financial models and analysis. It was developed in the area drained by the Mississippi River between the time steamships opened the vast natural resources for exploitation in the early 1800s and the completion of railroad networks in the last decades of that century. It combined the economic insights of John Law, a Scottish gambler turned French banker, with an extraordinary economic system based on dynamic self-organizing networks used by the Native Americans in the region, catalyzed by some innovations imported with natives of the Congo River and Niger River economies. The first person to publish an explanation in mathematical terms was the finance professor and banker Fischer Black.

A river network with dispersed population and difficult overland transportation induces a far more flexible and dynamic economic system than is found in areas where trading is dominated by roads and ports connecting towns. The American economic miracle was born in the futures exchanges of the West, not in the banks and stock exchanges of the East. It is no coincidence that poker was invented in the same time and place.

AN EXAMPLE OF THE TRADING GAME

Consider the price of a share of stock. An economist might point out that the stock represents an interest in the profits of a company and try to predict its value by analyzing the probable future profits and when they might be transmitted to investors. This is called *fundamental analysis*.

Finance professors emphasize a different view. They do not deny that stocks and other securities represent economic fundamentals, but valuation from first principles is too hard. No one seems to be able to arrive at a more accurate price than the current market price. Therefore, it makes sense to treat the stock price as a gamble, a number that can go up or down with some probability. This is called the *random walk theory*.

It's perfectly possible that both fundamental analysis and the random walk theory are sound. When a roulette ball is spun around the wheel, the laws of physics will dictate where it ends up. But the results are so hard to predict that for most purposes you can analyze roulette spins as random numbers. Claude Shannon (the father of information theory) and Ed Thorp (the mathematics professor who invented blackjack card counting) and their wives were just the first of a line of inventors of electronic devices that predict roulette spins. Claude also built a mechanical hand that could flip coins that landed reliably heads or tails, whichever he specified. For these people, roulette and coin flips are fundamental events to be analyzed by physics. However, most of us are content with treating them as random.

But there is another type of behavior that is important for trading that cannot be explained either by fundamental economics or by statistical theory. It doesn't contradict those views; it is just another way of viewing the same price movements. It helps some people but not others. It is sometimes called technical analysis, but that term has acquired a taint from people who use it outside its area of applicability and make it into a mystical faith rather than an everyday money-making tool.

One common traders' rule is that before any large move, the market takes out the stops. The best-known kind of stop is a stop-loss order (technically, a stop-*sell* order). An investor tells her broker to sell a stock if the price drops below a certain level. This is a technique for limiting losses from investing in stocks. There is also a stop buy, an order to buy a stock if it rises above a certain price. This is more popular with professional investors. The traders' rule does not just refer to formal stop orders filed with brokers or exchanges; there are also people who will choose to sell if a price falls or will jump in to buy if a price rises. Others will be forced to do those things—we call them "weak hands." An investor may have borrowed so much money to buy stock that if the price declines, his creditors will force him to sell. Or a portfolio manager who failed to buy a popular stock may be ordered to buy it by his boss if it continues going up.

To oversimplify a bit, suppose a stock is selling for $25 and there are stop-sell orders for a million shares at $23 and stop-buy orders for a million shares at $27. These orders will make for a nervous market. If the price starts falling, traders will want to sell before the million share orders to sell at $23 hit. So they'll start selling at $24, which will push the price down to $23.75, which will induce more selling, which could trigger the stops. As soon as one share trades at $23, a million stop sells become market sells (unconditional orders to sell at whatever price is available), and the price might drop to $22.

After the million shares have been absorbed, the price should start moving back up to $24. After all, there was no reason other than fear of the stops that pushed it down from that point. As it increases, traders will start to get greedy about the million buy orders that kick in at $27. Everyone will want to buy before those orders hit. That could push the price up to $27, triggering a million buys and pushing the price up to $28. The traders as a group will have bought a million shares for prices between $22 and $23 and sold them for prices between $27 and $28, for $5 million profit.

In a quiet market, the price will stay close enough to $25 that this will not happen. But as rumors come out about the stock, it will tend to be pushed up or down. Either way, it can trigger this windfall for traders. Only after the stops are taken out can the stock make whatever move is dictated by the economics.

Before I go on, let me caution you that making money in trading is not as simple as figuring out where the stops are and acting ahead of them. If the market took out all the stops all the time, no one would use stop orders. So this doesn't always work. Moreover, if you misguess the stop points, you could either miss the trades or end up being one of the stops yourself. Trying to profit from the stops is a little like stealing blinds in poker. It can work if you do it right, or it can cost you a lot of money.

My point is that the move from $25 to $22 to $28, before the eventual real move, had nothing to do with economic fundamentals, nor was it random. It was more like the outcome of a game, with winners and losers. Some traders sold and bought too soon, and they missed the profit. Others waited too long, with the same result. Some bought at one price, figuring the price was going back up, and were forced to sell at a lower price when the market surprised them. Each of these moves affected other traders: Some made money by guessing them ahead of time; others lost money by misguessing.

These effects are generally too small and short-lived for anyone but traders to exploit. Unless you deal directly with other traders, on an exchange floor or electronically, you will end up paying bid/ask spreads and commissions and getting your orders executed too slowly and at prices that are too unfavorable to make money from technical movements. Even among professional traders, many lose money trying to play these games. You may be fast, but someone else has a computer transmitting millions of precisely calculated orders in the time it takes you to do one. Or if you're the guy with the computer, it may make you $10 million in a month, then lose you $100 million in a second. It's a game, but a tough game.

If you want to understand financial markets, and their effect on the economy, you have to understand the trading game. Many short-term price movements are neither random nor caused by economic fundamentals. They're caused by investors buying and selling. This leads to predictable effects, such as stock prices being "pinned" to option exercise prices near option expiration, or sometimes forced away from them if the option holders have stronger hands than the option writers. These short-term movements affect the volatility and liquidity of securities, which affect their economic appeal to both issuers and investors. Small differences in trading characteristics lead to large differences in valuation, which affect capital allocation and investor portfolio choices. The trading game thus has tremendous influence on the economy and national mood. Moreover, the amount of money extracted by traders is a significant fraction of total wealth, and it is deployed far more dynamically than other pools of wealth. You cannot understand the economy without considering these effects.

GAMBLING AND FINANCE

The second part of the claim—that gambling acts as a financial market—is more controversial. The standard view of gambling is that it is a zero-sum game at best: Someone must lose whatever the winners win. At worst, when the game is organized by professionals, the house always wins, so it's a less-than-zero-sum game for the players. Therefore, the only sensible gambling is betting small stakes for entertainment. It's true that many people enjoy this kind of recreation, but it's not the gambling I'm talking about. This book concerns people who gamble for serious economic reasons. There are a lot of them, and they produce serious economic consequences.

The gross revenue from legal gambling in the United States is about two-thirds of the gross revenue of commercial banks, and the total amount wagered legally each year is about equal to total commercial bank assets. While there are no good statistics on illegal gambling, and it's not obvious how to compare the gambling and banking industries, it does seem as if gambling and banking are roughly the same size.

A bank gathers deposits from many people and invests that money in loans and securities. Viewed in isolation, a bank is zero sum in exactly the way a gambling game is. Any interest paid to the depositors can only come from interest paid by the borrowers. This was, in fact, a historical argument against banks and other moneylenders. Since money is sterile, charging interest is morally wrong.

However, no one today analyzes the bank in isolation. We always include the profit (hopefully) generated by the bank's loans and investments—real economic profit from real businesses. This allows the bank to return depositors' money with interest and pay its expenses. A bank is not a passive conduit; it can be a powerful engine of economic growth. A gambling game also gathers money from many people and delivers it to a few. At least some of those people use their winnings productively.

Several billionaires got their first stakes in poker games. Kirk Kerkorian funded his first business, the charter airline Los Angeles Air Service, with poker winnings. H.L. Hunt bet everything he had in a poker game and won his first oil well. Bill Gates, John Kluge, Texas oil mogul Clint Murchison, and corporate raider Carl Icahn all played poker for large stakes before they got rich. It's not just billionaires: Richard Nixon paid for his first congressional campaign with poker winnings and parlayed that into the presidency, where he continued to make risky bets but with less success. History is filled with people who began their routes to success with gambling winnings. You won't find as many equally successful people whose first stake was a bank loan or money raised from issuing securities. Even the losers can benefit. Writers from Dostoyevsky to Mario Puzo credited gambling losses for both the inspiration and the motivation to complete some of their greatest works.

Of course, there are many differences between a bank and a gambling game. People who borrow from a bank usually pay it back, but there's no requirement that winners at a gambling game do the same. There's no requirement for them to use the money productively, either. In that sense, a gambling game is more like a stock or commodity exchange, where participants transact with each other, winners keep their winnings, and losers bear their losses.

Another difference is that bank depositors expect to get their money back with interest, and they usually do. Gambling is more like an insurance company, which also takes money from many individuals and lends it out or buys securities. The insurance company repays only a few depositors, who get many times their investment. Most depositors get nothing. But gambling differs from insurance as well. Insurance buyers are passive (except for those planning fraud); they choose their bet but make no effort to help it win. In skill games like poker, gamblers actively try to win bets. That characteristic is shared with mutual funds, and even more by stock and other exchanges, where the payout for investors is a combination of luck and skill.

The difference between conventional financial institutions and gambling is of degree, not type. You can calculate a greater portion of the risk in the stock market than in a poker game. That's important, and people who forget it suffer. But a worse mistake is to assume you can calculate all the risk in the stock market or none of the risk in a poker game.

I don't expect to have convinced you by this point. Most people believe there is an essential difference between gambling and financial institutions. Some people think they know what it is; others think it's hard to define but real nonetheless. I will try to convince you in a later chapter. For now, just know that I'm entirely serious and that it makes a difference to risk takers. If gambling is a financial institution, it's important to learn whether the winners are economically productive. You would not deposit money in an uninsured bank that made bad loans, buy insurance from a company with foolish investments, or

invest in a mutual fund that picked poor stocks. Even worse are fraudulent institutions that don't invest at all, that just spend the money
you deposit. You must apply this same insight to gambling, or you
will surely lose.

The opposite of this idea is expressed by the tired cliché "If you
don't know who the sucker is at the table, it's you." I don't know who
said it first; I've seen it attributed to dozens of people. Regardless of
who said it, it's deeply stupid. Most con games are organized to make
the victim think that someone else is a sucker. So if you think you
know who the sucker is, you're most likely being conned.

The important question, whether you know who the sucker is or
you are sitting at a table filled with suckers, is why you are the one in
the position to fleece them. There's a lot of competition to exploit
suckers, so you should be thinking about where the competition is,
not where the suckers are. Is one or are all of the suckers pretending?
Is someone going to burst in and rob you? Or arrest you and fine you
all your winnings? Are you an intermediary sucker, collecting from
the little suckers, while someone else plans to collect from you?

Of course, you can try to make a living exploiting suckers. It's a
crowded field, but some people succeed. It has nothing to do with
gambling, however, and you will be hard-pressed to find examples of
people who tried it and ended up either healthy or wealthy. There are
a lot of smart and tough people in the world, and if you are a net loss
to everyone, someone is likely to decide to cut their losses at your
expense. And even if it does work, why would anyone want to spend
their life hanging around suckers? If you have to live off them, at
least do e-mail scams so you don't have to meet them.

Instead of looking for suckers, see if you can determine what productive economic activity is stimulated by your game. If you've never
thought about things this way, it's hard at first. But with a little practice, and the shedding of some prejudice, you can do it. You'll start to
see that it's much better to be sitting at a table of productive people
than at a table of suckers. If you also bring something to the table, it's
possible to win. You still have to learn how to play poker or trade, or
whatever other skills are necessary for the risks you choose to take.
Even in a good niche, you must win your money, one hand and one

trade at a time. Nobody gives you anything—not in my fields, anyway. But you're much better off with a plan that involves winning against strong players than one that relies on finding lots of suckers.

OPPONENTS

I wanted to write a poker book without using the word *opponent*. I've failed in the first chapter. But I won't use it often, and only with respect to other games or game-theoretic poker. You don't struggle *against* an opponent in poker; you play *with* a table of people. You don't win by dominating opponents. You win by finding a profitable strategic niche that it is in no one's interest to destroy. You must defend that niche, of course, but not at all costs.

Give me nine poker novices of average general competence, and in an hour I can teach them to beat the best poker player in the world, at a table with the nine of them against her. I don't mean by cheating—there will be no fooling with the cards or exposing cards or signaling, except through open betting. It is arguably unethical for the table to collude in order to beat one particular player, instead of each player individually maximizing his or her short-term profit, but a rule against this would be impossible to define, let alone enforce. More to the point, if you treat all the other players as opponents, you will encourage the table to organize similarly to what I would teach my champion-killers to do. They probably won't be conscious of this, but if they're any good at all, this will develop spontaneously.

This may seem to contradict David Sklansky's famous Fundamental Theorem of Poker:

> Every time you play a hand differently from the way you would have played it if you could see all your opponents' cards, they gain; and every time you play your hand the same way you would have played it if you could see all their cards, they lose. Conversely, every time opponents play their hands differently from the way they would have if they could see all your cards, you gain; and every time they play their hands the same way they would have played if they could see all your cards, you lose.

However, the two views are complementary, not conflicting (although I would prefer to use "other players" instead of "opponents" in the fundamental theorem). The mistake comes in reading into the fundamental theorem that long-term success comes either from making your opponents lose or by you gaining on every hand. What you want to do is gain overall; the other two goals are irrelevant.

To see the difference, suppose someone proposed a similar fundamental theorem of sales:

> Every time you charge less for your product than your customers are willing to pay, they gain; and every time you miss a profitable sale by trying to charge more, you lose.

This is true, and essential to remember for setting a disciplined pricing policy. The mistake would be to think that you want to keep your customers from gaining or that the best strategy involves no losses for you. In fact, you gain when your customers gain, and the best strategy accepts an optimal amount of losses greater than zero (usually, anyway; there are some cases in which the best strategy is to give your product away). If you forget the discipline of pricing, you lose, but if you treat your customers as opponents, you lose just as surely.

It might be objected that poker is a zero-sum game—in order for you to win, the other players have to lose. But that's true of a sale as well, if you focus narrowly on the single transaction. Every extra dollar the customer saves, the seller loses, and vice versa. But we all understand that the transaction is one small part of a broader web of economic activity. From a larger view, the transaction can—indeed, should—be profitable for both parties.

To be successful in poker, you also have to take a broader view. As in business, you cannot overlook the necessity of valuing every penny in every transaction, but you also cannot have faith in the old saying "Watch the pennies and the pounds will take care of themselves." It is true that in any one session of poker with a fixed group of players, the gains and losses will add up to zero (counting the house, if it is assessing a time charge or rake, as one of the players). But consider all poker games a gigantic network, like J.J.R. Tolkien's "one Road" (from *The Lord of the Rings* trilogy):

> He used often to say there was only one Road; that it was like a great river: its springs were at every doorstep, and every path was its tributary. "It's a dangerous business, Frodo, going out of your door," he used to say. "You step into the Road, and if you don't keep your feet, there is no knowing where you might be swept off to. Do you realize that this is the very path that goes through Mirkwood, and that if you let it, it might take you to the Lonely Mountain or even worse places?"

We can think of millions of players playing an eternal game. When anyone is ahead, he goes out and spends money in the outside world; when he is behind he stays inside and keeps playing. It's possible for every player to gain, in theory, anyway. In a broader economic context, a poker game can create money just like a bank does. To steal a phrase from George Soros, this is the alchemy of finance.

Unfortunately, things aren't this good. Not every poker player gains—the large majority of them lose, at least in an accounting sense. Nevertheless, to be successful, your goal cannot be to inflict maximum losses on everyone you meet at the table, any more than price gouging is smart business. Your goal also cannot be to avoid all losses. Avoiding losses is easy: Don't play. If you do play, play to win, not to not lose.

These are the two fundamentals of any risk-taking activity. On one hand, you must focus intently on every opportunity for gain and loss, and not let any slip away out of sloppiness. On the other hand, you must always act with a larger strategic vision that includes a chance for success. If, instead, you treat all other people as opponents, you will encourage them to act that way.

A lot of poker theory is derived from a two-player, single-hand, zero-sum model. I think most of the interesting parts of poker emerge only at a higher level—the entire table over a session. Part of this is my background in high-quality private games rather than tournament, online, or commercial poker. In private games you can take the longer view because players are not constantly coming and going. You know approximately how long the game will last, you don't have to worry about short-term winners leaving, but you also can't count on people hanging around for three days so you can get even.

A narrow focus on individual hands leads to random-walk results, with extremely high variance. Even the best players who use this approach have to endure huge swings in profit, and that's playing thousands of hours per year of rapid poker. To win consistently playing only 200 or 300 hours per year at a more leisurely pace obviously requires much more careful management.

That doesn't mean I'm right and other writers are wrong; it just means that we're talking about different kinds of poker. However, even if you play those different kinds of poker, this book is valuable. It offers a different kind of advice that can broaden your thinking about what you're doing. If you can see the game from a fresh angle, not already embedded in everyone else's play, you can come up with new ways to win.

HOLD 'EM ACES

I want to give a specific example of what I mean, because this book is intended to offer practical help, not airy generalities. The example requires some knowledge of poker, as given in Chapter 2. You can also skip the example and trust me, but that's not really in the spirit of a poker book.

There are three types of starting hands people play in Texas Hold 'Em: hands with aces, hands with two high cards, and hands with combinations (either pairs or suited connectors—that is, two cards of the same suit and adjacent ranks). These hands overlap: ace/queen, for example, is both an ace hand and two high cards; king of hearts/queen of hearts is both two high cards and suited connectors. In a rough average over many different games in my experience, a player who sees the flop has about a 40 percent chance of having one of these three types of hands. That adds up to more than 100 percent, due to overlaps.

The most important numbers for determining hold 'em strategy are these percentages applied to the table, not to individual other players. I have never seen a hold 'em game, even with the most expert players, in which one of these three types of hands was not overplayed, to the point that it almost never paid to play it. Which type to avoid is easier to determine and more stable than things like how loose or tight an individual opponent is, or whether she likes to play middle pairs. You might see two or three hands an hour from a single opponent. Even with some inferences based on how often he calls and what kinds of flops he folds on, it takes a long time to gather much useful information—and if he's any good, he's shifting frequently and being deceptive. Data on the frequency of ace versus high card versus combinations for the table as a whole are revealed almost every hand, and no one is trying to be deceptive about them.

Why is this so important? If two hands have aces, they obviously have 100 percent probability of sharing a card of the same rank. If two hands have two different cards ten or higher, there is a 62 percent chance they share a card of the same rank. If two hands are pairs or suited connectors, there is only a 7 percent probability they share a card of the same rank, and if they are both suited hands, there is only a 19 percent chance they share the same suit.

Anytime you are in a pot with other players who share cards, you have two advantages. They are each holding cards that would improve the other's hand, so they both have less chance of improvement. More important, it is likely that either both will beat you or neither will beat you. If both beat you, it doesn't cost you any more than if one does. But if neither beats you, you collect twice as much as you risk. Conversely, you don't want to be in a multiway pot sharing cards with another player (if there are only two bettors left, then it doesn't matter). This factor—whether you share cards with another bettor or whether other bettors share cards with each other—overwhelms most other considerations that make one hand different from another. If the other bettors are hoping for the same card, you want to be in with any playable hand. If you are hoping for the same card as another bettor, you rarely want to be in the pot.

Now, suppose you notice that the table plays too many high-card hands, suited connectors, and pairs, without enough respect for hands with aces. Obviously, you want to play all your ace hands and only the best hands of the other types (also, you prefer combinations in which the overcrowding causes less chance of overlap compared to high-card hands). Most poker theory focuses on individual other players and would tell you to go in with an ace only against other players who play too low a proportion of aces. But think instead about what happens if you play every hand as if it's impossible for any other player to be holding an ace. If anyone comes into a multi-way pot holding an ace against you, they will lose money. You'll lose money, too. If you defend your niche with vigor, you can become the designated ace player. Other players will rationally fold aces against you, leaving you alone in a profitable niche (you don't care what they do when you're not in the pot). If everyone knows you only play aces, no one wants to be holding an ace against you with other players in the pot as well. The table as a whole would be better off if someone challenged you, but no individual player would.

Okay, I admit that winning poker is not this simple. There are problems with this strategy—for instance, you're too predictable. Or you might lose so much money fighting over the ace niche that it's not worth winning, or you might pay a lot of money and lose the niche. You might encourage opponents to wait for ace/king or suited ace hands. My point isn't to play all your Texas Hold 'Em hands with aces in them; it's to remember that the game is not a sequence of independent hands, like spins of a roulette wheel, but a session in which it makes sense to invest money early to acquire a favorable position. A poker session is not a series of independent battles against individual opponents; success requires finding and defending a profitable niche at the table that it is in no one player's interest to dispute.

I will talk more about the forest than the trees, but you have to know trees as well. You still have to play each hand and each other player individually. But there's also a level above the forest—call it the ecosystem. Winning poker requires knowing why other people are at the table and how you got there yourself. If you want to play random-walk poker, without an unrealistically large bankroll or playing for trivial stakes, you need to understand the credit structure of the poker economy. If you plan to link a significant part of your life to the game, whether in terms of hours devoted or in terms of financial importance, I have some important things to tell you about the history and direction of the game considered as a financial institution.

TRUTH

I'm going to tell some stories in this book. I believe they're all true. When the names of the people matter, I use full names, like Bill Gates or Bob Feduniak. When they don't, I use real first names like Robert or Brian. In some cases, where the person might be embarrassed by a private story, I use nicknames like Dixie and Slick. The only possible confusion is with people like The Arm and Crazy Mike, real people I knew by nicknames. I will specify those occurrences in the text.

This book is about what I think today, not what I did in the past. I tell stories to help illustrate my points. I didn't make them up or consciously edit them, but I didn't go back and check against written records or the recollections of other participants. Memory being what it is, I might have transposed facts or inverted chronologies. That hardly matters, because it's what I remember, not what actually happened, that shapes my present thinking.

Poker books contain stories about hands, usually straight flushes beating fours of a kind, or one player holding absolutely nothing. Most of the money in poker changes hands when both players have pretty good, but not great, hands—maybe sevens and threes beating a pair of aces, or a pair of jacks beating a king high. For some reason, those hands don't often make it into the books. Just as hard cases make bad law, statistical freak hands teach bad poker. If you optimize your play for the hand when four of a kind comes up against a straight flush, you will be seriously miscalibrated for all but a few hands in your lifetime.

Another problem is that there is no such thing as an interesting poker hand. The play makes sense only in the context of a session. Telling about individual hands is like reviewing a book by picking out four or five of the interesting words it uses. Actually, Amazon.com does exactly that with its "statistically improbable phrases" and "capitalized phrases," and you can see for yourself how useful it is. Even the simplest poker decision involves consideration of past and future hands.

The same thing is true of trading and investing. People often ask me for a stock tip or whether it makes sense to be long or short the dollar. If you think that way, you've lost already. You need a strategy, and a trade or investment decision can be evaluated only in the context of that strategy.

Despite that, there's no way to write this book without discussing some real poker hands and real trades. The question is, how to do it without being misleading. It would fill this book if I listed all the considerations that go into even one hand. I'd have to put in everything I knew about everyone at the table, everything that affected my judgment about what cards people had, every past hand, and my thoughts about future hands. But that could give the impression that I sat for two hours mulling over subtleties before folding a worthless hand. I rarely go through even a few seconds of formal calculation or conscious weighing. Afterward I can reconstruct the factors that went into the decision, but that makes it seem much more organized and deliberate than it is. If I asked you how you decided to wear what you're wearing right now, you could probably think of dozens of things that influenced your choice, but you probably didn't spend a lot of conscious effort weighing them.

There's another misleading aspect to this kind of account. I was a baseball umpire in high school. Once in a while the runner would be safe, I would see him as safe, and I would call him safe, but looking at myself from above I would see that I was calling him out. These were the clearest and most definite calls I made. All the while, one part of my brain was telling me, "No, you're supposed to call him safe." I can't explain why I did it; every conscious part of my brain said "safe," but my body was clearly signaling "out." I've done the same thing in trading and poker. I never know why I do what I do, and I am reminded of that fact only when what I do is exactly the opposite of what my brain ordered. Otherwise, I ignore the difference to maintain the fiction that I am in charge of my life.

In baseball, an umpire can never change a call. Maybe in the World Series, where the game really mattered, you would; I don't know, no one ever asked me to umpire the World Series. But in amateur games, changing one call just means people will argue every call, and no one will have any fun. Some umpires practice payback. I just figure the bad calls are random pieces of luck, like bad hops on grounders. Oddly enough, I have never gotten an argument on that kind of bad call, the ones from another dimension. However obvious the mistake, the added authority your body gets when disobeying your brain intimidates people. On some deep level they realize that if my body won't obey *my* brain, what chance do *they* have of influencing me?

In poker and trading, it's too late to change the call. You just factor it into your calculations and go on from there. If you're shaken, you recite this aphorism from James Joyce's *Ulysses* three times: "A man of genius makes no mistakes. His errors are volitional and are the portals to discovery." If the decision works, it was an unconventional masterstroke. If it doesn't, it was a devious misdirection to keep other players off balance. It's never a mistake.

Therefore, when I tell you about a poker hand, I can't pretend to describe what I thought at the time. The best I can do is reconstruct a scenario based on what I remember about the few seconds of conscious thought, consistent with what I actually did. Again, that's fine for illustrating my points, but it's misleading if you interpret it as how I think during a poker game. I don't know how I think in a poker game, and I don't know how my thoughts affect what I actually do.

Finally, there's the trivial point that I don't remember every card of every hand I've ever played. Since it's tedious to write "I held a middling pair, probably sixes to nines, with some cards that don't matter except there were no straight or flush possibilities," I will just go ahead and write "I held seven of clubs, seven of diamonds, king of spades, nine of diamonds, and three of spades." I will follow a similar convention for trading.

CHAPTER 2

Poker Basics

Is it a reasonable thing, I ask you, for a grown man to run about and hit a ball? Poker's the only game fit for a grown man. Then, your hand is against every man's, and every man's is against yours. Teamwork? Who ever made a fortune by teamwork? There's only one way to make a fortune, and that's to down the fellow who's up against you.

—W. Somerset Maugham, *Cosmopolitans*

Poker is a family of games that share hand ranks and betting rules. It can be played with as few as two people. Six is the most common number in home games; nine or ten is usually a full table at a commercial establishment. In recent years, online play has become popular.

To play poker, you need a standard deck of 52 cards; some games use the joker. There are four *suits* (spades, hearts, diamonds, and clubs) and 13 *ranks* (ace, which can be high or low, king, queen, jack, then ten through two). Unlike bridge, the suits have no order in poker: Two hands that are identical except for suits tie. Also, the order in which you receive the cards seldom matters; you can rearrange your hand as you like.

POKER HANDS

In poker games that use a wild card, the best hand is *five of a kind*. For example, if the joker is wild, five aces is the best hand.

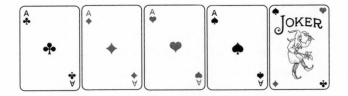

With a single wild joker as a fifty-third card, and no draw, you will see five of a kind only once in 220,745 five-card hands. In many poker games, the joker is not completely wild; it can be used only as an ace or to complete a straight or flush. Some poker games allow cards other than the joker to be wild.

The next best hand, which is the best hand possible without wild cards, is a *straight flush*. It consists of five cards in sequence, all of the same suit. For example:

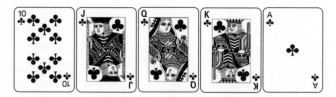

The ace is always allowed to be high, so the highest straight flush (called a *royal flush*) is:

In most games, the ace is also allowed to be played low; this is also a straight flush:

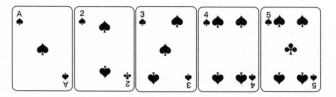

Despite the presence of the ace, it is the lowest straight flush because the ace is being used as a low card. You cannot use the ace as both high and low—this round-the-corner straight flush is not recognized in conventional poker (it is a flush, but not a straight flush).

Two straight flushes of the same rank tie, since there is no order ranking among suits.

A straight flush will come up in 1 five-card hand out of 64,974, without a wild card or draw. All further odds are stated under those conditions. Straight flushes are more than 20 times as common in seven-card games like Seven-Card Stud or Texas Hold 'Em; you'll see one every 3,217 hands.

Four of a kind, also known as *quads*, is the next ranking hand. If two players each have four of a kind, the higher four wins (aces are high). So:

beats:

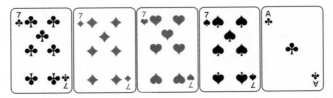

If two players have the same four of a kind (as can happen in games with community cards), the higher fifth card (called a *kicker*) wins. So if the board in hold 'em is:

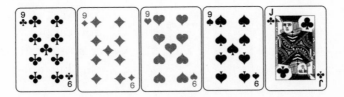

then your:

beats my:

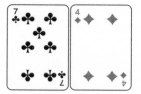

Your best five-card hand is four nines with a queen kicker; mine is four nines with a jack kicker. My three jacks don't matter; only five cards count. If, instead, you had:

we would have tied because both of us would have had four nines with a jack kicker. You'll see four of a kind in 1 five-card hand in 4,165 or 1 seven-card hand in 595.

Below four of a kind comes a *full house*. This consists of three of one rank and two of another. Among full houses, the higher set of three wins, with the higher pair breaking ties. You get 1 full house per 694 five-card hands, versus 1 per 39 seven-card hands.

Next comes a *flush,* five cards of the same suit that are not in sequence. Flushes are ranked by highest card, then next highest, and so on.

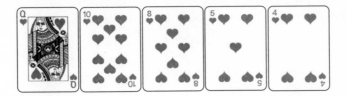

beats

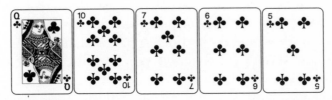

One in 509 five-card hands is a flush, and 1 in 33 seven-card hands.

Flushes are followed by *straights*—five cards in sequence that are not all of the same suit. Straights have the same rules as straight flushes for breaking ties. You'll see 1 straight in 255 five-card hands, and 1 in 22 seven-card hands.

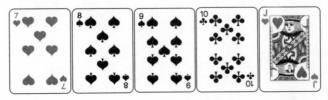

Three of a kind is the next best hand. These are called *trips* or (if at least one of the cards is a hole card in stud or community card games) a *set.* The higher three of a kind wins. In a tie, we look first at the highest kicker, then if necessary the second highest. Trips show up in 1 in 47 five-card hands and 1 in 21 seven-card hands.

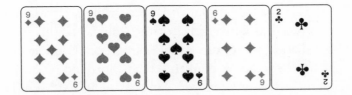

Two pair follows in the rankings, and the higher high pair wins. If those are the same, we look at the higher second pair. If both pairs are the same, the highest kicker wins. In five-card poker you get two pair once in 21 hands, and 1 out of 4.3 in seven-card games.

Next comes *one pair*. For one pair, the highest pair wins, with ties broken by the three kickers in order. A pair is about equally likely in both five- and seven-card poker—1 per 2.4 in five-card hands, and 1 per 2.3 in seven-card hands.

Finally, hands with no pair, straight, or flush are ranked the same way as flushes. These appear in 1 out of every 2 five-card hands, but only 1 out of 5.7 seven-card hands has nothing better.

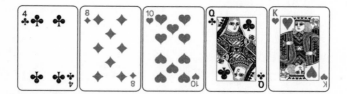

BETTING

Poker is not poker unless it is played for stakes of some value to the players. For one thing, the card play is too simple to hold anyone's interest. Beyond that, the entire point of the game is the betting. This is one similarity between poker and finance.

Betting can be done with money, but chips are more commonly used. Home chips are traditionally plastic in white, red, and blue. Values can be assigned as convenient for the stakes, but the ratio of five whites to a red and two reds to a blue is traditional. Either one player (usually the host) can act as banker, selling chips and redeeming them at the end of the game, or all players can be issued a fixed amount, with winners and losers settling up after the game. Commercial card rooms issue their own clay chips, which are heavier and have security features to detect counterfeiting. While there are differences among establishments, a common color denomination is white or blue ($1), red ($5), green ($25), black ($100), purple ($500), and orange ($1,000). Limit signs are usually color coded to the appropriate chips.

Table position is very important in poker. It is advantageous to have good or cautious players seated to your right and poor or reckless players on your left. In many games, players arrange themselves and move only if a player leaves. Serious players often assign seats by dealing one card to each player: The highest card deals, the next highest sits to his right, and so on around the table. Extra cards are dealt to break ties. By tradition, after an hour of play any player can request a new deal for seats. Most commercial establishments allow players to choose seats in the order in which they arrive. When a player leaves, any player at the table can take that seat before it is offered to a new player. Tournaments assign seats randomly.

In some commercial establishments, such as Las Vegas and Atlantic City casinos and northern California card rooms, the dealer is an employee who does not take part in the play. In others, such as southern California card rooms and many smaller places, the players deal for themselves. In either case, one player is designated as dealer for each hand to determine playing positions. That player may be designated by a *button,* a small object used for the purpose. The dealer position is therefore referred to as "on the button." The deal passes to the left after each hand.

The betting begins before any cards are dealt, or at least before any player has looked at cards. There are many variations and elaborations of these systems to create a pot before players see their cards. In most home games, each player places a white chip in the pot. This bet is called an *ante.* In commercial games, the most common arrangement is to use two blinds instead of antes. The player to the dealer's left puts up the *small blind,* equal to half the limit on first-round raises if this is a limit game. The player to the left of the small blind puts up twice as much. This is called the *big blind.* Other arrangements are possible—different numbers and amounts of blinds or combinations of blinds and antes. Some games allow more complicated predeal bets such as *straddles* and *kills.*

The difference between an ante and a blind is that a blind is actually a bet. The player to the left of the blinds, after looking at her cards, must either match the big blind, raise, or fold, putting no money in and taking no further part in the hand. In an ante game without blinds, the player to the left of the dealer can *check* (bet zero) and remain in the game because no bets have been made in that round yet. In an ante game, the player to the dealer's left opens the betting. He can check or bet. In a blind game, the player to the left of the last blind acts first. She can bet or fold. In either case on subsequent rounds, the first remaining player from the dealer's left opens the betting, except for games in which exposed cards determine the betting order.

LIMITS

Almost all poker games today have some kind of limit on the bet. The most common is a *fixed limit* game. All bets and raises must be for a specified amount, which usually doubles on the later rounds. For example, a typical limit game might be $100/$200 Hold 'Em, meaning the small blind is $50 and the big blind is $100. Any player calling the big blind must put up $100 to match that bet. If she wants to raise, she can only put up $200—$100 to call and $100 to raise, no more, no less. A player raising her must put up $300—$200 to call and $100 to raise, no more, no less. On the last two rounds of betting, any bet or raise must be $200.

In other cases, the limit is a *spread limit*, meaning that the player can bet or raise any amount up to that number. Some games limit the number of raises to three or four per round. That rule is usually waived if there are only two players remaining in the pot or sometimes in the last round of betting.

Other games are *pot limit*, meaning you can raise as much as is in the pot (including any amount you have to put in to call a previous bet), or *table stakes*, meaning you can bet as much as you have on the table (in this case you are not allowed to put money on the table or take it off during a hand). Table stakes is now often called *no limit*, but in true no limit someone can raise you any amount of money and you have 24 hours to raise it in cash.

The betting moves around to the left in strict order. Each player in turn can call by matching the sum of all previous bets and raises since his last action, raise by calling and then adding more to the pot, or fold. The betting round ends after one player makes a bet or raise and everyone else still in the hand either calls or folds. You are never allowed to reraise your own raise (the partial exception is the last blind, who can raise even if everyone else folds or calls the blind). At the end of every betting round, every remaining player in the hand has put the same amount of money in the pot in that round (and since the beginning of the hand, unless there were uneven antes).

Once money goes into the pot, it never is taken out, except by the winner or winners of the hand. Some games do not allow *check-raising*—that is, betting zero at your first opportunity but raising after some other player bets. Check-raising is also called *sandbagging*. Even when allowed, some players regard it as unfriendly, but serious poker players cherish it as an important tactic.

The situation can arise that a player is raised more than the amount he has in front of him. In modern games he is almost always allowed to go *all-in*. That means he bets all of his chips. The amount that was previously bet, which he was unable to match, is segregated in a side pot. The remaining players can continue to bet in the side pot among themselves. At the end of the hand, the remaining hands are exposed. The best hand takes the original pot. The best hand, ignoring the all-in player's hand, takes the side pot. It can happen that A goes all-in, while B and C continue to bet. C eventually folds. When A and B reveal their hands, A beats B, so he gets the original pot and B gets the side pot. If C's hand is better than A's, she could argue that she should get the original pot since she matched all of A's bets and has a better hand. While many players have argued this, poker rules give A the pot. If you fold against any player, you can never share in any pot for that hand.

MECHANICS

In home games, players often throw their chips in the pot, make change for themselves if necessary, and grab the pot if they win. If there is a professional dealer, players place the chips they intend to bet in front of their stack, but not all the way into the pot. The dealer checks the amount and pushes the chips in the pot at the end of each betting round, distributing appropriate change. At the end of the hand, the dealer pushes the chips to the winner. Players never touch the pot.

Commercial establishments generally have rules to prevent *string betting,* whereby a player bets some chips, looks for a reaction from another player, then adds more chips. If you say nothing, once you place an amount in the betting area, that is your entire bet and you cannot get change, except that placing a single chip of any denomination is assumed to be a call and you will get change if it exceeds the call amount. If you say anything, you are required to adhere to it, so if you say, "I raise $100," the amount you put in is irrelevant; you will be required to place the call amount plus $100 in the pot. To prevent the verbal equivalent of string betting, if you say, "I call and raise $100," the dealer stops listening after the word *call* and you have not raised the bet. These rules may be enforced strictly or not at all.

Another aspect that causes trouble in commercial card rooms for some casual home players is that you are responsible for protecting your own cards. If you do not place a chip or some marker on top of your cards, the dealer may scoop them up, assuming you have folded. If another player's cards touch yours, your hand is dead, even if it is the winning hand. If your cards get out of sight of the dealer, your hand is dead. You see hold 'em players cup their hands over their cards and lift the corners; if the cards leave an imaginary plane extending up from the table's edge, the hand is dead. You cannot fan your cards in front of your face and lean back in your chair.

The commercial game moves more quickly than home games. If players are paying by time, they are in a hurry; if the house is collecting a percentage rake per pot, it is in a hurry. Even experienced home players are well advised to watch for a good while before playing, start at extremely low stakes, and inform the dealer (if any) of their inexperience. Online play is even quicker, but you don't have the physical issues of cards and chips, and the software prevents you from doing most illegal things. Also, you can practice with simulators before you risk money. Many players play in several online games at once.

YOU GOTTA KNOW WHEN TO . . .

The most popular form of poker today is Texas Hold 'Em. In this game you make the best five-card hand you can with two cards dealt to you face down and five community cards (called the *board*). Only the five cards you use matter. If two players tie, their sixth and seventh cards are irrelevant; they just split the pot.

To begin a hand of Texas Hold 'Em, each player is dealt two cards face down. These are called *pocket cards* or *hole cards*. There is a round of betting. If at least two players are left in the hand (if there is only one player left in any poker game at any time, she wins, and that hand is over immediately), the dealer burns a card (moves the top card in the deck to the bottom without revealing it) and deals three cards face down. Burning the top card prevents players from learning one of the flop cards from a possible scratch or smudge on the back of the top card; the top card is burned before all turns.

These three cards are called the *flop* and are turned up simultaneously. The reason for revealing the cards simultaneously, rather than simply dealing them face up, is to prevent players from observing any *tell* (facial expression or other sign giving a clue about a player's cards or strategy) from players' reactions to individual cards.

Another betting round follows, then a fourth "turn," or "fourth street" card, is dealt face up. After a third betting round, the "river" or "fifth street" card, is dealt face up. There is one final betting round. If two or more players remain in the hand, the last player to raise reveals his hole cards, with the other players going around in turn revealing their cards.

The usual rule in poker is that the cards speak for themselves. If you have a straight but don't see it, and you announce "pair of jacks," your hand is still a straight and beats three of a kind. Still, it's a good idea to be sure of your hand and announce it clearly, especially if there is no professional dealer to watch out for your interests.

This phase is called the *showdown*. Many players are sloppy about the showdown and reveal cards in any order, or throw their cards away without revealing them (conceding after seeing a better hand). These are considered minor violations in home games. Most commercial establishments allow them unless any player objects. It is legal to reveal your hand even if there is no showdown, but traditionalists frown on the practice. Players are supposed to pay money to see your hand. It is a major violation to look at someone else's discarded cards—this could get you kicked out of a card room or tournament. It is even worse to reveal your cards during play or make any statement at all that could give information to a player. The exceptions are when you and one other player are left in a hand, you can reveal whatever you want, or when everyone is all-in so no more betting action is possible. Another important rule is one player to a hand; you are not supposed to get advice from anyone while you are playing a poker hand.

Texas Hold 'Em is among the easiest poker variants to learn, especially for players with experience at other games of strategy. It is the best for spectators because you can follow the action intelligently without seeing the hole cards. (I think watching poker while seeing the hole cards, as it is usually shown on television, is as boring as watching a taped football game when you know the outcome, but obviously lots of people disagree with me on both counts.) Texas Hold 'Em is also one of the few variants that play equally well for small limits, high limits, and no limit. Its popularity is also due to its prominence in the World Series of Poker, the oldest and most prestigious annual championship.

AND HE ANSWERS: "OMAHA"

The other popular community card game is Omaha. The rules are the same as in Texas Hold 'Em except you get four pocket cards and must use exactly two of them in your final hand. As an added twist, it is often played high-low, meaning the best and the worst poker hands split the pot (in most Omaha games, the low hand must be an eight low or worse by rule, but straights and flushes do not count).

There are several different ways of deciding the pot in high-low games. Omaha usually lets the cards speak. That means at the end of the hand, each player shows his or her hand. The highest hand that can be made wins half the pot and the lowest hand that can be made wins the other half. A player can win both, either by using different cards for high and low or with a wheel:

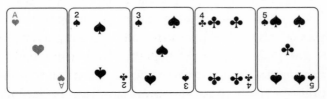

which is the best possible low hand and also a straight. An example of an Omaha hand that might win both high and low using different cards is you holding:

with:

on the board. You have three kings for high and eight/five/four/three/ace for low. Only a pair of aces (for three aces) or a jack/ten (for a straight) can beat your high, and only a four/two or five/two can beat your low.

Other high-low games make you declare, usually by taking two chips below the table and bringing up some in a fist. When everyone's fist (everyone remaining in the hand, that is) is above the table, fists are opened. A high-denomination chip means you are going high, a low-denomination chip means you are going low, and both means high and low. Another system is no chips for low, one for high, and two for high-low. In this case the usual rule is that if you go high-low and lose either way, you are out of the pot and it is divided among the remaining players as if you had folded. If all the players go high-low and no one wins both high and low among all the hands, the pot is divided among all the players.

These games can get complicated. You have to guess whether other people are going high or low. With luck, you can pick up half the pot without beating any hand. Or you could have the best high hand at the table, but go low because you're not confident of it, and lose to a better low hand.

STUD

Another popular poker variant today is stud poker games. Five-Card Stud came first and may have been the first poker variant. It was played by modern rules in the 1850s, and references to the name date to the early 1800s (possibly even before the game was called *poker*). In it, one card is dealt face down to each player, followed by one card face up. There is a round of betting, then a second face-up card is dealt to each player, and so on until each player remaining in the hand has five cards (one down, four up). This is a memory-intensive game, since cards are revealed early in hands that fold quickly. It is not apparent until later in the hand which of those cards were important.

Most of the time, players will fold unless their hand can beat at least all the exposed cards on the table. That means on their first two cards they need a pair or a card equal to or higher than all exposed cards. Paying careful attention to the cards with this rule in mind gives you quite a bit of information about the likely hole cards of other players, and about your chance of improving.

For example, suppose you are playing at a table of 10 people. Everyone antes one chip and the following hands are dealt:

You: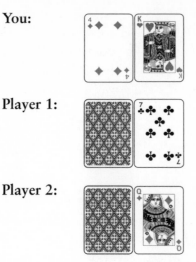

Player 1:

Player 2:

Of course, your four is hidden to the other players. You bet one chip, and two players call. Everyone else folds, showing low cards. Player 1 should have an ace, king, or seven; player 2 should have an ace, king, or queen. You're not sure, of course, but that's the most likely guess. On the next round:

You: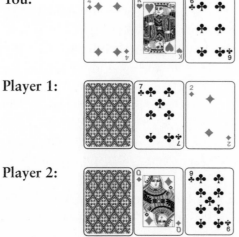

Player 1:

Player 2:

You bet another chip, and both players call. Then you get:

You: Player 1:   Player 2:

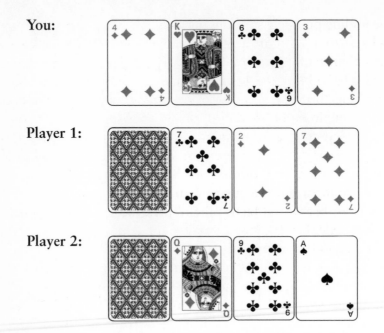

Player 1 bets one chip (in stud poker the betting is usually started by the best hand showing, while in hold 'em and draw the betting order remains fixed by table position relative to the dealer on all rounds; in some games the last raiser opens the betting on the following round). Player 2 folds.

You want to figure your chance of winning this hand. You need a king on the last card to have a chance, and even then you may not win. You have seen 17 cards, the 10 exposed cards shown here (including your hole card) and 7 up cards from the first round. That means there are 35 cards you haven't seen. If 3 of them are kings, your chance of getting a king is 3/35 = 8.57 percent. With 17 chips in the pot and 1 chip to call, you need 1 chance in 18 of winning, or 5.56 percent, to justify a call.

However, you have to consider what player 2 could have had. She should have started with an ace, king, or queen in the hole. She would never have folded a pair of queens or aces against sevens betting one chip, so she probably had one of your kings. That drops your chances of pairing from 8.57 percent to 5.71 percent. That's close to the folding point already, but it gets worse. Of the three cards player 1 is likely to have in the hole, a seven beats you for sure, a king reduces your chance of pairing to 2.86 percent, and an ace, your best hope, gives him a 7/34 = 20.59 percent chance of beating you if you do get your king (because 7 cards—2 remaining aces, 2 remaining sevens, and 3 remaining twos—out of the 34 cards are left after you get a king). So your chances of winning are either 0 percent, 2.86 percent, or 5.71 percent × (1 − 20.59 percent) = 4.54 percent. You might have misfigured one or both of the hole cards, but it does not make sense to call. If someone held a gun to your head to prevent you from folding, your best bet would be to raise, representing a pair of kings (and a reckless style, betting into a possible three of a kind).

If you have a good memory and can follow this kind of logic, Five-Card Stud reasoning is trivial. What isn't trivial is that *immortals* are very common—hands that the holder knows cannot possibly be beaten (the terms *nuts* and *nut* are often defined the same way as *immortal,* but sometimes are used to mean very strong hands that are not total certainties). Five-Card Stud only plays well with no limit, which means you must avoid at all costs facing a possible immortal. If there is a card another bettor might have that makes him sure of beating you, he can bet any amount and you will probably fold, even if there is only one such card. But if you remember that the key card was exposed on the first round and immediately folded, you can turn the tables. You also have to be very alert for situations in which you might have an immortal. This kind of thing makes Five-Card Stud very dull for gamblers and cardplayers, but it makes for the purest mano a mano confrontations, which some players consider the essence of poker. An evening of Five-Card Stud is hours of tedium and rote brain work, punctuated by occasional high tension.

Seven-Card Stud became popular around 1900. In this game, you get two down cards and one up before the first betting round, then three more up cards, each followed by a round of betting, and finally the seventh card face down and one more betting round. It is often played high-low and sometimes with wild cards (cards that can be used as any rank or suit) or additional rules such as that low spade in the hole splits the pot.

Seven-Card Stud calls for the widest variety of poker skills and is probably the most difficult poker variant to learn. You need more memory than a Five-Card Stud player because more cards are exposed and the deductions about hole cards are more complex. You also need to be aware of immortals, although they are not common. There are many strategic possibilities, but they can sometimes be enumerated and calculated, depending on the hand. That puts it between Texas Hold 'Em and Omaha as a strategic game. It can be played limit or no limit, and the choice makes more difference in terms of play than for other games.

DRAW

The other major form of Poker is Five-Card Draw. It is still a popular home game, but is popular commercially mainly in California. Each player is dealt five cards face down, after which there is a betting round. Each player remaining in the pot is allowed to exchange some or all of his or her cards for new ones (some games limit the draw to no more than three or four cards, but serious players would rarely draw four or five cards, anyway). Another common rule is that the first bettor must have a pair of jacks or better. Draw poker plays best with limits and often uses wild cards.

The only information you have about the other players' hands in draw poker, other than the general strength you may or may not be able to infer from the betting, is the number of cards drawn. Players generally draw three cards to a pair but sometimes keep a high card as a kicker and draw two. That reduces the chance of getting three of a kind, but if you get two pair, it's more likely to be a high two pair. More important, it adds some deception, suggesting you might be drawing to three of a kind.

With three of a kind you might draw two, or you could keep a kicker and draw one. Unless there are two wild cards, there is no point to keeping a high kicker rather than a low one, since it makes no difference to the hand. Even with two wild cards it's unlikely that two hands will have the same three of a kind so that the ranks of the other cards matter. The reason to draw one is to represent your hand as a draw to a straight or a flush.

Generally, you draw flushes or straight only when you have four cards already and, if it's a straight draw, only when your straight is open ended (four consecutive cards that can make a straight at either end). In rare cases, it makes sense to draw to an inside straight:

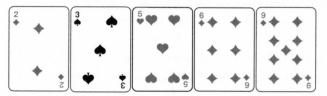

where only one rank of card can complete the straight (throw away the nine and hope for a four in the hand shown here). Only four cards can complete this hand, versus eight for an open-ended straight. Inside straights are also called *gut-shot* or *gut straights*. Players will sometimes draw two cards to "monkey" straights or flushes, when they have only three suited or sequenced cards, especially when the cards are high ones. This is mainly a bluff of having three of a kind, but once in a while you complete the hand, or get two high pair or three of a kind. Having a wild card makes straight and flush draws more attractive.

Draw poker requires no memory and little strategic thinking. It's mainly a game of straight calculation, and those calculations are pretty simple. It's the only poker game for which you could write out a complete strategy on an index card. It is the most psychological poker game—the edge consists of guessing how strong other players' hands are. It's important to keep track of how, and how often, players bet different hands, and how they vary their draws.

BASIC STRATEGIES

Poker players are generally divided along two dimensions. Tight players contribute little money to the pot; loose players contribute a lot. Aggressive players raise and fold a lot; passive players mostly call. It's important not to confuse these things. There is a stereotype that tight players are passive and loose players are aggressive, but if anything, the reverse is more common. Any of the four combinations is possible. You can play good poker tight or loose or in between, but you cannot play good passive poker. You can't play poker not to lose; you have to play to win.

Beginners almost always play loose, so beginner manuals usually recommend playing tight. That's useful because it slows down your losing until you can learn to play aggressively. However, an advantage of loose play is that it makes for a lively game. Other players like it. So if getting invited to good private games is important to you, develop a good loose style. Popularity doesn't matter in tournaments, where people have to play you, like it or not, and it's less important in commercial establishments and online, where one more tight player probably won't kill the table.

The essential thing is to vary your degree of tightness. The one fatal flaw in poker is predictability. If you're tight, make sure you play loose on occasion. If you're loose, tighten up once in a while. When you learn to control your degree of tightness and adjust it to game conditions and to disconcert other players, you're playing poker.

You don't have to choose one extreme or the other. There are two intermediate strategies. One is to enter more pots than a tight player but fold earlier than a loose player. The other is to be tight about getting into a pot but continue betting longer than a tight player would without improving. I think it's generally a mistake to split the difference, entering an intermediate number of pots and staying an intermediate amount of time in them. Better to play half your hands pure tight and the other half pure loose.

You always want to be aggressive in poker. That doesn't mean betting a lot; it means using all your options. The other players at the table should never be confident about what betting action you are going to take or about what cards you must have to justify your previous actions.

There are three ways to be aggressive, and it usually doesn't make sense to combine them, as they tend to cancel out rather than reinforce each other. You can be aggressive in your hand selection. This is what people tend to think of most as aggressive poker. A bluff is an aggressive play because you are raising with your weakest hands. But it's also aggressive to fold a moderately strong hand and to call with a very strong hand. If you do any of these things predictably, it's passive play, but if you mix them up enough, it's aggressive. With hand selection aggressiveness, you're unpredictable from hand to hand, but once you play a hand a certain way, you tend to maintain that front throughout the hand. So if you bluff, you play the hand from start to finish exactly like a strong hand. If you call early with a very strong hand, you keep betting weak until the end of the hand to encourage other players to raise.

Instead, you can be aggressive in your betting. With this strategy you can pick your hands straightforwardly, but you use all possible betting patterns. You do not maintain consistency throughout the hand; you may act strong at some points and weak at others. The classic example of this is the check-raise, when you check with a strong hand, hoping someone will raise so you can raise back. Again, it's passive if it's predictable. If you slowplay all your very strong hands, you won't win. An aggressive bettor switches apparent strength constantly throughout the hand.

Finally, you can be aggressive by reacting more strongly to other players than to your cards. You can play cards and bet straightforwardly, except that you are basing your actions on what you think of the rest of the table. If you read that one player has a weak hand and another really wants to fold, you'll bet your fair hand. If you think someone has a very strong hand, you'll fold your strong one. The classic example of this is the blind bet, when your strategy is so determined by other players that you don't even need to look at your own cards. Random blind play is passive, as are predictable responses to other players.

Actually, aggressive reaction players seldom play blindly or with the idea that they know what other players hold or will do. This strategy is usually based more on table sense—that there are times to go in with any playable hands, and times to stay out unless you're absolutely sure of winning. There are times when a raise will make people fold, and times when it will attract more action. There are times it makes sense to invest a lot of money to win big pots, and times when it makes sense to steal a lot of little pots cheaply. As the mood and strategy of other players change, profitable niches open and close. The alert aggressive reaction player can always have a cozy home.

The reason it doesn't pay to mix these strategies is that each one is used to make your actions unpredictable to other players. Combining them is like shuffling an already shuffled deck. It doesn't make things any less predictable. But it is hard to maintain focus and not degenerate into playing randomly. Keeping a clear aggressive tactic in mind leaves you free to concentrate on adjusting to the proper degree of tightness and also to pay attention to cards and other players.

CALLING

Although the unpredictability of different types of aggressive players springs from different sources, it has the effect that they fold and raise a lot. There's a useful poker overstatement that it never pays to call. If you have the advantage, raise; if you don't, fold. That's not true; there are situations in which you should call. But there are only three of them, and you should be sure one applies before you do call. If you're unsure, it's almost always better to fold or raise. Even if you are sure, you should fold or raise once in a while for deceptiveness. Many players' first thought when they're uncertain is to call. That's never right. Calling is not a compromise between folding and raising; it's a narrow tactical response to specific situations.

My views on this subject have sometimes been misquoted as "never call." I don't say that. In the first place, even I admit there are some poker situations in which a call makes sense. More important, I don't care about the frequency of calling. You can call often if you like—there are perfectly good strategies that make a lot of calls. The essential thing is to have a good reason every time. The occasional fold or raise based on a hunch won't kill you in poker, but thoughtless calling will. The theoretical mathematics of why a call can make sense is often invoked in situations where a careful analysis of the probabilities doesn't support it. A lot of calls are made because people (a) hate to give up when there's still a chance to win, especially when there are more cards to come and other players may be bluffing and (b) don't like to risk more than necessary. Either one of these is a fatal flaw in poker.

The simplest calling situation is when you know that each new chip you toss in the pot has negative expected value, but you have overall positive expected value because of the money in the pot already. For example, suppose on the last betting round there's $12,000 in the pot, and the one other remaining player bets $4,000. If you call and win, you win $16,000; if you call and lose, you lose $4,000. So you have to win one time out of five to make this call worthwhile. That way, out of five hands you'll win one $16,000 and lose four $4,000s to break even.

Suppose you think your chances are better than one in five— they're one in four. So out of four hands, you'll win one $16,000 and lose three $4,000s for $4,000 net profit, or an average of $1,000 per hand. But you also think the other player knows that your chances are one in four. That means if you raise, she will call or raise further. Each new dollar that goes into the pot costs you money. If you raise to $8,000 and she calls, then you're betting $8,000 to win $20,000. If you win one and lose three, as you expect will happen in the long run, you lose $4,000, or an average of $1,000 per hand.

What's happening here is that you had positive equity in the pot that existed before the other player bet. There was $12,000, and you had one chance in four of winning it. That's an expected value of $3,000. But in order to collect that equity, you have to call a bet that is to your disadvantage. Considering just the new $4,000 the other player bet, over four hands you will win $4,000 one time and lose $4,000 three times for a negative expected value of $8,000, or $2,000 per hand. That negative expectation gets subtracted from the $3,000 pot equity you started with, to leave you with $1,000. So you are calling a bet you don't want to make, in order to collect on the equity you had before the bet. Although you had the worst of the new bet, and certainly didn't want to raise it, it was worth calling it.

That's the first reason to call—the money in the pot already makes your odds good enough, even though you are losing money on each new dollar bet. But this situation does not happen as often as most players think. Early in the hand there are so many variables that it's seldom wise to stay in unless you think you have the best hand or are bluffing. You also don't know for sure what your chances of winning are or what another player thinks about her chances. A raise might make her fold; a fold might save you money. If she doesn't fold, it may make you more money next hand, when you have her beat and want to push the pot higher. If she's a good player and could have raised more, you have to ask why she didn't take all, or at least more of, your pot equity. Even when your call will be the last bet of the hand, when you think you've probably lost but there's enough money in the pot to make it worth betting on the 1-in-10 chance that you've won, don't forget to think about whether a raise, even now, might have a 1-in-10 chance of making the other player fold with better cards than yours; if not, it might not make you money with one last raise on the next 10 hands when you do have winning cards. After that, don't forget to think about folding. Is the 1-in-10 chance of winning really 1 in 20 or 1 in 20,000? Will a fold now encourage the table to bet higher against you all night? With all these considerations, you won't find too many times at the poker table that it makes sense to let your chips drain passively into the pot to protect what you think is your equity.

The second reason to call is the opposite. Instead of sacrificing current chips to protect past equity, you're investing them in the hopes of getting future equity. For example, suppose in hold 'em you have:

and the board at the turn is:

You think one player has a pair of sixes in her hand and the other has two clubs. Under that assumption, there are 4 out of the unknown 42 cards (neither of the other players can have a seven or an eight if you're right about their holdings), for 4/42 = 9.52 percent chance of your getting a full house. There's $100 in the pot, suspected flush bets $100, and suspected three sixes calls. If you bet, you're putting up $100 to win $300, with a negative expectation of $62.

However, if you do get a seven or an eight, you think you beat both players' hands. Suppose if you get it, one or the other player would call a $1,000 bet from you. Now you're putting up $100 to win $1,300, and have a positive expectation of $33. It's only $100 you're putting up because you'll fold if you don't make the full house, and the $1,000 you bet (if you do) is riskless according to your assumptions. You wouldn't want to raise before you find out whether you'll get the full house, because that has negative expected value.

While this is all true mathematically, again it's rare that you can count on terrific additional value from making your hand. Players will think about the chance that you have that hand, or a pair of sevens or eights. They might not call a $1,000 bet, unless you've set that up carefully with prior bluffing play (in which case, you have to charge some of the equity in this situation to depreciation of that asset). Moreover, you're not really sure of your reads. Why is three sixes calling what you think is a club flush, and why is the club flush only betting $100? Maybe three sixes is a bluff and the flush didn't fill, and you could take the pot with a simple raise. Maybe one of those hands is a pair of eights and you cannot win, and maybe you'll get your seven, bet $1,000 on your sevens-over-eights full house, and get raised $10,000 by an eights-over-sevens full house. Or maybe you'll get raised $10,000 as a bluff and fold the best hand.

The last reason to call is to keep other players in the pot. If you have a very good hand, you can sometimes make more money by letting other players stay in. If they improve, they may give you enough extra money to make up for any small chance of them actually beating you. This does happen, of course. But you will be surprised how often the player who will call the first bet will call a raise also, and how often a player who won't call a raise won't put any more money in the pot on the next round, anyway (unless, of course, she improves enough to beat you). You also lose some hands you thought were safe. Finally, if this is the only time you call, other players will know it indicates a stronger hand than a raise. The other two calling situations won't be confused with this one. So if you do this, you also have to call with weaker hands for deception. I know that sounds weird— that the natural call is with the strong hand, so you have to call with marginal ones to keep from being predictable—but it's true.

The nonreason is actually the most common reason to call in poker. Because it so seldom makes sense, you do it precisely because there's no reason. It's more important to be unpredictable in poker than it is to always have a sound mathematical reason for your actions. But remember that you can play good poker and never call, but you can't play good poker and always call.

TAXES

I'm including a brief sketch of gambling income tax law because it has a tremendous effect on the organization of poker in the United States. When one person gives money to another, generally it is treated one of two ways. If it is an economic transaction—a sale or a wage or anything else done for consideration—the recipient owes taxes on the money as income. It may or may not be deductible to the giver, depending on a lot of complex rules, but the basic idea is that money spent to make more money is generally deductible (the government likes you to make more money because you pay more taxes), whereas money spent for most other things generally is not, except for certain basic living expenses and a laundry list of other stuff.

However, if the money is treated as a gift, it is never taxable to the recipient. In certain extreme cases it can trigger gift taxes to the giver—these are basically estate taxes assessed early to prevent people from giving away all their money before they die.

In principle, we could treat gambling either way. We could call it an attempt to make money, in which case winnings would be taxable net of losses. Or we could treat it like gifts and say the winner need not pay taxes but the loser cannot deduct (and if he loses enough that he seems to be trying to avoid estate taxes, he might even have to pay tax on his losses).

But we don't. Because gambling is viewed as bad, the government taxes it in an extraordinary, inconsistent way. The sum of all gambling winnings for a year, totaled over all winning sessions rather than net of losses, is income and fully taxable. Gambling losses are deductible only up to the amount of winnings, and only as an itemized deduction. The last basically means that if you have a relatively low income, you have to give up your exemption for basic living expenses to claim gambling losses. The deduction is most useful for taxpayers with big mortgages in states with high income taxes.

There is an exception. If you claim that gambling is your profession, you can deduct losses against winnings like any other profession or business. However, the Internal Revenue Service (IRS) has been hostile to people who claim gambling as a profession and have any other job. The IRS appears not to believe in gambling as an income supplement, only as a full-time job. In my experience, most people who take the professional gambler route successfully don't have other jobs and hire good tax attorneys. One other niche some people seem to have used successfully is claiming that gambling is part of a larger self-employment activity that includes writing, teaching, and so forth. I don't know if that has ever been accepted by the IRS, but I do know people who have filed that way and not been challenged (yet).

This system works for three nearly empty sets of people:

1. *Those who win every session.* They have to pay taxes on their winnings, but since they never lose, the taxes are a reasonable percentage of their income.
2. *Those who lose every session.* They cannot deduct their losses, but at least they don't have to pay again to the government.
3. *Gamblers with no other jobs* who have enough money to live on plus pay a tax attorney.

Therefore, most people ignore the law and report neither their winnings nor their losses, or else they net them together before reporting. One problem with this is that you could get caught. I think this is a serious problem for people who play online poker and other gambling games. Many people ignore the risks, figuring that so many people do it, they will not be singled out for prosecution. Another argument is that the people running the online poker rooms are making so much money, they would never provide the IRS with information about their customers.

I heard exactly the same arguments throughout the 1990s about banks that offered debit cards and trusts in offshore locations with strict bank secrecy laws. The IRS estimated that a million taxpayers were taking advantage of these schemes, and some major law and accounting firms defended their legality (however, although some schemes were legal in theory, in practice many clients were using them illegally, and other schemes were inherently illegal). The off-shore banks were making lots of money, and seemed to have every interest in protecting their clients. Then John Mathewson, one of the pioneers of the business, was arrested and agreed to finger his customers to the IRS in return for avoiding prison. Many of the most prominent authors and promoters, including Terry Neal, Jerome Schneider, and Eric Witmeyer, followed suit.

The IRS sent out lots of bills, offering taxpayers the option of avoiding criminal and civil fraud penalties if they agreed to furnish all information and pay back taxes plus interest and a 20 percent penalty, and pay quickly. I suspect the IRS will someday force online casinos to disclose lists of social security numbers and account balances. Every player will get a letter with a huge tax bill. This will be most surprising to people who lost all their money. You might have deposited $100 in an online casino and gradually gambled it down to zero over a few months. But you didn't go straight down—you had plenty of $20 winning sessions and $25 losing sessions. Added up, you might have made $1,000 and lost $1,100. So you get a bill for $300 in taxes, plus penalties and interest, for the $100 you deposited and lost. Rakeback bonuses could double the tax pain. The fact that the play took place offshore is irrelevant (and legally dubious, anyway) because U.S. taxpayers owe taxes on their worldwide income. Not only do people apparently thoughtlessly play online, they sign up for other companies to download and keep track of all their play statistics. That makes it even easier for the IRS to track things, and harder to claim that you didn't know your results.

Even if you play only at places that keep no records, you are vulnerable. The IRS catches most tax evaders when friends and family inform on them for the reward money. Moreover, when one person is caught, he is often persuaded to name others. However, I think you have more protection here. The IRS has not shut down either casinos or state lotteries, which it could do anytime it wanted by enforcing the letter of the tax code. I think some decision must have been made not to do that. I have never heard of it targeting a private poker game, either.

The second problem with ignoring the law occurs if you play in casinos, especially in tournaments. The IRS will withhold 28 percent of any large winnings, and you will have to report them on your return (which could result in paying more or less than 28 percent in taxes). For many players, 28 percent of their largest winnings is much greater than their net income for the year.

As a result, poker players tend to fall into one of four groups:

1. *People who make most of their living from poker and claim professional gambler status.* They pay taxes on their net winnings. These people need full records of their play, which must be made available to the IRS in an audit. This makes many tax evaders reluctant to play with people from this group.
2. *People who make most of their living from poker and ignore the tax laws.* Some of these people file no returns at all. Many of them do most transactions in cash and avoid bank accounts or giving their social security number. Assets are kept hidden in cash and are hard to seize.
3. *People who have other jobs and accept the disadvantage of paying tax on every winning night but not being able to deduct losing nights.* The only way you can do this profitably is to be a very consistent winner. The only other way to afford this is

to have a very high paying other job relative to your poker stakes.

4. *People who have other jobs and ignore the law.* This is pretty easy to do because you have a normal tax return without the gambling. Unless someone informed on you and the IRS chose to pursue the case, it's hard to see how you would get caught. Still, you are committing a serious crime and could get a very unpleasant surprise.

Players in group 1 often exploit their tax advantage by high-variance play, the kind of thing that leads to random-walk results with large standard deviations. In casino games, players in groups 2 and 4 can't afford to risk the 28 percent withholding from large winning sessions without the ability to net large losing sessions against it. In private games, players in group 3 cannot afford to have many losing nights, even if they're ahead at the end of the year.

I think this is a serious issue for poker. In other forms of gambling it just increases the negative return to the player. That's unfair, but it doesn't distort the game. In poker, we'll never have open championship play until the tax law is changed to treat gambling consistently.

CHAPTER 3

Finance Basics

To cover all of finance in a single chapter, we're going to have to simplify. The world consists of only two things: people and capital assets. *Capital* has so many different meanings that it results in more confusion than clarity. In this context I mean assets (good things) used to make money. So if you have a car you drive around in, it's an asset, but not a capital asset. The same car owned by a taxi driver, or by a business, is a capital asset.

At this level of abstraction, we're not going to worry about government. It's just another business, holding capital assets, collecting revenue, and delivering goods and services. Its pricing policy is unusual: It tells its customers how much to pay and decides for itself what goods and services to deliver in return. Nice work if you can get it.

ECONOSPEAK

I do have to warn you about terminology. The words for the things I'm going to discuss in this chapter were invented by economists. Economists are clever people who take innocent delight in defining words as exactly the opposite of their normal English meanings. We've already seen *goods and services*. Well, goods need not be good and good things need not be goods. A sunset is not a good because nobody pays for it. A bottle of pain reliever capsules with cyanide in it is a good because somebody does. I'm not even going to mention some of the things that pass for services in the economy.

Anyway, businesses deliver *goods* and *services* to people—excuse me, to *households*. Of course, households don't have to own a house or hold anything. It's just shorthand to remind us that a lot of economic activity takes place outside the money economy. If a mother gives food to her child, that's not considered an economic transaction because it takes place within a household. If you spend all weekend cleaning your house, nothing economic happened, but if you pay someone outside your household to do it, it's a transaction and counts in the statistics.

Households get money to buy the goods and services, mainly by delivering *labor* to businesses and receiving wages in return. The labor example I use that resonates with students is to imagine the final exam, when I'm sitting in the front of the room doing a crossword puzzle and listening to my iPod, while the students are sweating, cursing, punching calculator buttons, and writing furiously. I'm laboring because I'm being paid. They're not because they're not.

COMMERCIAL BANKS

Okay, finally we get to the finance part. Businesses make profits, meaning the revenue they receive for selling goods and services exceeds the wage income they pay out. The excess can be used to purchase assets or labor from households to increase the stock of capital assets, or it can be returned to households through payments on financial instruments. Although this is the aggregate direction of the flow, many individual households earn more money than they spend. The surplus can be used to buy more assets for consumption (this includes just hoarding the extra money) or it can be sent back to the business sector.

I'm going to omit the large part of financial services that are consumed entirely within the business sector. Banks and other financial institutions do all kinds of things to help companies do business with each other: exchange foreign currencies, write letters of credit, authorize credit lines, and so forth. Because we're flying at 20,000 feet, those business services are no different from legal or janitorial services. In that sense, finance is just another business. There is a smaller, but still important, part of finance that operates entirely within the household sector. A credit union, for example, accepts deposits from its members and makes loans to them.

For our purposes, the important part of finance is when financial intermediaries stand between households and businesses. Banks are one familiar institution. We call them *commercial* banks if they accept deposits from the public, although deregulation is erasing this distinction. The deposits are lent out to businesses or used to buy securities (they can also be lent out to households, as with mortgage loans, but we're ignoring that). Businesses repay (we hope) the loans with interest and the securities go up (we hope) in value, so the bank can pay depositors their money back with interest, either in cash or in the form of transaction services such as free checking accounts.

An insurance company is exactly the same thing, except that it doesn't pay its depositors back according to the amount of money they deposited. Instead, it pays based on whether they die or have automobile accidents. From a financial standpoint there's little difference. A mutual fund has a different system: It pays investors back according to how much money it makes, but again it's just a variety of commercial bank. A hedge fund is just a mutual fund that is subject to lighter regulation because it refrains from advertising itself to the public and insists that its investors be rich. Hedge funds charge much higher fees than public mutual funds, but only if they make money, and they engage in much more sophisticated investment strategies. Not all of those strategies are risky; most hedge funds pitch moderate risk approaches.

INVESTMENT BANKS

A different type of financial institution is an investment bank (although, as I said, the distinction between investment and commercial banks is fading as more and more institutions take on both characteristics). The main job of an investment bank is to provide financial services to businesses, which we ignore except for one particular service. Investment banks act as underwriters, meaning they raise new capital for businesses by creating and selling new securities.

The two most important corporate securities are bonds and stocks. There are many hybrids, variations and combinations, and some entirely different types, but if you understand bonds and stocks, you've got the basics. Bonds are loans; they make periodic interest payments and return the principal amount at a stated maturity. If the issuer (the company, that is, not the investment bank) fails to make payments, bondholders can force it into bankruptcy. In the United States, that generally means bondholders and other creditors get the main voice in how the company is run, or whether it will be sold to make partial payment on the debts. In some other countries, bankruptcy is more difficult or less creditor-friendly, making bonds of issuers in those countries less attractive to investors.

The investors who buy a company's stock get to elect a board of directors to oversee the running of the company (as long as it stays out of bankruptcy court). In principle, the board acts to maximize shareholder wealth, although we could spend the whole book discussing the complexities in that arrangement. The shareholders are entitled to the residual earnings of the business, after all expenses and bondholders are paid. The company could send shareholders checks (called *dividends*), use the extra money to buy up shares in the market (which increases the value of the remaining shares, sort of like an automatic, tax-free dividend), or reinvest the money to make the business larger. Some stocks pay high dividends; others, no dividends at all (in which case, the price better go up or holders will be unhappy).

EXCHANGES

The third important type of financial institution is the exchange. Examples are the New York Stock Exchange and the Chicago Board of Trade. This is where households and businesses can come to buy and sell securities like stocks and bonds, and also things like commodities, foreign currencies, and entirely made-up securities called derivative contracts. Not all exchanges are physical buildings where traders gather face-to-face. Most trading these days is done electronically, either directly from institution to institution (this is called the *interbank* or *dealer network*, also *over-the-counter trades*) or through private companies that set up exchanges as for-profit businesses.

I want to highlight two particular kinds of derivative—two of the simpler ones—because I discuss them a lot in this book. A *call option* is the right, but not the obligation, to buy a specific thing for a specific price at (or sometimes at or before) a specific time in the future. The thing is called the *underlying,* the price is called the *strike* or *exercise price,* and the time is called the *expiry.* For example, a call option might give you the right, but not the obligation, to buy 10 ounces of gold (the underlying) for $4,000 (the strike price) at or before January 1, 2007 (the expiry). A *put option* is the same thing except it gives the right to sell the underlying at the strike price.

One person creates the option, which is called *writing* it. She always receives money; the option buyer or holder always pays. The amount the option sells for is called its *premium.* The premium is paid at the time the option is written and is never refunded, whether or not the option is exercised.

The curious thing about this third sector is that it seems unnecessary. All the other financial institutions collect money from households, send it to businesses, and return the profits, less expenses, back to households. But pure trading just moves money from one entity to another without obvious economic effect. If I buy a stock on the New York Stock Exchange, the issuing company doesn't get the money; another investor does. If I enter into a long cattle futures contract and cash out three days later, I'll make or lose money, but the cattle I owned—or had economic exposure to, anyway—for a few days won't be any different as a result; in fact, they were never specifically identified.

This view was largely true until the settlement of the American West. Exchanges were minor economic afterthoughts, more often associated with disaster or scandal than useful function. But in the dynamic self-organized network economy that emerged a century and a half ago, the exchange became the core institution. The trading characteristics of a security became more important than its underlying economics. The virtual economics began to drive the physical economy rather than the other way around. How and why that happened, and what it means today, is the subject of this book.

THEORY

A half century ago, finance was a purely descriptive field, like biology before the theory of evolution. Students learned what a letter of credit was and what documents were needed to issue a corporate bond, but there was no meaningful theory. A group of professors—most notably Franco Modigliani, Merton Miller, Jack Treynor, John Lintner, and Harry Markowitz—began trying to change that. The work with the broadest application was Markowitz's Modern Portfolio Theory, called MPT in the business.

The hard part about teaching MPT today is explaining why it is not obvious. That's an impressive testament to its success. All it says is that investors care about the statistical properties of their portfolios. Today no one would think of buying a mutual fund without thinking about its expected return and standard deviation of return. More sophisticated investors examine other statistics such as the Sharpe Ratio and beta.

However, a little thought will indicate that most things people buy are not evaluated by statistics. If you can measure or estimate the value of something accurately enough, its statistical properties don't matter much. Even if that's not true—say, when you choose a career or a spouse—there aren't a lot of statistics that can help.

So when Markowitz asserted that investors care about statistical properties, he was really making two statements, one negative and one positive. First, that research and analysis could not produce value estimates reliable enough for decision making. Second, that there were enough high-quality data for useful statistical analysis. These things were just beginning to become true in the mid-1950s. Before the 1930s, there was enough nonpublic information available that research could unearth good and bad values. Investors wanted inside information to bet on sure things, not statistics about historical returns. After the reforms of the 1930s, it took about 20 years to build up enough statistics to understand the market. It also helped that computers were becoming available to do the job.

The other half of MPT is that investors think at the portfolio level. They don't look for good individual securities; they look for securities that fit well with the rest of their investments. Some people buy a shirt because they like it; other people think about the other clothes they have that it would go with and for which they don't currently have the right shirt. Markowitz said that investors shop for a wardrobe, not a shirt. But he didn't say that investors match their portfolios to broader life assets, such as careers, houses, and spouses. MPT says that financial investments are evaluated in connection with all other financial investments, but not with everything else.

MPT does not require that markets be efficient. Every investor could have her own views on security prices and select the appropriate portfolio, given those views. Investors can be wrong about the statistical properties. Securities can be mispriced. Therefore, MPT can never be proven right or wrong, except in the irrelevant sense as a statement about investor psychology (in which case it's clearly false—investors care how much money they made or lost, not about abstract statistical properties). MPT is important because important features of the market are explained most simply if it's true. In other words, security prices move as if investors care about the statistical properties of their portfolios, even though investors don't.

A few years later, Eugene Fama made an essential advance to put finance on a sound basis. He investigated the results of assuming that security prices incorporate all information—in other words, that you cannot use any information to predict future security price movements. Without the Efficient Market Hypothesis (EMH), you can explain anything as a disagreement among investors. He sold stock A to her at $50 because he thought it was worth less than $50 and she thought it was worth more. Stock A went to $52 because more investors wanted to buy it. If you can explain anything, you explain nothing. Whatever happens, your theory covers it, so it never has to be changed. Of course, it also cannot predict; anything is possible in the future.

So Fama asked, "What happens if all investors agree about statistical properties of securities and try to form good portfolios?" Then he checked to see whether security prices moved according to that prediction. It's important to realize that no one thought the market was efficient; it was just a way to study things rigorously. If Fama could document the deviations from efficiency, there would be something to study, hence the possibility of learning. It came as a massive surprise that markets were so close to totally efficient that it was questionable whether there were any deviations at all. There are some anomalies, which could be inefficiencies, or could be data errors, or could reflect the need for more sophisticated theories. But no one ever found an anomaly without starting out with EMH. People criticize efficient markets all the time, but no one has come up with an alternative way to study finance. If you like to argue opinions forever with no possibility of data to resolve the issue, you hate EMH. If you would like to make some progress and actually figure things out, learn things, then you need EMH. Whether or not you believe the market is efficient has nothing to do with that.

William Sharpe, John Lintner, Jack Treynor, and Fischer Black independently came up with versions of the Capital Asset Pricing Model, or CAPM (pronounced "Cap Em"). There are dozens of other versions, which I had to memorize for my finance PhD qualifying exam at the University of Chicago. Lintner was probably first, although Sharpe's version was communicated more clearly and was the most influential. Treynor's and Black's version, based on equilibrium, turned out to be the most useful.

All three versions give a formula for relating the expected return on any asset to its systematic risk, known as *beta*. Systematic risk means risk related to broad market movements, as opposed to idiosyncratic risk that affects only some companies or industries or sectors. CAPM says that only systematic risk is rewarded by increased expected return. This is important because it says risky projects do not need higher expected returns to be chosen over safer projects, unless the risky project requires the stock market to go up to succeed. If a company is choosing between a high-risk and a low-risk research project, it should not penalize the high-risk one, because the success of a research project is not related to the market. But if it is choosing between two marketing projects, one of which is riskier and will do better only in economic good times, at the same expected return the company should prefer the safer project. However, if the riskier marketing project does better in bad economic times, it would be preferred to a safe project.

FINANCIAL CHALLENGES

One of the reasons I wrote this book is to try to attract a broader range of people into finance. I think it's a great field, but it needs new blood. The advantages are well known—high pay, interesting work, and if you make a mistake, well, it's only money; nobody dies. Too many people are entering the field for the safe money, and not enough for the challenges. At the moment the field has far more than its share of opportunities for breakthroughs, including ones that can make you rich, others that can make you famous, and still others that would do immense social good.

♦ We fail to provide even minimal financial services for at least half the world. This includes poor people, independent people, and even most rich people. Middle-class conformists are well served, but that's not everybody. Better financial services could make huge progress toward alleviating the miseries of poverty and social ostracism, and could make wealth concentrations more productive.

♦ We lack a basic theory of corporate finance. We don't know why firms organize as they do, nor do we know how they should be financed or overseen. A better theory could help businesses do a better job for employees, customers, investors, and communities. I don't think we do such a terrible job of corporate finance now, but it's all based on traditional knowledge.

♦ We don't really understand risk. We know it sometimes causes disasters but that it's essential for all the good things in life. We have some rough ability to tell good risk from bad risk. But a deeper understanding is needed.

♦ While our financial models have become very good at pricing securities, they require assumptions that clearly conflict with how security prices actually move. This creates some minor technical problems, but people have learned to ignore the underlying inconsistency. I think this has to be addressed eventually, and when it is solved it will reveal hidden worlds of opportunity.

- ◆ The new techniques of finance can be applied productively to areas of human interaction that have resisted money exchange. I don't mean by putting a money value on everything and trading it; I mean by integrating insights from gift and gambling exchange to the mathematical machinery of modern finance. The possibility for increase in happiness from this is far greater than from anything else I know.
- ◆ We have little control over the economy. I do not believe that monetary or fiscal policy help. It is reassuring that there seems to be persistent, unlimited long-term growth, but it would be nice to know why, especially in case it stops. Also there are areas in which that might not be the best policy. Humans should be able to choose how much and what type of growth they want. On the darker side, there seems to be persistent, growing inequality among and within groups of people. Again, we should be able to choose the degree of inequality we consider acceptable.

No doubt others would have different lists. My point is that finance is at a very exciting time when a relatively small insight can trigger a massive realignment of thought. This in turn could lead to the solution of an age-old problem or the creation of an incredible, unimagined opportunity. You want to be in a field at a time like this. Even if it doesn't work out, you will meet lots of other talented, interesting people. They'll go out and find the next set of challenges and invite you along for that adventure; or if you find the right place first, you'll have lots of allies to join you.

FLASHBACK

WALL STREET POKER NIGHT

The Wall Street in the chapter title is not the physical street that runs "between a river and a graveyard" near the southern tip of Manhattan. The last major financial institution left there several years ago, a year before 9/11. The New York Stock Exchange and New York Federal Reserve are still nearby, but physical floor trading of equities is no longer an important part of the financial markets and the center of Fed activity has shifted to Washington. There's still a financial district downtown, but except for Goldman Sachs, the headquarters of the large firms have moved to midtown Manhattan or farther away.

In the 1980s and early 1990s, there were plenty of high-quality poker games in the Wall Street area. Some took place in private clubs that no longer exist. Others were played in luxurious dining rooms on the premises of the big banks. The few rooms like this that survived cost cutting are reserved for customer entertainment, and it is now unthinkable to gamble on corporate property (gamble with cards, that is). In the summer, there would be games on yachts.

No doubt someone plays poker on the physical Wall Street, but I haven't been to a major game in the area for 10 years. Today, traders and other financial types who are serious about their poker are likely to play in midtown hotel rooms, private apartments or townhouses on the Upper East Side, or homes or country clubs in Westchester or Greenwich. Last night's game took place in the Tower Suite of the Mark Hotel. It's a spectacular setting with gorgeous views of Central Park and midtown. It was a rolling game, with some of the traders starting play early, about 5 P.M., while the bankers trickled in between 8 and midnight. Most people play for five or six hours. The game broke up at quarter to five the next morning, an hour after I left. The hotel is convenient for this kind of game, especially since some of the late stayers nap and shower before heading back to work without going home.

I haven't been playing much poker this summer because I've been too busy writing this book. I did attend the 2005 World Series of Poker, but only to get interviews. I didn't have the focus for tournament play, and I didn't do well when I took a seat in some side games.

A couple weeks ago, I sent drafts of the book to some of the players, so I'm gathering comments as well as poker chips. I would love for them to go on the record, but everyone refuses. It seems silly—most of them are on some kind of public record as poker players; some have won major tournaments. Most of their colleagues know they play. But Cao Chong sums up the opinion of the group that having coworkers know in general that you play is different from being identified in public as having played at a specific game. Playing in Las Vegas on vacation is not the same as playing after work in New York. You never know when exposure could come back to haunt you. I've tried to minimize the use of pseudonyms in this book—there are only three outside this chapter—but everyone here tonight will be identified by nickname. Some of them appear in other chapters under their own names.

The Players

I've known Cao Chong the longest of any of the players, over 20 years. He was one of the original Liar's Poker team described in the Flashback that follows Chapter 8. In fact, he went on to rewrite the rules of the game, civilizing it with the stipulation that everyone must challenge the last bid and share in the result. He became a very successful trader and now runs a hedge fund. He is among the best mathematicians I know. He is also writing a book on poker, but the highly mathematical kind that only 10 people in the world are going to understand when it is published posthumously; however, those 10 people will revolutionize the game.

Among the players I've never met is The Kid, a college student who won $350,000 playing online poker last year. He's here to play, of course, but also to hunt for a job. Poker has always been a way for ambitious young risk takers to prove their skills and get the attention of traders. Like everything to do with poker, it has exploded in the last few years. It used to be that students would play in serious games near their college, and someone would recommend them to someone on Wall Street who played. Today, kids show up fresh from tournament victories or online triumphs, and many have never played in this kind of private game. The Kid has—or else has the skills to fake it perfectly, which would be even better. On top of his poker and charm, he's got the IQ and education to get in. He'll probably be running a major bank in a few years. If not, he can make a living playing poker.

If you are an aspiring trader, you don't have to learn poker to get a good job. You do have to demonstrate some risk-taking aptitude. Risk management is not a hidden talent you discover miraculously when entrusted with other people's money. If you have it, it shows up young.

The mistake most applicants make is to think you have to demonstrate extreme risk—risking your life or a prison sentence. People who do that without commensurate expectation of gain are thrill seekers. What I listen for is someone who really wanted something that could be obtained only through taking the risk, whether that risk was big or small. It's not even important that she managed the risk skillfully; it's only important that she knew it was there, respected it, but took it anyway. Most people wander through life, carelessly taking whatever risk crosses their paths without compensation, but never consciously accepting extra risk to pick up the money and other good things lying all around them. Other people reflexively avoid every risk or grab every loose dollar without caution. I don't mean to belittle these strategies; I'm sure they make sense to the people who pursue them. I just don't understand them myself. I do know that none of these people will be successful traders.

The kid is not the youngest player tonight—that honor goes to Ma Liang. Cao Chong is typical of the Chinese people who used to come to Wall Street. On the day he was to be sent to the countryside, almost certainly for a life of hard physical labor and poverty, he received word that he had a place in university, if he could get there in 20 hours. He rode an old bicycle over dirt roads through an unlit night, and he made it. He went on to get a PhD in physics and then a job on a trading floor in New York. I can't imagine how he did it.

Ma Liang's life offers an extreme, and pleasant, contrast. He seamlessly connects Beijing with Hong Kong and New York, drifting easily through each without seeming to have a plan, but probably with a very subtle plan. I'm not sure what his connections are, but he seems to know everyone. He's fantastically diffident about it—he doesn't drop names; you just see him at the head table, or shaking the hand of the guest of honor, or standing off to the side of the publicity photograph.

He works for a private investment company and plays poker with an unmistakably Texas accent. He declined the invitation to our last game, on September 1, 2005, but showed up unexpectedly. I later learned he was supposed to have spent the night at the White House, but the visit was canceled due to Hurricane Katrina activity. Coincidentally (I hope), Hurricane Rita hit Houston today. A lot of people in the room spent the day trying to keep in touch with partners and customers from that city. A well-known hedge fund run by former Enron traders relocated to Las Vegas for the duration, a confluence that probably sums up the modern financial system for some critics. Methane, a former natural gas trader who is now a senior utility executive, is livid that the New York Mercantile Exchange invoked force majeure at Henry Hub. That means sellers of the natural gas futures contract do not have to deliver to that location due to the hurricane, saving them (and costing contract buyers) the high price of alternative delivery pipelines.

Kotha is a softs trader (softs are agricultural products, as opposed to metals and energy). He is evasive about his background but concedes that he has some roots in northern India, or possibly Jammu, Kashmir, Pakistan, or even Tibet. Given that no resident of the region seems to agree with any other resident where the borders are, perhaps evasiveness is a good survival trait. He objects to my statement in the book that Fischer Black was strongly opposed to gambling. He claims he saw Fischer with Ed Thorp playing the horses at Saratoga in 1992. Ed was running regressions on a handheld calculator and Fischer was placing the bets, and they were doing very well.

Maybe a dozen other people show up during the course of the evening. Only one player from our group had a money finish in this year's World Series of Poker (considerably more than his entry fee, but not final table). He was supposed to show up about 9 P.M., after a 7 P.M. dinner with some other players at Alto. They ordered the tasting menu, which means they didn't finish dinner until midnight and arrived too cheerful with wine to play. Some modern players are almost puritanical—they treat poker as a competitive sport and would never drink or have fun during a game. No one in our group would play drunk, but no one would play if it weren't fun. We have some conversation beyond smug anecdotes from winners and "shut up and deal" from losers. Players are concentrating on the game, but that does not impede civility.

Nevertheless, none of these people are my friends. I find that hard to explain to non–poker players. It seems obvious to me—why would I want to win money from my friends? There is a mutual respect and some collegial feelings. In some ways I trust them more than my friends (but not in all ways). I certainly do them favors, and I expect favors in return. But even Cao Chong, the player I know best, is somewhere between professional associate and friend. There is a closeness with people you play serious poker against, but there is a distance as well. I was invited to the Alto dinner—something I would rarely pass up, still less when someone else is paying. But I had a quieter meal with non-poker friends at Capsouto Frères, the best restaurant in Manhattan that no cab driver can find. I dislike eating with someone before winning from him, and I dislike more accepting a meal from someone and then losing to her.

Economics

Since I insist on analyzing the economic underpinning of all poker games, I have to apply this tonight. Why are these people here? You have to be a very good player to get in. Why not find an easier game?

It's simplest to see from the perspective of a poker player—like me, for instance. When I started playing seriously in college, I sought out games with the reputation of having good players. I played in easy games to make money, but I also tried to find tough games to measure my ability. Some of it was competitive instinct: If you're good, you want to prove it against other good people. But it was also self-protection. I had to find out if there were better players than me out there. If there were, I wanted to find them when I was alert and looking for them. If I couldn't beat the tough game, I'd stick to easy games and learn to avoid the better play-ers. If I could beat the tough game, I could play with confidence. There's no way to know how good a player you are except by measuring against others. This was even more true in the 1970s, without as much poker theory available and no computer simulators to let you practice, record, and analyze 100,000 hands. This urge to measure myself led me not only to serious games at Harvard, but to Gardena, California, and other commercial poker sites known for top professional play. There is so much randomness in poker that measuring yourself against one other player is impossible. You can only hope to measure yourself within a network or community of players that has demonstrated superior play over hundreds of millions of hands, far more than any one person can play.

The process continues. If you win consistently at one level, one of the other consistent winners will introduce you to a better game. But it doesn't go on forever. In the book and movie *The Cincinnati Kid,* there is one person, known as The Man, who everyone knows is the best. It doesn't work that way. Of course, you can say there really is The Man, but I was never good enough to learn about her. I can't prove you wrong, but I've played with enough top players over enough years that I'm confident that the process ends at a regional level. In Boston, for example, there were maybe five games I played in at one time or another that were generally considered among the best. There may have been an equal number that I never attended. But there weren't a hundred games of this caliber in the city, and there wasn't one universally acknowledged best game. These games were also the best in New England—the top players from other cities in the region would show up from time to time.

It didn't go any farther than that. The best players in Boston stayed in Boston. They didn't head for Houston or Los Angeles or Las Vegas to get better games. They had jobs or other reasons for staying in the city. Similarly, the best business executives in Boston didn't hang out in China-town or in the Italian or African-American parts of town or crash Harvard student games. Mostly people played with people they felt comfortable with. There was some intercourse among these games. As a student, I played in several of them and also visited games in other cities that were supposed to be good. Players from different games, either within the city or from out of town, would show up occasionally. There was enough of this to make it clear that no one game or type of game had a monopoly on good poker. Las Vegas professionals didn't clean out the locals at serious private games, but they didn't get cleaned out, either. The same thing was true of private players on trips to casinos and card rooms.

Serious poker players face a lot of challenges. The games are often illegal. You have to collect debts and avoid being cheated. Poker players are known (or reputed) to carry a lot of cash, which makes them robbery and burglary targets. Sticking together in a poker network helps enormously. You can learn the safe places to play and safe people to play with, and get the introductions necessary to assure other people you are safe. The network can help you collect winnings and avoid legal trouble. Players in commercial establishments have the house to look after them, in ways I will discuss in subsequent chapters. But private game players have to stick together to look after themselves.

The Game

Tonight's game is no-limit Texas Hold 'Em with $25 and $50 blinds. Most people buy in for $5,000 to $20,000. This is not like casino and card room games, where many players make the minimum buy, then buy more chips if they lose, and even switch tables in order to cash chips in if they win (most casinos prohibit selling chips back to the house without leaving the game). There is a mathematical advantage to holding a small stack. If you go all-in, the other players keep betting, with no risk to you. The best hand may fold rather than call a bet made by another player, allowing you to win your pot. When playing in a commercial establishment, some players consider it part of the game to exploit advantages like this. But in most of the serious private games I know, players are expected to put everything they care to risk for the game on the table, and stop playing if they lose it. Most people quit if their stake falls below a convenient playing level—say, $500. There are no formal rules about buy-in amounts or rebuys; the conventions are honored voluntarily. If you like a different kind of game, there are plenty available.

This makes the stakes a little smaller than the same dollar levels in a commercial establishment. You rarely get to an all-in showdown, except when one of the bettors started with a small stack. A relatively high proportion of the time, someone going all-in has an unbeatable hand, so no one else will call. Players do bluff all-in, but if you do it once and get called, you're finished. That's the same as in a tournament, of course, but after losing a tournament you can enter another one or join a side game. In this game, if you're finished, you're finished for the night. If you lose more than rarely, you won't be invited back.

I have noticed that the stakes of the private poker games I play have remained pretty much constant over the years, adjusted for inflation. In college in the mid-1970s, typical buy-ins were $1,000 or $1,500. That grew steadily to the current $5,000, in line with the Consumer Price Index. It might seem odd that as I got richer, I didn't seek higher stakes. There are people playing tonight who measure their wealth in the hundreds of millions and people who don't have a hundred thousand. Nevertheless, we all find this a comfortable stake level. Poker is best when the stake is meaningful, but not so large that fear and greed come into play. The money should focus your mind, not blind you.

People who have a thousand times as much money don't spend a thousand times as much on dinner or clothes or rent. Therefore, $5,000 does mean something to multimillionaires—at least the ones I know—in relation to their everyday decisions. On the other hand, anyone with the poker skill and contacts to get into this game can get her hands on $5,000 somewhere. So the stake does not exclude anyone who would otherwise be invited, but it doesn't bore anyone, either. Gamblers like to ratchet up the stakes as much as possible; serious poker players like to get the stakes just right.

Despite the layoff from poker, I am not rusty. I arrive a little after 8 P.M., buy in for $5,000, and lead the table with $37,500 by 3:30 A.M. No one has left ahead by much, so there's plenty of money in play. I've had a steady increase—one good hand an hour with lower-level break-even play in between. I haven't been behind all night, nor have I needed exceptional luck on the river. All in all, a near-perfect poker night for me. Then comes the biggest hand, and my last. In the big blind, I'm dealt:

That's not the strongest hand in hold 'em, but it's the most versatile. It has enough high-card strength to form good pairs, two pairs, and trips, plus the maximum number of straight and flush possibilities. If you get a straight, it has to be the highest one unless there's a ten or jack on the board.

Cao Chong is under the gun and bets $500. He gets three callers before it gets to me. This is shaping up to be a strong hand. It's perfect for me. I put up $450 for a pot that totals $2,525. Either the flop will give me at least four cards to a flush or open-ended straight or it won't. If it does, I've got something like one chance in four to win, and possibly win a lot. If it doesn't, I'll fold.

The flop comes down:

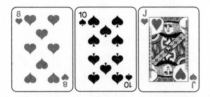

This reverses things. Instead of having a drawing hand, one that can improve with the right cards, I've got a strong made hand, two pair. The flop sets up lots of straight and flush possibilities, but no one can have a flush already. It's possible someone has a straight with queen-nine, but that's not a likely hand to make or call a $500 bet (nine-seven is even less likely). There could also be people out there with high pairs, queens or better, that could beat me if any pair shows up on the board. Another worry is a hand like queen-jack that would beat me if another queen comes down. Any pair could turn into trips. With four other players in the pot, there are too many ways to lose if everyone stays in until showdown. But it's quite likely I have the best hand right now and have the advantage over any single player individually.

It's important to contrast this situation to one where I need one card to make a great hand—say I held the ace and another heart with the flop above. In that case, I want to play against as many bettors as possible, since I'll likely beat them all or lose to them all. With the jack-ten that I have, I'll most likely lose to exactly one of the other players. My goal is to get the pot down to zero or one other player—I don't care much which it is. Since the small blind folded, I open the betting, and I go all-in. Everyone calls.

That's not as surprising as you might think at first, because there's $2,525 in the pot, and some of the players have small stacks. Methane is holding:

That gives him an open-ended straight draw, three cards to a flush, and a chance of taking it if an ace shows up with another card to form a pair either in his hand or on the board. The straight is the best possibility and on this hand could easily lose to a flush or higher straight. But he has only $1,500, and with everyone else calling, he likes his odds. Another player has a pair of kings and also about $1,500. Kotha thinks his ace/six of hearts is worth betting $3,000.

This, of course, is exactly what I didn't want. Against only these three hands, however, I still have a positive expectation. I have a little better than one chance in three of beating all of them, which gives me an $8,000 profit, versus about one chance in three of losing $3,500 and one chance in three of losing $500 net by beating Kotha but losing to one of the other two.

All this changes when Cao Chong lays down:

Now the only way I can win the hand is if the turn and river cards are the two remaining tens in the deck—1 chance in 741. I have 6 chances in 741 of tying (nine of clubs or diamonds with seven of clubs, diamonds, or spades). None of that happens, and to make matters worse, Cao Chong has the most money of the four of them, a little over $10,000. That gives him over $28,000 and leaves me with $27,000—a $22,000 profit for the night and a good time to walk away.

CHAPTER 4

A Brief History of Risk Denial

Risk in Finance and the People Who Pretend Not to See It

At some time in the distant past, after the invention of language, two strangers who could communicate met for the first time. I don't know what they said, but two good guesses are "Wanna bet?" or "Wanna swap?" Gambling and trading are two of the oldest human activities. In fact, some researchers trace these activities to animals, bacteria, and even single genes. Both of these activities involve risk, one of the most important and least understood puzzles life throws our way.

In premodern societies, gambling was the preferred way to make decisions when adequate facts were not available to make informed choices. Stone Age societies throw sticks, stones, or bones—or examine animal entrails—to decide where to hunt or whether to move on. The Bible and other ancient sources make frequent references to casting lots to determine God's will.

Recreational gambling got less respect. In general it was tolerated but discouraged. Playing with instruments God gave us for the most serious social decisions seemed impious. Monotheism introduced the idea that we should passively accept whatever fate God dealt. Gambling seemed to be a refusal to do that. Financial transactions were viewed similarly. Buying and selling of real assets was acceptable, but strong moral suspicion attached to pure financial transactions such as charging interest, money changing, speculation, buying or selling insurance, and dealing in securities.

I'M SHOCKED—SHOCKED—TO FIND THAT GAMBLING IS GOING ON IN HERE!

Attitudes to finance began to change in Renaissance Italy, and the change accelerated during the Reformation in northern Europe. As the size and risk of purely financial transactions increased, the gambling element became harder to ignore. Financiers had a choice between claiming that gambling is good and claiming that finance is not gambling. Most of them chose the latter (in theory, anyway; in practice, a good many of them were serious professional gamblers on the side).

Some of this is just euphemizing, the way Hollywood producers who spice their movies with carefully calibrated amounts of good-looking young people running around in their underwear claim they are not pornographers, or people who alter their moods with caffeine, nicotine, or alcohol say they do not use drugs. Gambling, pornography, and drugs are for sleazy lowlifes—nothing to do with buying stock, reading D.H. Lawrence, or taking Prozac prescribed by an MD.

If you like to make these distinctions, it's fine with me, but don't blind yourself to the reality of the associated businesses. This chapter is not about silly things people said to avoid using the word *gambling* with respect to finance; it's about silly things people did.

Let's start with an easy one: British premium bonds. These are the most popular individual investment in Britain—23 million citizens own $50 billion worth (£27 billion). They are sold by the National Savings and Investments agency of the British government. Each £1 invested in these bonds gets you a number, and every month there is a lottery drawing. Two lucky numbers collect £1 million first prizes, and there are over a million other prizes, going down as low as £50. There's only about 1 chance in 24,000 of getting anything at all in a given month, but unlike a regular lottery ticket, the premium bond does not have to be torn up after the drawing; it has a chance of winning again next month.

I hope no one will argue that premium bonds are anything but a prepaid strip of monthly lottery tickets. Nevertheless, from the government's point of view, they are just like any other government bond. The government gets money today and pays out interest every month to the bondholders. Instead of paying the same amount to every bond, as is the usual practice, the government pays 50 to 1 million times face value on a million bonds, and nothing at all on 26 billion other bonds. That doesn't matter to the government, only to the bondholders.

The National Savings and Investment web site offers two choices: "guaranteed returns" and "high potential returns." The guaranteed returns are standard investments such as fixed-rate government bonds and savings certificates. There are two options for high potential returns: the premium bonds and the "guaranteed equity bond," a similar bond for which the payout is based on the performance of the stock market rather than a lottery drawing.

Conventional financial theory says there's a world of difference between the (gambling/bad) premium bond and the (investing/good) guaranteed equity bond. From an investor's point of view, the only difference is distribution of payouts. The premium bond is riskier than the guaranteed equity bond if you buy only one, but safer if you buy a large number. Whereas the premium bond has a known expected return, you have to guess about the guaranteed equity bond, but it appears to be about the same. A major disadvantage of the guaranteed equity bond is that it will deliver its highest returns when most people are least likely to need them—when the economy is good, there are plenty of jobs, and other investments are doing well. From the government's point of view, there's no difference at all. It gets money today and either distributes monthly interest payments to bondholders via lottery or invests the monthly interest payments in the stock market according to a complex formula and returns the winnings (if any) to bondholders.

But you could argue that the difference is that the guaranteed equity bond causes the government to invest the monthly interest payments in the stock market. That means the government is buying stocks from other investors. Those other investors might take the government's money and make real investments—say, buying newly issued stock directly from companies. In that case, the guaranteed equity bonds resulted in real money being devoted to real economic effects. But what if that didn't happen? What if the government didn't buy stock? What if the people who sold stock to the government just spent or hoarded the money, and the people who bought the guaranteed equity bonds used money that otherwise would have been invested in real economic activity? Then the guaranteed equity bond has exactly the opposite effect, taking money that was used for investment and devoting it to gambling.

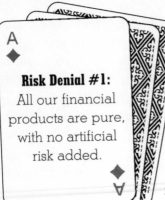

Risk Denial #1:
All our financial products are pure, with no artificial risk added.

If all of this is sounding impossibly abstract, you're right. The simple truth is that no one knows the effect of offering premium bonds versus guaranteed equity bonds versus straight bonds versus straight stocks. There's no grand theoretical answer, or if there is, no one has found it yet. The bald truth is that both these products, and all retail financial products, are designed for their appeal to investors, not their subtle effect on the economy. If investors like to gamble—and most people do—issuers will find ways to accommodate them.

Virtually all financial products and institutions have some deliberately added risk, beyond anything that can be justified as naturally arising out of life or economic activity. Some of it, like the lottery numbers drawn in premium bonds, is done to increase appeal to investors, the way packaged food often slips in a lot of sugar and salt. Economists are often uncomfortable with this fact because conventional utility theory argues that investors shouldn't like the extra risk. We'll see the hole in that argument in the "Utility Belt" chapter (Chapter 10). But as a result, many economists prefer to ignore premium bonds entirely and deny the existence of risk additives in other financial products. If you want to make a living in finance, or use financial products wisely, you have to understand the additives.

Not all food additives are to make the food more appealing to consumers; preservatives and stabilizers are there for the convenience of the packager. Of course, "preserve" and "stable" sound nice—you wouldn't say "we put stuff in this food so even bacteria won't eat it." Financial institutions add risk to assets for the same reason: so people won't consume or hoard them. Other additives ensure the correct amount of clumping in food—you don't want some things to crumble or other things to cake up. Adjusting the risk in exchange markets, rather than the assets themselves, changes the distribution of wealth among investors. If security ownership is too concentrated or too dispersed, it causes real economic inefficiencies. The polite phrase for this processing is *capital formation.*

A capital asset is one held for the purpose of making money. That's got nothing to do with the asset; it's all in the mind of the owner. The father of a friend of mine was a General Electric engineer who carried two identical pens in his shirt pocket protector. He bought one himself for personal writing and took the other from the office for company work. Both pens were assets, but only the second one was a capital asset. In order for the economy to grow, people have to be persuaded to use assets to make money, rather than hoard them or use them for personal enjoyment. An important role of financial institutions is to encourage this kind of thinking.

Risk Denial #2:
It's capital
formation,
not gambling.

One of the best ways to form capital is to concentrate assets. Suppose 1,000 people each have $1,000 under their mattresses for emergencies. Talk them into holding a lottery and letting one lucky person win the entire million and—voila!— instant capital. Nobody keeps a million bucks under their mattress; most people would invest it. Some people would spend it, but that's okay, too. Spending adds to business profits, and the profits add to capital. Moreover, increased business profits encourage other people to invest. There's another advantage, too: The 999 losers will engage in economic activity to rebuild their emergency funds, which is going to create more capital as well.

Conventional economics treats the stock market as a convenience for people who want to buy and sell stocks—sort of an eBay for stocks. But that doesn't begin to explain either the number or the volatility of stock market transactions. Only a tiny fraction of stock market trades are to change the exposure of an end investor to the market; most are zero-sum bets of one investor with another. If the stock market as a whole goes up 10 percent during the year, the average investor, of course, makes 10 percent. But individual investors will have returns all over the map, from –100 percent (losing all their money) to +1,000 percent or more, by picking winners and day-trading. If you want to understand the stock market, the *volatility* around the mean is a lot more important than the mean 10 percent. That's what all the traders are excited about, that's what stock market analysts write about, that's what people sue about, and that's what mutual funds (except index funds) advertise. That's why the stock exchange was built and why it makes a difference. That's the secret to making a living there or using it wisely as an individual.

Another capital formation trick relies on gambler psychology. If you put your money in a checking account, it stays the same every day. You'll put money in or take it out according to whether you need it. That's not much good for capital—most investments require having money for an extended period of time, and they have uncertain return. If you put your money in a mutual fund instead, the fund will either go down or go up. People hate to sell at a loss, so if the fund goes down, they'll do without rather than sell the fund to get money to buy things. If the fund goes up, people want to put more money in mutual funds—after all, they just made money.

Another use of gambling in capital formation is most important during bad times. When the economy is bad, there are almost no good fundamental investments. Of course, this is precisely the time it's most important to encourage people to form capital. If you don't, the bad times will never end. Most financial market transactions are zero sum. A bond has a borrower and a lender; any money the borrower makes comes from the lender. If I buy euros with U.S. dollars, someone else is on the opposite side of that trade. If I sell my GM stock to invest in Ford, again someone is on the other side of that. Therefore, even if the average return on investments in the economy is negative, a lot of smart or lucky people will be making money. In the 1970s, for example, when stock and bond prices were falling, commodity prices were going through the roof. In the 1990s, we had a run of years in which leveraged interest rate bets won big. When that crashed, emerging market investments took off. When they crashed, Internet stocks soared. Whatever happened, there was some attractive new sector to convert your excess funds into capital. If no one gambled against the grain in good times, there would be no winners to inspire people in the bad times.

I don't claim that gambling is essential for capital formation. Some day, a sensible economist may open a "health food store" institution that serves financial products with no added risk. Fully informed investors may maximize utility by converting parts of their income into capital. Some people might claim this has already happened, citing low-cost index mutual funds as examples. I think there's more added risk than meets the eye in those, but I agree that they involve less risk than active mutual funds or direct stock trading. But I think there's a reason that gambling has always been the dominant technique for capital formation, and I expect it to continue for the foreseeable future. If you want to understand the financial markets, you have to understand the risk additives.

Financial institutions are responsible not only for capital formation, but for capital allocation as well. Which projects will get the scarce capital? You might think that these decisions should be made by committees of experts, with degrees and extensive business experience. It turns out that those people do a terrible job of it, whether they are employed by the government or in the private sector. This is especially true in dynamic sectors of the economy. Capital allocation is more like a game than an art or a science, and games players seem to do the best job of it. Successful financial markets have to attract traders with the right kinds of skills, which

Risk Denial #3:
Traders are
order clerks.

means devising the right kinds of games. Economists tend to assign traders passive roles, filling orders and providing liquidity to cover short-term imbalances. Real traders are not like that at all. They are essential and highly paid participants at the core of financial markets. In fact, they are the only essential. With good traders you can form and allocate capital without a building or regulations or centralized information. Without good traders, those other things are no more efficient than government-run programs.

Traders have important roles even after they stop trading. Fortunes made buying and selling securities have underwritten economic revolutions. The impact of this money is much greater than fortunes gained in business or other ways. Former traders have also moved on to new jobs that influenced the economy without direct investment.

HEDGING BETS

Risk denial led to absurdities such as the refusal to use probability theory to price life insurance until the 1830s. For 250 years before that, the basic mathematics had been applied to games of chance, but insurers had to claim that life insurance was deterministic sharing (determinism and sharing were popular among Protestant religious leaders) rather than a bet that you would die. After all, everyone dies, so life insurance is not a bet but an investment.

This was not just a verbal formula; the refusal to use mathematics led to huge mispricings. Government annuities were sold at the same price to people of any age. Insurance companies failed to gather the statistics that would lead to rational actuarial predictions.

Risk Denial #4:
It's not gambling;
it's hedging.

After enough losses, some anonymous genius came up with the answer. Insurance, the revised argument goes, shares the same mathematics as dice or roulette, but it differs in an essential respect. Gamblers create risk artificially for entertainment, while insurance allows people to hedge risk that occurs naturally. So insurance companies can use the mathematics the dice players invented without being sinful gamblers.

Thus was invented the concept of *hedging,* making a bet that is risky in itself but reduces your overall risk. It sounds great, but it fails more often than it works. Many financial disasters can be traced to people who thought they were hedging. The problem with the idea of hedging is that it depends crucially on the scope of your analysis. When you look at a larger picture, what seemed to be a hedge turns out to increase risk.

The other trouble with the hedging explanation is that it isn't true. Life insurance does not hedge the risk of dying—it has no effect on that. In principle, it could be used to reduce the financial consequences on your dependents if you die early. If that's what people used life insurance for, then young wage earners with lots of dependents would need a lot of life insurance, while single and retired people would need little or none. About half the people alive today will consume more than they earn over the remainder of their lives. They should hold negative amounts of life insurance (a life annuity is a form of negative life insurance—you get paid for living longer rather than for dying early).

The numbers show that the amount of life insurance held is unrelated to the amount of risk that is supposedly being hedged. If anything, there is a negative correlation: People who need a lot of insurance are less likely to have it than people who need negative insurance. In the United States, the aggregate amount of life insurance held is roughly equal to the financial exposure of individual families, but it's held by the wrong families. Overall, life insurance exaggerates the financial impact of people dying early; it does not hedge it.

I'm not against insurance. Some people do buy it to hedge. Every day someone's house burns down, and she collects from an insurance company to cover the loss. Some young wage earners scrimp on their budgets to afford enough insurance to pay off the mortgage and put the kids through college if the grim reaper calls early.

But let's be realistic. Most people, including most college graduates and most wealthy people, play the lottery. Many people spend large amounts—$50 or $100 per week. For amounts like this you can buy insurance policies with payouts similar to large lottery prizes. Typically, the state takes 55 percent of the lottery player's dollar off the top, then the federal government takes 28 percent from any wins (plus the state dips again). For serious players, there is another tax. Because they use smaller prizes to buy more tickets, the state's effective share rises from 55 percent to about 85 percent. So for every lottery dollar spent, the serious long-term player expects to get back about 10 percent.

Doesn't it make sense that at least some of them would prefer to buy a life insurance policy on a convenient spouse for the same amount that will pay off with certainty and gives them back an average of two or three times what they pay in, or more, instead of 10 percent? What if the premiums were tax deductible, unlike lottery tickets, and the winnings tax advantaged? Wouldn't it be crazy if none of them did it? The demographic evidence suggests that people who hold otherwise hard-to-explain amounts of life insurance are similar to heavy lottery players, except they are richer.

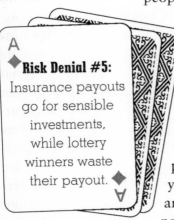

Risk Denial #5: Insurance payouts go for sensible investments, while lottery winners waste their payout. ♦

Proceeds of voluntarily purchased life insurance are spent more like lottery winnings than as if they were replacing the lost income of a wage earner. Life insurance holders get good press and lottery ticket buyers get bad, so you might think the insurance payouts are placed in sensible investments to support widows and orphans, while lottery winnings are wasted in wild debauch. In fact, both of them tend to be used to make permanent increases in the social status of relatively young people (for example, sending children to college) and to make a permanent lifestyle change for older people (for example, selling the suburban house and buying a condo in Florida). For most purchasers of each product, it is the only financial product likely to accomplish the goal. Life insurance is more sure, but it requires someone to die to collect. It makes the most sense when the desired lifestyle change is only for one.

Once insurance companies accepted gambling analysis, they funded enormously useful research about risk. On one hand, the development of actuarial science led to important progress in the field of Statistics, with a capital "S." On the other hand, companies gathered volumes of data about the risks people face in everyday life, statistics with a lowercase "s." Hundreds of millions of people were allowed to make bets that improved their lives. They got reasonably fair odds and didn't have to break the law to bet. Tax rules were skewed in their favor instead of heavily against them, as with casino gambling and poker.

A RANDOM WALK DOWN WALL STREET

It took another century and a half before stockbrokers admitted the stock market was a random walk. Like insurance, resistance to gambling analysis was not just a verbal formulation; it led to mispricing. Today, financial theorists agree that stock dividend yields should be lower than bond yields because stocks can appreciate (bonds will pay back either the promised amount or less—in that sense, they can only go down, so an investor needs a higher promised return to make them attractive). But until Modern Portfolio Theory was invented in the 1950s, stock dividend yields were higher than bond yields because stocks were considered to be riskier. Moreover, stock portfolios were improperly diversified and no one computed track records of managers because diversification and statistical performance measurement made sense only if stock price movements were random. Refusal to acknowledge the randomness of stock price movements created tax loopholes and irrational legal rulings.

Risk Denial #6:
We're not gambling; we're investing.

The stock market claim looks particularly silly in light of the history of financial institutions. From the lottery to raise the funds for the founding of Jamestown, Virginia, in 1607 to the lottery used to pay the interest on Dutch loans to the United States during the Revolutionary War, the development of the United States was funded by gambling. Wars, churches, universities, and public buildings were all paid for by lotteries. The government encouraged private businesses to raise capital via lottery. As the financial system evolved, businesses began to issue stocks and bonds instead, so lottery brokers became stockbrokers. The two forms of finance coexisted throughout the 1800s. They even reinforced each other. Lottery companies sold stock, and bucket shops sprang up where customers could place bets on stock and commodity prices, without any underlying ownership. Only in the latter part of the century did people start to distinguish sharply between respectable investing and gambling, elevating the former and despising the latter.

When stock market professionals finally embraced tools developed for gamblers, they needed a defense. They couldn't claim that people bought stock to hedge other, naturally occurring, risks in their lives. Instead, they claimed that the risk was inherent to economic activity and the stock market simply allocated it to willing risk takers. This helped the economy grow by providing risk capital and meant that the inevitable losses from bad luck and miscalculation would be assigned to the people most able to bear them.

Like the insurance defense, that makes some sense until you think about it. Starting a business is risky—it might succeed or it might fail. If you put $100 into a new business, it could turn into $1,000 or zero. But if you put $1 into each of 100 businesses, you're much more likely to come up with something in between. You can't eliminate risk this way, but you can reduce it. This is called *diversification*. Like hedging, it's true enough in principle, but it is dependent on the scope of your analysis. Relying on it has caused more financial pain than gain.

If the stock market existed to convert inherent economic risks of individual businesses into safer diversified portfolios, most of the activity would center around new issues of stock. This is a tiny fraction of stock trading, and it takes place outside the stock market. Most of the risk experienced by market participants comes from short-term buying and selling of stocks with each other—risk that has nothing to do with raising capital for businesses or, indeed, any economic activity. Young people, who have the longest time horizon over which to diversify risk, should slowly accumulate index funds, then slowly withdraw from them after retirement. In fact, most money is put into the stock market by older people. Until fairly recently, among people who owned stock, the most common number of companies held was one.

In this case, practice is moving toward theory. Index fund investment is growing, and more young people are building up positions in the stock market. However, portfolios are still very far from what theoretical models advise, and the vast majority of research and news reporting about the stock market concerns the quest for undiversified short-term gains (hot tips) rather than diversified long-term returns. That makes no sense if the purpose of the stock market is to spread out unavoidable economic risk, but perfect sense if the purpose is to let people gamble.

If the stock market is supposed to allow investors to diversify business risk, no business should issue more than one kind of security. In fact, many companies have multiple classes of stock, some of which represent different types of bets on the underlying businesses (in other cases, the classes differ only in control rights). They can issue many different types of bonds, preferred stocks, warrants, and other securities as well. A few years ago, "tracking" stocks were popular, in which a company allowed investors to bet on individual subsidiaries. None of this promotes diversification of existing risk; it just creates new gambles for willing investors.

Intraday trading is the whole point of the stock exchange, and it serves no diversification purpose. If you sell a stock at 11 A.M., you get your money at the same time the next day as if you had sold at 10 A.M. or 3 P.M. There's no reason the exchange couldn't accumulate all buy and sell orders for the day and execute them all at one price at 4 P.M., the way mutual funds do. We wouldn't need all those brokers shouting and instant messages relayed to Blackberries and breaking news stock market shows on every minute the market is open. All the intraday trading is day traders making negative-sum bets with each other. Serious long-term investors would be perfectly happy to buy or sell once per day, and probably even less frequently in most cases.

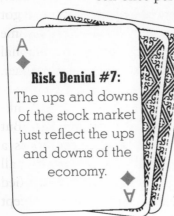

Risk Denial #7:
The ups and downs of the stock market just reflect the ups and downs of the economy.

Of course, without intraday trading, the stock exchange wouldn't be the stock exchange. The very essence of stock trading to a trader has no importance to an economist.

Another problem is that stock prices seem to move up and down far more than makes sense in economic terms. The extreme example of this was October 19, 1987, when the stock market fell almost 25 percent in one day, with no significant news. In less than three weeks, from the highest to the lowest point in October, the market fell by 40 percent. It's hard to explain that as inherent economic risk, and equally hard to tout the benefits of diversification when 1,973 stocks on the New York Stock Exchange go down and only 52 stocks (and mostly small, obscure ones) go up.

None of the largest stock market crashes on record were associated with any obviously significant economic news, either before or after the fact. Five of the top ten declines to date happened in the second half of October, with one more on November 6. In a modern economy no longer based on agriculture, that's easier to explain based on investor psychology than on economic fundamentals. If anything, October is a time of year of relatively little economic news: few extremes of weather, no major seasonal activity like Christmas or income tax day, uneventful times in construction and agriculture. U.S. elections are typically held in early November, but none of the crashes were in a presidential or otherwise significant election year.

For people who didn't like the "inherent risk of economic activity" argument, stock professionals had another argument. This one made more practical sense, but less theoretical sense. The claim is that investing in stocks is not gambling because the stock market has a positive expected return. Where is the gamble if the long-term investor always wins?

Everyone had always thought that when two people made a bet, both were gambling. In this new formulation, only the guy who got the worst of it was the gambler. The other guy was fulfilling some noble economic duty. In a reversal of older morality, the professional sharp was in the right and his or her hapless sucker was the sinner. Welcome to the 1980s, the decade when greed was good.

There are sensible reasons and some historical support for thinking stocks have a higher expected long-term return than bonds. But the case is by no means certain. Even if you accept it, there is a tremendous amount of risk in the stock market, even eliminating all the artificially added stuff by holding a low-cost, widely diversified index fund, and even over a time period of 20 years. So I can't accept the likely positive expected return as an essential difference between the stock market and gambling.

FOREIGN INTEREST

The next place to admit to gambling was the market for interest and foreign exchange rates. As with insurance and stocks, denial that rates were random caused serious mispricings. The government encouraged banks to issue 30-year mortgages to home owners at fixed rates, funding them with deposits that could be withdrawn at any time. That obviously meant that if interest rates went up, the banking system would be in huge trouble, since its revenues (the income from the mortgages) were fixed but its expenses (the rates it had to pay on deposits) would go up. The solution until 1980 was Regulation Q, a rule that set a maximum amount on short-term interest rates. That makes perfect sense if you think of interest rates as something the government sets, but if interest rates are random you're asking the banks to make a trillion-dollar bet with government money. Of course, Regulation Q failed, and the government was forced to spend hundreds of billions of dollars bailing out the banks. And only a miraculous efficiency in the government-run cleanup effort and some good luck kept the trillion handle off the price tag. Japan suffered far more—political unwillingness to write the check took the most dynamic economy in the world and mired it in almost two decades of recession.

Not only did governments try to legislate interest rates; they used their central banks to try to set foreign exchange rates. The final nail in that coffin was driven by George Soros, a famous hedge fund manager. Great Britain insisted the pound was worth 3.2 German deutschmarks. George kept selling pounds at that price until the country gave up on Black Wednesday, September 16, 1992. George

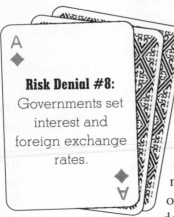

Risk Denial #8:
Governments set interest and foreign exchange rates.

made several billion dollars, England lost 10 times that amount, and the pound fell to 2.9 deutschmarks. Even with the advantages of controlling the printing presses and making the laws, governments were no match for determined speculators.

Central banks still influence interest rates and foreign exchange rates, but none are bold enough to get in the way of a determined market move, or even a determined hedge fund manager. Everyone knows that unpredictable market forces are more powerful than governments. Foreign exchange and interest rates are random.

An economist would explain that the government manipulates the value of money in order to manage the economy, to keep it from growing too fast or too slowly. I don't believe this works; central bankers use outdated and imprecise information to guide unpredictable tools. There is no doubt the process injects a lot of risk into the economy. No one can be sure what one currency is worth in terms of another, or what the currency will purchase in the future. Traders wait breathlessly for Federal Reserve Board announcements, which often trigger frenzied trading and market volatility. Those risks are artificial. We could virtually eliminate them by going back to the gold standard. The fanatic secrecy and delicacy associated with Fed decisions remind me more of gamblers ensuring a fair shuffle than scientists reaching open consensus about how to tune a precision machine.

I think that risk stimulates the economy. The fed is doing its job by being unpredictable, not by being right about the economy.

Now it was even harder to distinguish financial markets from gambling. With insurance and stocks, there was some physical external risk the markets could use to claim they were not generating their own randomness so people could bet. But what physical external risk caused interest rates and foreign currency exchange rates to move up and down so much? Interest rate trading volumes were far larger than the total outstanding amount of bonds. Foreign currency trading dwarfed exchanges to support export and import.

FUTURES AND OPTIONS

Next in line were the commodity exchanges. Commodity contracts are agreements to exchange a fixed amount and grade of some commodity, such as wheat or pork bellies, at a specified location, for a fixed amount of money within a fixed delivery window in the future. The classic example you will find in finance textbooks is a farmer who uses the contract to sell his wheat. For example, suppose he has a crop he expects to harvest in June. It's now early April, and the price for June delivery is $3.00 per bushel. He can lock in that price today with a commodity contract, or he can wait until June and hope the price goes up. If he does that, however, he could lose if the price goes down. On the other side, a miller knows she needs to buy wheat to grind in June, so she can also lock in the $3.00-per-bushel price today rather than taking a chance on the price going up. Viewed in this light, commodity contracts are the opposite of gambling. The farmer and the miller use them to avoid gambling with each other.

It should come as no surprise at this point that the farmer story is a fairy tale. Almost no farmers use commodity exchanges, nor did they in the past. Millers and other processors of agricultural products do, but they generally sell the commodity in the future instead of buying it. That looks as if they're doubling up so they make twice the profit if the price of wheat falls but take twice the loss if it rises. The vast majority of traders have no connection to the physical commodity at all—they don't grow it, transport it, or process it. The only time they use it is when they buy a loaf of bread in the grocery store like anyone else.

Futures markets are vital to the economy and were even more vital in the past, but not because they help farmers strike price bargains with millers. In a simple story, a crop steadily gains in value as it moves from being in the ground on a farm to harvest, then to movement to a city for processing, through cleaning, grinding, and packaging in final consumer goods. If that's true, there's no need for futures markets. At each step of the way people can make economic decisions based only on current prices.

Risk Denial #9:
Derivatives aren't
gambles.

That kind of "myopic" planning works well when there aren't any options for shipping and processing, when change is slow, and when infrastructure is already in place. None of those conditions applied in, say, 1880 Kansas City. Myopic planning would have led to alternating shortages, when the city's expensive processing facilities are idle, and glut, when commodities are rotting on the sidings. The economic solution to this problem required deliberately added randomness to the commodity prices, induced by exchange manipulation. Without that randomness, the supply network could not be robust and dynamic, and the people to run it would not have bothered to come.

How can options be portrayed as anything but gambling? An MIT professor named Robert Merton shared the 1997 Nobel Prize in economics for coming up, in 1973, with an original argument. Options aren't gambling games, he said, they are *derivatives*. Merton's argument was highly mathematical, but the essence is simple. It is possible to re-create the option payoff by buying and selling the underlying security, and the return on that strategy can be computed in advance. Therefore, an option is just a convenient packaging of other financial transactions and should sell for the same price as the "replicating portfolio."

To see how this works, suppose the Yankees are playing the Braves in the World Series and it's tied 2-2. The first team to win four games wins the series. Therefore, whichever team wins two out of the next three games will win. A bettor approaches you and wants to bet $100 that the series will go the full seven games. Assuming you can bet on each individual game at even odds, what is the fair price for this bet?

You can bet $100 in the sixth game against whichever team wins the fifth game. If you lose that bet, the same team won the fifth and sixth games, the series is over in six games, and you don't have to pay off on the seven-game bet. If you win that bet, the series is tied 3-3 and will go to seven games. In that case you will have $200, so that is the fair payout for the seven-game bet. Figure 4.1 shows the results of betting on the fifth game. You end up with $0 if the series ends at six games and $200 if it goes to seven, just like making the seven-game bet.

Figure 4.1

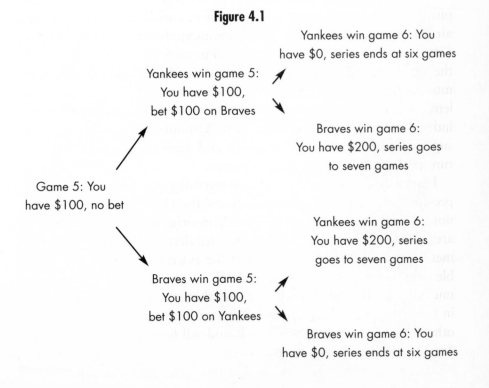

Yankees win game 6: You have $0, series ends at six games

Yankees win game 5: You have $100, bet $100 on Braves

Braves win game 6: You have $200, series goes to seven games

Game 5: You have $100, no bet

Yankees win game 6: You have $200, series goes to seven games

Braves win game 5: You have $100, bet $100 on Yankees

Braves win game 6: You have $0, series ends at six games

This seems similar to the argument that if each game is a 50/50 coin flip, the probability that the series will go to seven games is 0.5, so $200 is a fair payout for a $100 bet. But that argument is a gamble. It depends on the probability of each team winning, while Merton's argument depends instead on the betting odds, which do not have to be the same as the probabilities (although you wouldn't expect them to get too far out of line, or smart bettors could get rich). Moreover, the probability argument is just a long-run expected value; Merton's argument guarantees the bookie will have the $200 to pay off every time.

What if the betting line is not even? Suppose betting on the Braves pays 2:1 (for each $1 you bet, you win $2 more if you win) but Yankees bets pay 1:2 (for each $2 you bet, you get $1 more if you win). Now the hedge is a little more complicated. In the fifth game, you bet $25 on the Braves. If they win, you have $150, which you bet on the Yankees. If the Yankees win, so you have to pay off on the seven-game bet, you have $225. However, if the Yankees win the fifth game, you lose your $25 bet, so you have $75, which you bet on the Braves. If the Braves win the sixth game, so you have to pay off on the seven-game bet, you will have $225. So now the fair price for the seven-game bet is $225, and you still have no risk (see Figure 4.2).

This example may be a bit tedious to go through, and I've got some more coming up. But they are crucially important to understanding modern derivatives markets. If you can follow them in World Series betting, you know the basic principle that drives financial engineering.

Although no one seemed to notice it at the time, the riskless hedge argument was a complete reversal from all other financial markets. Insurance companies, stock exchanges, and foreign exchange and interest rate dealers all argued that their *customers* were not gambling. These financial institutions admitted that they acted as casinos, taking lots of bets from customers and relying on diversification to cancel most of the risk. But it wasn't evil gambling, even though it used the same principles, because the customers were engaging in prudent and socially useful activities.

The options markets ignored the question of what the customers were doing. They claimed that options weren't gambling because there was no gamble. The exchanges weren't acting like a casino, diversifying many customer bets. They were acting like a sports bookie, setting

Figure 4.2

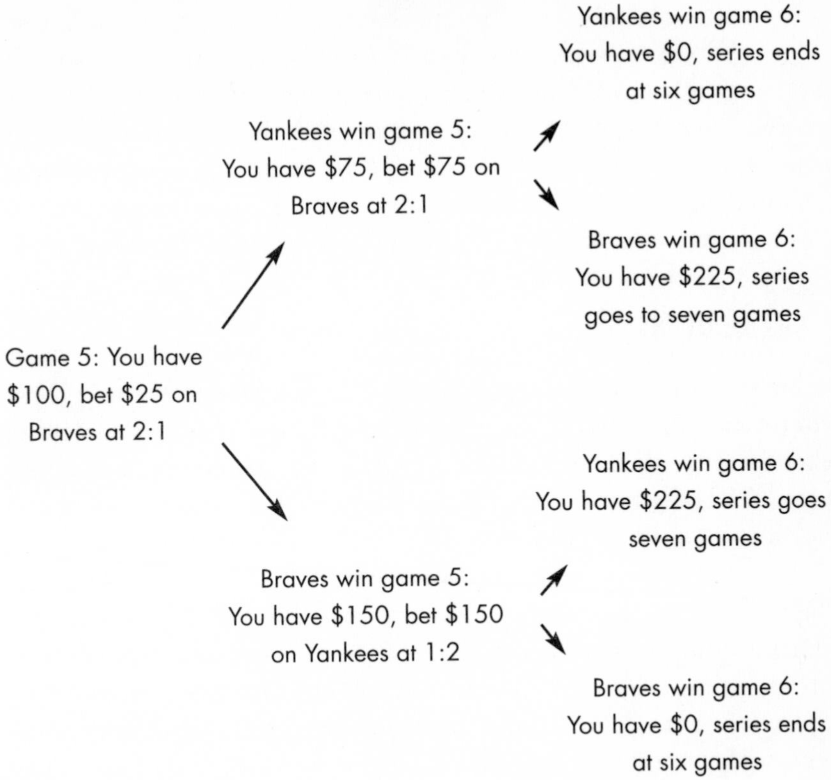

Yankees win game 6:
You have $0, series ends
at six games

Yankees win game 5:
You have $75, bet $75 on
Braves at 2:1

Braves win game 6:
You have $225, series
goes to seven games

Game 5: You have
$100, bet $25 on
Braves at 2:1

Yankees win game 6:
You have $225, series goes to
seven games

Braves win game 5:
You have $150, bet $150
on Yankees at 1:2

Braves win game 6:
You have $0, series ends
at six games

the line so that they made money whichever team won the game. Options dealers didn't care whether the stock went up or down, for the same reason a sports bookie doesn't care if the Yankees or the Braves win the World Series. As long as the bet amounts are equal on both sides, the exchange and the bookie make a riskless spread.

In one sense, this is a more honest argument. It doesn't invent silly nursery stories about what customers are doing. But in another sense, it's much more dangerous. It says that derivatives aren't gambling because there is no risk. Putting perfume on risk and calling it hedging is silly, but denying that it exists at all is insane.

The refusal to admit options were gambling led to the inevitable disaster. If you believe options are derivatives, then you can buy or sell any amount with no risk, as long as you offset the trades with borrowings and transactions in the underlying stock.

Remember, you quoted $225 for the $100 bet that the series would go seven games. You bet $25 on the Braves in the fifth game and lose. Now you have $75, which you expect to be able to bet at 2:1 on the Braves, so you win $225 if the series goes to seven games. But suppose when you try to place that bet you find out that the odds on the Braves have dropped down to even (1:1)? Now if you bet the $75 on the Braves you will get only $150 if they win, so you will take a $75 loss. If you don't know what the future betting odds will be, derivatives have risk.

THE CRASH OF '87

That big risk came home to roost on Monday, October 19, 1987. I was out of town at the time. My wife and I had decided to take a three-day weekend to hike through foliage and stay in an upstate inn. The previous week had been bad in the stock market, and there was a pronounced nervousness. On Friday morning, October 16, Deborah suggested that we sell our stock. I wanted to get away early to beat traffic, and I uttered the famous last words, "Let's talk about it on Tuesday."

I'm not going to talk about the complex causes of the crash, nor the frightening events of Tuesday, when the market almost failed completely. At the time, people focused on portfolio insurance, program trading, and lack of circuit breakers—none of which appear to have been significant factors, in retrospect. Underpriced put options, which led people to invest in the stock market without assuming risk, were vastly more important.

What is truly amazing is the sudden paradigm shift in all financial markets. From the first exchange-traded options in 1973 until October 16, 1987, all options on the same underlying for the same expiry date had been priced assuming the same-size move. If prices deviated a little bit, dealers came in and took advantage of the difference until it disappeared. This was true not just in the stock market; it held for commodity, interest rate, and foreign exchange options as well.

As soon as options resumed anything like normal trading—certainly by Thursday, October 22—that assumption had disappeared without a trace. It happened in all markets simultaneously, without comment or explanation. Now if the $20 put traded on one volatility assumption and the $25 call traded on a different one, nobody rushed in to take advantage of the "discrepancy." No one talked about it, but portfolios that had been treated as riskless a week earlier were assigned significant amounts of risk capital.

To see what I mean, let's go back to the example of betting on the World Series. Pre-1987, the assumption that you could get 2:1 odds betting on the Braves meant the seven-game bet was worth $225. The same assumption means a $100 bet on the Yankees to win the series should pay off $135. To match this payoff, you bet $40 on the Yankees to win game 5. If they win game 5, you bet $30 on them in game 6; otherwise, you bet $60. If the Yankees win games 5 and 6, you have $135. If they lose games 5 and 6, you have $0. If they split, you have $90, which you bet on the Yankees to win in game 7, collecting $135 if they do and nothing if they don't (see Figure 4.3).

Suppose that the seven-game bet paid $225, but betting on the Yankees to win the World Series paid $180 instead of $135. Precrash, everyone treated this as an opportunity. If the seven-game bet was priced correctly, betting on the Yankees to win the series was a great bet. If the Yankees series bet was correct, the seven-game bet should pay only $201, so getting $225 was good as well. To take maximum advantage, let's bet $1,500 on the Yankees to win, getting $2,700 if we are right, and $1,200 on the series to go seven games, also getting $2,700 if we are right. If we win one of the two bets, we break even. If the Yankees win in seven, we make $2,700. The only risk is if the Braves win in six, in which case we lose $2,700. But we don't want any risk. We're going to put together a hedging strategy to make sure we profit at least $500 whatever happens (see Figure 4.4).

Our hedge betting produces a profit of $3,200 when the Braves win in six. We lose both of our original bets, costing us $2,700, but our net profit in this case is $500. If the Yankees win in seven, we lose $2,200 from our hedge but win both our original bets, for a profit of $2,700. Again, we have a net profit of $500. In all other cases, we make $500 from our hedge and break even on the original bets. We have a riskless profit, an arbitrage. More important, we don't care what the odds are on Yankees-Braves games. We might change our initial bets and our hedging strategy as a result, but there's always an arbitrage profit when (a) you can bet on the Yankees to win the series at 0.8:1, (b) you can bet on a seven-game series at 1.25:1, and (c) you

Figure 4.3

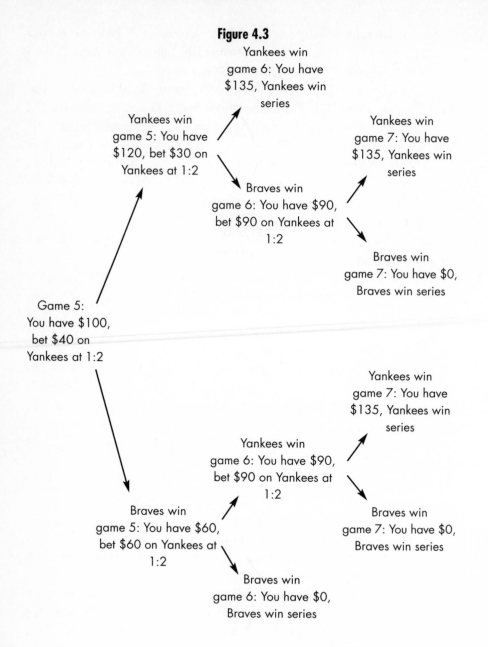

Yankees win game 6: You have $135, Yankees win series

Yankees win game 5: You have $120, bet $30 on Yankees at 1:2

Yankees win game 7: You have $135, Yankees win series

Braves win game 6: You have $90, bet $90 on Yankees at 1:2

Braves win game 7: You have $0, Braves win series

Game 5: You have $100, bet $40 on Yankees at 1:2

Yankees win game 7: You have $135, Yankees win series

Yankees win game 6: You have $90, bet $90 on Yankees at 1:2

Braves win game 5: You have $60, bet $60 on Yankees at 1:2

Braves win game 7: You have $0, Braves win series

Braves win game 6: You have $0, Braves win series

Figure 4.4

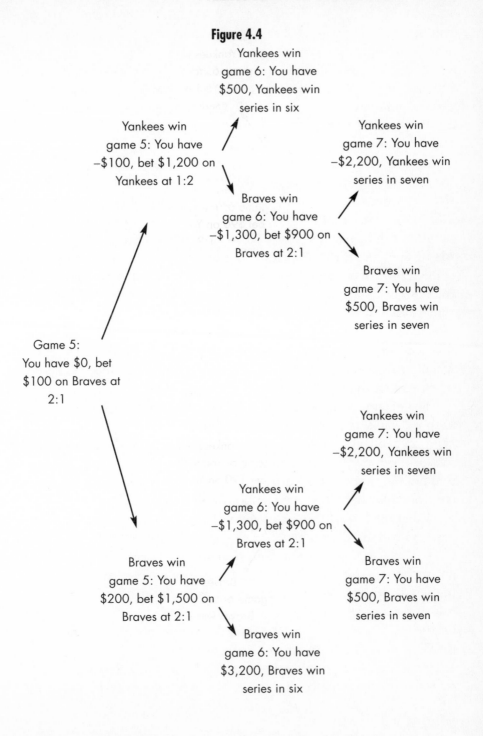

can bet on individual Yankees-Braves games all at the same odds. It was (c) that bit the market.

Of course, once you find something like this, you bet more and more, borrowing whatever money you can. That drives the profits down; instead of betting $2,700 to make $500, you're betting $5,400 to make $250, then $10,800 to make $125. The prices of the seven-game bet and the Yankees series bet get driven closer to theoretical parity.

Suppose you had been doing this for five years, doubling your bets for half the profit every year, until 1987. You've got to game 6 with the series tied 3-3, meaning your hedge has lost $1,300. Adding the cost of your original bets, you are $4,000 out of pocket. You don't mind that, however, because you've already won the seven-game bet for $2,700, and if the Yankees win game 7, you have another $2,700 coming in. You go to place your $900 bet on the Braves, only to be told the odds are no longer 2:1. The entire Yankee pitching staff came down with the flu and the betting odds on the Braves have moved to 1:2. The best you can do is bet $1,800 on the Braves and take a $400 loss whoever wins. Only by this time, it's not a $400 loss when you expected to make $500, it's 32 times the loss ($12,800) when you expected to make $\frac{1}{32}$ of the profit ($16).

The amazing thing was that as soon as this happened, the payouts snapped back to $180 and $225, and no one said anything about it being an arbitrage. Derivatives were gambles after all, and people got to work to monitor and manage the risk. The more accurate derivative pricing made the securities far more precise levers of financial control and ushered in a new era of financial engineering.

This is the closest thing to a miracle that I ever expect to see. The markets collapsed, completely and unexpectedly, but when the dust cleared, everything was rearranged in a stable formation. Imagine if an earthquake hit San Francisco and the Embarcadero floated into the bay to form a nice island with all the buildings intact—and the rest of the city slid around, but everything ended up in a convenient location. Then imagine no one talked about it; they just went about their business as if nothing had happened.

By the way, for people who want to go one more step in understanding financial math, there were two main quantitative solutions to the new derivative pricing problems. If we accept that it is correct to pay $180 for a $100 bet on the Yankees to win the series, and $225 for a bet that the series would go seven games, then we can explain things by assuming different odds for each game. In this case, if the Yankees are 2:1 favorites in games 5 and 6, but 1:3 underdogs in game 7 (perhaps the Braves' star pitcher will be ready for that one while the Yankees will have run out of rested starters). This is called *local volatility* because we know in advance the odds of every game, but they're not the same for all games.

The alternative is to assume that the game odds are partially random. We know the odds for game 5, but not for games 6 and 7. We might find that we have to place our bets at 3:1 or 1:1 for game 6— we don't know in advance. This is called *stochastic volatility*. Local volatility preserves the riskless hedge; it's more complicated, but there is one. Stochastic volatility means that the derivative is no longer a derivative—its price does not depend only on the underlying; it can move up or down on its own account. There is no more riskless hedge.

Although both these models are used in different areas of finance, they tend to give opposite recommendations for hedging and strategy. This has led to fruitful research into the nature of risk and unlimited employment opportunities for quants. Volatility does change, but it is neither stochastic nor predictable. Basic theoretical breakthroughs are needed before we will understand its nature. The grand unification challenge in theoretical finance is to come up with a model that aligns the predictions of local volatility models, stochastic volatility models, and actual future price movements (at the moment, neither model is good at that).

Of course, there were casualties of the 1987 crash. Some of the chess, poker, bridge, and backgammon players in the options markets lost most of their money; a lot of others lost as well. One particular story of relevance to poker concerns Roger Low, one of the three best backgammon players of the 1970s, who had been recruited in options trading by Ron Rubin, whose exciting story will be told in detail in Chapter 7. Roger had hired another backgammon champion, Erik Seidel. Both Roger and Erik tapped out big-time in the crash. Erik switched to poker and became one of the top players. Roger got off the trading floor and opened the Parallax hedge fund. Bridge champion Josh Parker also moved upstairs (that means he started trading large block orders over the telephone instead of smaller lots on the floor) and later joined the Gargoyle hedge fund with two other bridge champions. Mike Becker, also profiled in Chapter 7, struggled for a few years to help his traders survive, then moved to Florida to play tennis and golf. These were the three choices for games players in the 1990s and later: Move into more mainstream financial jobs, go back to making a living at games, or quit with the money you already made and do whatever you want. It's still helpful at many financial firms to have some serious games success on your resume, but it better be in the "hobbies and interests" section, and you have to make clear to most interviewers that you have put away childish things.

For financial quants, the revelation was that risk had a price. There was a stable, liquid, rational market for risk. Options weren't riskless, but they weren't incommutably dangerous, either. Finance was demonstrated to be gambling, which shook things up, but when the shaking stopped, it turned out to be possible to compute the odds. That made it a rational game that people could play with limited risk and reasonable odds of winning. That changed the world forever.

FLASHBACK

GARDENA AND THE SINGLE HETEROSEXUAL MALE

In June 1976, I walked into my first commercial poker establishment. There wasn't much commercial poker in those days. New Jersey would not approve casino gambling until November of that year. Nevada casinos offered poker, but it was a minor afterthought, and they enforced a 21-year-old age minimum. I was 19. There were legal games offered via various loopholes in different parts of the country— Indian reservations and casino boats and so on—but none of them attracted serious players from outside their immediate vicinity. The Mecca for commercial poker in those days was the Los Angeles suburb of Gardena, California.

No Stud-Horse Allowed

The close of the nineteenth century saw antigambling laws passed in all U.S. states and at the federal level. California's 1885 statute outlawed "banking and percentage games" and specified "faro, monte, roulette, lansquenet, rouge et noire, rondo, tan, fan-tan, stud-horse poker, seven-and-a-half, twenty-one, hokey-pokey." Unfortunately, this is the last recorded use of "stud-horse poker," except when quoting this statute. Based on a few citations from Colorado mining towns around 1880, it appears to have been a briefly and regionally popular casino game that used poker hands, possibly similar to the modern three-card poker. It was not a poker game.

The myth somehow arose that California prohibited stud poker as a game of chance, but allowed draw poker as a game of skill. This is not true, and in any event, the distinction between skill and chance is not relevant under California law, although it figures in common municipal statutes. The clear intention of the 1885 statute is to outlaw gambling as a business, while allowing private groups of citizens to gamble.

Nevertheless, when the city of Gardena decided to allow commercial card rooms in 1931, it specified only draw poker. Possibly, the town counsel at the time misinterpreted the state statute. His real legal master-stroke to evade the spirit of the law is that the house charged by time played; it did not take a percentage of the pot. Legally, the card rooms claimed they were renting seats. What players did at the table was their own business. It didn't hurt that the American Legion and Veterans of Foreign Wars ran three of the six establishments. Posts of these organizations escaped liquor, cabaret, and gambling laws all over the country.

Robert called the place "Gardena of Eden" for its primacy in American poker at the time. He was a lawyer from San Francisco who had paid his way through Stanford by managing a poker room. He had started as a player and moved up to dealer and then manager. But in Gardena card rooms the quality of the top level of play was much higher. Robert was a consistent winner in San Francisco, but could not hold his own at the top-limit Gardena games ($100/$200 with a $2,000 minimum buy-in at the time, $350/$700 in 2005 dollars). I had met him at a private game in Boston the previous year. I played well that night, and he suggested I go west to test my skills.

I had a place to stay, since my brother Daniel was a student at Cal Tech at the time. The school is in Pasadena, about 25 miles northeast of Gardena. But it still took me over a year to get from campus to card room. I found a Cal Tech student named Tom to go with me. He claimed to be a regular player, but I started losing confidence when he pronounced the place "Gardenia," like the flower, or perhaps he thought it was a Spanish name, "Gardeña." However, he knew the way to the Horseshoe. We were denied admittance because I had no proof of age—or none that would prove I was 21. We drove to the El Dorado, where no one checked. Tom and I walked up to the boardman and asked for seats. Mine was available immediately; Tom's initials were put on the board to wait for an opening.

The Subculture

I played regularly enough, at high enough stakes, to recognize some of the players and employees. I tried a few other card rooms, but spent most of my time at the El Dorado. I didn't try the Horseshoe again, but no other card room asked for proof of age.

I did find my expert players eventually. One of the best at that time was Crazy Mike. That's not a made-up nickname; that's what everyone called him. If that makes you think of a cheerful eccentric, always joking around, you're mistaken. His manner suggested serious clinical issues, and his play was wildly erratic. He was among the best players I've ever seen, but I honestly didn't think it was an act, and I still don't know for sure. Anyway, he apparently calmed down, because people now call him the "Mad Genius" and tell jokes about his antics. I was shocked to recognize his picture about 15 years later as Mike Caro, the celebrity player and author.

Oddly enough, I met another great player who wrote a poker book. I don't know if Gardena in 1976 was like Paris in the 1920s, or if I was just lucky. This guy was called "One-Armed Bandit" or just "The Arm." He was a Japanese man about 30, with an extremely aggressive style and manner. He bet a lot of hands and picked up a lot of antes and small pots. When I met him, I was surprised to see he had both his arms. Playing him, it was later explained to me, was like pulling the arm on a slot machine. He usually took your money, but once in a while you could hit the jackpot. I didn't see him pay off many jackpots.

I got a little friendly with The Arm because we shared an interest in poker theory. Casual acquaintances at Gardena would often tell you quite a bit about themselves, often more than was usual in the outside world, but questions were discouraged strongly. People told what they wanted, and nothing more. So I met a lot of people, but learned few last names. I got a blow-by-blow description of one guy's divorce, and I didn't even learn his *first* name. He went by "Blackie," but he wasn't black.

The Arm told me he was an "autoethnographer." That doesn't make a lot of sense. Ethnographers write about specific human cultures, typically in places like Papua New Guinea, where The Arm would later make his professional reputation. So an autoethnographer writes about his own culture, but that's just a writer. I didn't take it seriously, but six years later he came out with the book *Poker Faces*, with me in it. He analyzed the Gardena poker players as a separate culture, beginning slyly with a quote from Marco Polo: "and I only wrote half of what I saw." And he put *autoethnographer* in the dictionary.

The roots of the Gardena culture are in something sociologists call the single heterosexual male subculture. All complex societies develop these for men who do not settle down with women and raise families. Sometimes these groups are needed for wars or settling frontiers; in other times they hang around poolrooms and racetracks and bars and social clubs and volunteer fire departments, or whatever the local equivalents are. They live in single-room-occupancy hotels or barracks or YMCAs or cheap apartments or self-built cabins in the woods. Young unmarried men often spend some years in this culture, and older married men often visit for an evening. There are females associated with this subculture— sometimes they are prostitutes or other sex workers, other times they own and run the gathering places, or they can just live on the periphery of the culture. Males will have sex with them, and the subculture supports them economically, but they do not enter into traditional monogamous mutual-support arrangements.

The "heterosexual" part does not refer to what the men do in the bedroom or bus station restroom, still less to what they lust for in their hearts. It just means the culture is not supportive of homosexuality. It's not a good place for one romantic young man to find another—sexual taboos are if anything stronger than in mainstream society. You can be a homosexual, but don't let anyone catch you practicing. Anyway, homosexuals often have a separate subculture that better meets their needs. Although sex data are notoriously unreliable, what empirical evidence there is suggests the incidence of homosexuality in this subculture is lower than in the population as a whole.

Gardena had advanced from that subculture in several respects. First of all, maybe 10 percent of the players and a third of the employees were female. Second—and this is a point I think The Arm and other researchers missed—it was very intense. It's true that people went out to dinner, and watched sporting events on TV, and chatted a little; also there were various hangers-on and railbirds watching the action. But for the most part, people came to play poker. They played with speed and concentration, something people don't do when the results don't matter. Bars don't charge rent for their stools; regulars can nurse drinks as long as they want. You can hang around all day at a racetrack, and all day and all night at a social club. Most of the people in a poolroom are not shooting pool at any given time. But in Gardena, you played poker seriously.

Still, the similarities were greater than the differences. A loan shark, a fence, and a bookie, along with the other usual cast of characters, were available in every card room. There were the same social rules, quick friendships in which people revealed only the part of themselves they chose. There was no expectation that even a close card room acquaintance had the right to ask questions or give advice. There was the same indiscriminate mixing of social classes and manners, and the same timeless sense that the place existed in a different dimension from the everyday world.

I'm not going to tell you that I understand everything about Gardena on the basis of a few dozen visits, reading some academic studies, and talking to some regulars. I'm just going to argue that you can understand some otherwise puzzling facts about the place if you think of poker as a financial institution rather than a card or gambling game.

All human activities have layers of meaning. If you ask why someone got married, the answer could be couched in terms of evolutionary biology, cultural anthropology, or economics; or you could say they fell in love or she got tired of dating or he had a shotgun at his back. All these answers can be true at once on different levels. Evolutionary biology might explain why marriage rates go up when there is a relative shortage of young men, as after a war. Cultural anthropology might explain why people marry at younger ages in rural areas than they do in urban areas. Economics might explain how increasing participation by women in the paid workforce affects the median age differential between husband and wife. The individual factors might explain why Harry married Sally. And neither Harry nor Sally needs to know or care about the explanations.

Similarly, if you asked why the poker was so intense and the stakes so high in Gardena, there are many answers from "the players like it that way" to theories based on sociology, psychology, or economics. I'm going to address only the economics. The other approaches may be true as well, and understanding them may help you in poker or in life. But you'll have to read about them in other books.

Never Ask of Money Spent, Where the Spender Thinks It Went

California poker rooms have been studied more intensely than any other gambling culture. I think it has to do with the number of nearby universities and the extraordinary education levels of a significant minority of the players. All that observation and data have failed to examine the financial aspects of Gardena, but they can still help us pinpoint who brought money in and who took it out.

To see the big picture, start with a simplified breakdown of the Gardena poker economy in a snapshot view. The proportions of different types of players varied throughout the day and year. You got different mixes at 10:00 A.M. on Christmas morning than at 4:00 A.M. on a Tuesday in June than at 10:00 P.M. on an October Friday. Things also changed over the years and, to a lesser extent, among different card rooms. At an average time, for example, about 70 percent of the players were at least somewhat familiar to the boardman; 30 percent were newcomers or people who played very rarely. However, that 30 percent represents many more individuals than the 70 percent, because the 30 percent changed all the time, while the 70 percent had a half-life of about four years (that is, if you look at the regulars today and four years from today, about half the group will be the same people). The numbers here include all the people in the card room—employees and railbirds as well as players—at an imaginary average point frozen in time. (See Figure 4.5.)

At the top of the social hierarchy, about 2 percent played for high stakes and were perceived as winning consistently. An equal-sized group played for high stakes but played wildly and lost consistently. These people were by far the biggest losers in the card room. Call the first group the winners and the second the action players. For every winner there were five people, 10 percent of the total population, who played in the high-stakes games and were perceived as break-even or losing players. They played more conservatively than the action players and lost less when they lost. I'll call these break-even players. So a typical high-stakes table had one winner, one action player, and five break-even players. Another group, about the same size as the break-even players, won consistently, but at lower stakes. These subsistence players sometimes exchanged places with the break-even group.

Figure 4.5

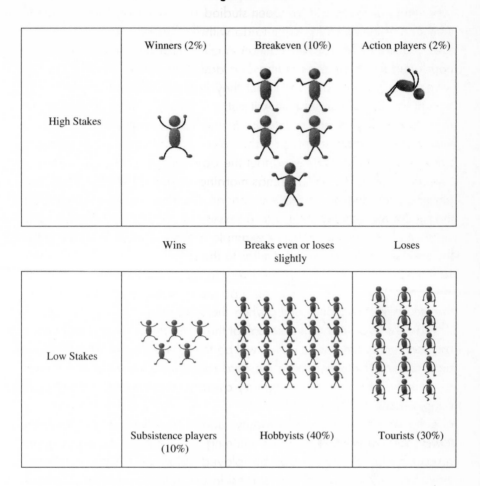

At the bottom of the hierarchy was the 30 percent consisting of strangers, or tourists. As a group, they lost even more consistently than the action players. In between were the 40 percent perceived as breakeven or losing regular players at lower stakes. Call these the hobbyists. That leaves 6 percent for nonplayers. Of course, these are just rough estimates of a typical card room at a typical time. These groups are not well defined, except for the action players. The others fade into each other by degrees, and players move among them.

Money flows from the right-hand column to the left, from tourists to subsistence players and from action players to winners. The middle column contributes slightly to the left as well. Subsistence players in the lower left sometimes move back and forth with break-even players in the upper middle; this moves money from low-stakes games to high. Otherwise, most players tend to stay in their boxes, although a few tourists become hobbyists or subsistence players, or even move up to become break-even players and winners. Occasionally, people move down as well, although most people prefer to leave rather than accept a reduced status.

In the 1970s, a typical club had gross revenue of about $5 million per year, mostly from the seat charges but with some contribution from the sale of food and drink. It was home to about 10 winners and 50 subsistence players—the winners taking home about $50,000 per year and the subsistence players about $10,000 each, for a total of $1 million. The poverty line in 1975 was $5,050 for a family of four, and the median family income was $13,719. However, for reasons we will see, the incomes of the successful players were higher than they seemed.

That makes $6 million for card room revenue and winnings that had to be made up by the losers. I said there were typically about 50 subsistence players per card room, and at any given time there were about five times as many break-even players and hobbyists. But that represents many more people—say, 1,000 instead of 250—because the second group played about a quarter as many hours per week. There were three times as many tourists as subsistence players at any time, but that represents an even greater multiplier—say, 5,000 people instead of 150. There's really no way to know the difference between four people who come in once each and one person who comes in four times per year, especially if she visits different card rooms. These people had to contribute an average of $1,000 each. The actual amounts varied wildly. Some tourists showed up once and won, and some break-even players had a substantial profit for the year. Other players dropped $10,000 or more.

If you measure over a shorter interval than a year, you get more total wins and losses. For example, if you stood outside the cashier's cage and measured the total wins and losses of every player over every session for a year, you would get something like $100 million won and $105 million lost. Since any given player will win or lose on different sessions, a lot of that money gets offset to total the $1 million won and $6 million lost over the year. This is what makes it so hard for a poker player to tell whether she is a winner or a loser, and still harder to see whether another player is winning or losing. Measured over hands, the numbers are probably another 20 times larger—$2 billion won and $2.006 billion lost, if you add up the money won and lost on every pot.

A Miniature Global Economy Laid Out on a Baize Oval Table

If we view Gardena as a financial institution, we want to know the capital ratio: How much actual cash were players willing to lose, versus how much of the floating pool of wins and losses was available for productive economic activity? A bank, for example, might lend out $12 for every $1 it has in capital. It can do that because the money lent out is either spent or redeposited in the banking system. If it's spent, it will again be either spent or redeposited. Every dollar lent out comes back in as a deposit, so it can be lent again. In theory you could use $1 of capital to fund every loan in the world (and people have tried that), but in practice you need to keep enough capital back in case someone wants to make a withdrawal. In fact, you need to keep enough capital so that everyone has complete confidence they can make a withdrawal whenever they want, or there will be a run on the bank and you will have no liquid capital left. In most countries today, the capital ratio is monitored by bank regulators, and the government guarantees the deposits.

It's important to understand that the money created by bank multiplication is real money—it has the same economic effect as if it were bills or coins. Only if the banking system fails does it disappear. A bank creates economic activity by using $1 of risk capital to fund $12 of productive loans. It can be profitable. The 1970s version of the 9-6-3 rule in banking is to lend money at 9 percent, pay depositors 6 percent, and be on the golf course by 3 P.M. If you start a bank with $100 in capital, lend out $1,200, make a 3 percent lending spread or $36, you have a 36 percent return on your $100 investment, and you get to tee off before the course gets crowded.

It's actually not quite that easy, but banks can make a lot of money. It's not just banks that create money. The economist John Kenneth Galbraith pointed out the economic importance of what he named the "bezzle," the total amount of money embezzled at any point in time. Since both the embezzler (correctly) and the embezzlee (incorrectly) think they have the money, both will live and spend accordingly. As long as the embezzlement is undiscovered, there is more money in the world. When it is discovered, it has a depressing effect on the economy out of proportion to its amount, because embezzlers tend to be dynamic spenders and wised-up embezzlees tend to the opposite extreme.

To figure the card room's capital, we can ignore the tourists, action players, and hobbyists. These groups were losing about as much as they were willing to lose. If they lost faster, they would just leave earlier. The card room itself was not willing to lose: If profits declined, it would change management or close. Even though card rooms financed 25 percent of Gardena's city budget, they couldn't count on any government or other external support.

Winners would probably play until they lost their entire bankrolls, which I would estimate at half a year's income, or $250,000. The subsistence and break-even players would quit before losing that much, so maybe they would kick in another $250,000 among them. If the entire $2 billion of hand wins and losses were available for productive investment, I estimate the card room had a capital ratio of 0.025 percent. Each dollar of risk capital generated $4,000 of hand wins and losses. Obviously, not all the $2 billion is available for economic activity, and there's a tremendous amount of guesswork in that estimate. But it's apparent that the card room operated on less than 1 percent of the capital of even a shaky bank. This, of course, is its economic appeal to people who are short of money.

This level of capital ratio is not unknown in economic history. For more than a century, the southern and western United States had soft money banks. These banks would take in small amounts of capital and lend it out 100 or 1,000 times. They failed frequently, but they also did more to develop the natural resources of North America than the hard money banks. Soft money banks arose spontaneously when people gathered on the frontier. They lent the money needed for development.

If the town succeeded, the bank prospered and became a hard money bank. The investors who had put up the bank's risk capital became extremely wealthy. If the town failed, pretty much everyone went away broke, anyway. The only difference is that with the soft money bank, there was a chance to succeed. If regulation had insisted on 8 percent capital ratios, no one would have supplied capital to start a bank. Note that the California poker card rooms began and gambling was legalized in Nevada at the same time Congress effectively outlawed soft money banks.

Nor Tie to Earths to Come, nor Action New

One clue to how the Gardena bank worked is the action players. Why did these people come back day after day and lose money? They were not bad players—at least not all of them. They often were big winners for a night, since wild play can lead to large wins. I also noticed that many of them were experts at other games, like bridge or chess, something that was not common in the card room. Despite their skill, they provided the lion's share of the losses that kept the community going and a substantial portion of the large pots. They played like gamblers, not like poker players.

Every action player I ever met at Gardena was a professional or owned a local small business. Academic studies make the same point, although no one seems to have considered the obvious implication. I didn't see all the action players do business at the card room, but I know many regulars went to the auto repair shops, appliance outlets, and clothing stores owned by action players. Others rented apartments from them or did casual work for their companies. If you saw the movie *Rounders,* think Joey Knish, the character played by John Turturro. There were card room doctors, dentists, lawyers, and accountants.

Any community needs merchants, professionals, employers, and landlords, and Gardena players had special needs. Many, especially among the subsistence players, first came to the card room after a traumatic life event: divorce, job loss, bankruptcy, or health problem. This trauma could leave them with debts, tax liens, and no credit. Making some cash off the books in casual labor and spending it with merchants who didn't ask questions could be extremely convenient. The employer and the merchant could save on taxes, possible royalty payments, and investor paybacks. Professionals could get business without the credentials and office overhead necessary to compete for non-poker-playing clients. Both parties to these transactions knew where to find each other and valued their respective standings in the Gardena community. A poker-playing landlord could trust a subsistence player because he could collect the rent whenever the tenant had a good night—if necessary, whenever the tenant had a good hand. The player might be over her head in debt and a long-term loser, but she's still going to walk out some nights, or at least finish some pots, with a few months' rent in cash. As long as you're the first to get to her, you collect. But an outside collection agent will have no success.

Leaving your money in the poker game was sort of like depositing it in a bank. It had the advantage of being private, tax free, and creditor proof. It had the disadvantage of being uncertain. Imagine if you tried to withdraw money from a normal bank, and the teller pulled out a deck of cards and started dealing to determine whether you got your money. That would be inconvenient, but it would keep you safe from court-ordered withdrawal to pay your creditors. Even the IRS couldn't go into a Gardena card room and demand your back taxes from people to whom you had lost money at poker. And since you deposit money on the same terms, half the time you win and get the money credited to your account and keep the cash; on average, you break even.

Well, okay, you don't break even unless you're an above-average player. The house takes a cut. But Swiss banks at the time offered similar services for rich people with numbered accounts. Those accounts paid a negative interest rate. Regular banks pay positive interest, but will hand over your account information and cash to anyone waving a court order.

To ease the inconvenience of not always getting your money back, many Gardena players relied on card room loans. These were always done at no interest (the loan shark was not a poker player and offered an entirely different deal).

Losing players for the session would search the card rooms for winners, with whom they had borrowed and lent before. Money was available based on presumed solvency and poker-playing ability. If a guy had shown up four times a week for the last three years, and bought $2,000 worth of chips each time, and seemed to win more than he lost, he could borrow money. If he started owing too much or paying back too slowly, or stopped showing up or buying so many chips, or seemed to be losing too much, the credit disappeared. Trust was not based on income or assets, as in a normal credit transaction, but on variability. If someone had money at least some of the time, which he would as long as he could get credit and wasn't a terrible player, he could be trusted, so he could get credit. Gamblers devote the kind of effort to keep gambling as home owners devote to keep their houses. It is a strong and ancient bond, worthy of respect from any financial credit professional. Many regulars owed tens of thousands of dollars to some players, while they were owed tens of thousands of dollars by others.

The house was also a source of credit, selling chips without immediate cash payment to some regulars in defiance of the law. Regular players could also count on being hired as shills or proposition players, and sometimes they could get jobs like Robert did. The whole system was set up to conserve the small amount of available capital, so everyone could get by.

You Took Little Children Away from the Sun and the Dew . . . for a Little Handful of Pay on a Few Saturday Nights

Some of the hobbyists made use of the card room economy. For others, poker seemed mostly a social activity. The house seemed to value them, striving to make them comfortable and keep them from going to rival card rooms. Although they didn't lose much as a group, they kept games going consistently for tourists who might walk in, and they used the restaurant steadily, which kept overhead down. Also, the card rooms seemed anxious to preserve a friendly image, advertising good meals and companionship rather than excitement and sex, like Las Vegas did at the time. If the hobbyists went away, the card rooms might look more threatening to the city of Gardena.

Both subsistence players and hobbyists tended to be older—most were over 65. They had some kind of outside income, which they supplemented through poker (subsistence players) or from which they funded poker as an entertainment expense. My guess is that these groups combined gained much more than they spent at Gardena. For one thing, they could take advantage of the tax-free discount goods and services available from other players. For another, they could spend all day socializing in comfortable surroundings with moderately priced meals, without the expenditure for front (clean clothes, a decent apartment, etc.) required in other social situations.

In Las Vegas, the loser is king. Casinos fall all over themselves to offer airplane tickets, free rooms and food, fancy shows, and other inducements to losers. That's why it seems odd that Gardena treated the tourists badly. There was no effort to attract them or to turn them into regulars, and no concern if they disappeared or went to a rival card room. The clubs don't run beginner's classes or other things to make it more comfortable to play. Gardena is not a place to play poker for fun.

Perhaps the clubs have figured out that it's too expensive to compete for tourists. These players generate steady profits, but they seem to come without encouragement. The biggest reason casinos lose money (yes, casinos often lose money) is that they go crazy competing for the losers. A monopoly casino, or a small group that cooperates to restrain competition, is a much better investment.

To complete the contrast with Las Vegas, the card rooms cater to winners as if they were star athletes. Las Vegas sets the rules to prevent winning. If someone outsmarts them—for example, by card counting in blackjack—the casinos do everything they can to exclude them. In Gardena, winners are treated with extra consideration, they are lent money or given employment as house players if they fall on hard times, and they get the most favorable rulings from floormen. If a winner considers changing card rooms after a bad spell, the house will bend over backward to prevent it, including offering to forgive all debts. Las Vegas does that only for losers.

Winners help the club's reputation, of course, which does attract some long-distance players (like me). But their main function is to protect the community from tourists. Most tourists can be handled by the hobbyists. If they start to win, the subsistence pros can take over. But if that doesn't work, each card room needs to have some of the top players in the world to bring in. The house may not rearrange seating to accomplish this, but if a tourist keeps winning, he will come up against his match. If that weren't true, top poker players from all over the world would keep showing up in Gardena until the game had such negative expectation to the community that it would fall apart. The winners are the hired guns elected sheriff to keep other gunmen away.

The most influential theorists in poker today—David Sklansky, Mason Malmuth, and Mike Caro, for example—made their names in these card rooms. This explains the focus on beating individual opponents. That was their main job. They could accept high-variance, random-walk results because they were embedded in a secure credit system (not secure like a portfolio of AAA bonds and a vault filled with gold, but secure enough to mean that if their abilities kept up, they would always have a stake). They didn't have to worry about the larger economic infrastructure; the card room did that for them.

This kind of environment makes for superlatively refined one-on-one competitive skills, but not the kind of balanced outlook needed in other poker situations. This isn't to say that the theorists don't have that balanced outlook, just that Gardena did nothing to encourage developing it.

Winners are mainly younger men, almost always divorced or never married. They are the best-educated group within the community. Unlike most of the other regulars, who have arrived at their destinations in life and will likely go down rather than up in the future, winners are usually on their way to something. Some want to become more successful professionals; others want to write books, or finish school, or invent something. Another reason the house is nice to them is that they leave sooner than other regulars, so they must be constantly replaced.

The biggest demographic difference between the winners and the break-even players is that the latter group is mostly married and includes some women. They also tend to be a bit older, less well educated, and less ambitious. Some of them may move up to become winners (also true of a few subsistence players), but most will not. Some make substantial income in private poker games and use high-stakes Gardena games to hone their skills. Others seem to be keeping one foot in the Gardena community as an escape route if the other part of their life turns bad.

This overall picture may be pretty depressing. The tourists are fleeced, and the hobbyists are just passing time away in windowless smoke-filled rooms with a red light every half hour to mean money is due. The subsistence players are eking out a very marginal living, and the action players are keeping noncompetitive businesses afloat with cheating. The break-even players are devoting tremendous skill and energy, and losing money in the process. Only the winners seem to have a good deal, and they are mostly trying to get somewhere else. However, consider the alternatives for many of these people.

We're going to dig a bit deeper into the poker economy, to find less depressing niches that make it work at least as well as your local bank, for you and for the community at large.

CHAPTER 5

Pokernomics

*How Poker and Modern Derivatives Were Born
in a Jambalaya of Native American and West
African River Traders, Heated by Unlimited
Opportunity and Stirred with a Scotch Spoon*

Everything I have ever found useful in economics I've read in two
books. Both were written by people with sophisticated mathematical skills, theoretical and practical, yet both use only simple qualitative arguments. They are deceptively deep, easily understood on
first reading by people without prior knowledge of economics, but
full of additional insight to experts upon careful rereading. John
Law's 1705 work, *Money and Trade Considered with a Proposal for
Supplying the Nation with Money,* is the clearest statement of the
economic question, and 290 years later Fischer Black's *Exploring
General Equilibrium* gave the answer. In between, you will find some
brilliant writing and clever reasoning, and their opposites as well, but
nothing I have personally been able to apply with profit. This isn't a
point I care to argue. If someone else finds practical guidance in the
works of Adam Smith or Karl Marx or John Maynard Keynes or any
other economist, I'm happy for them.

John Law died over two centuries before I was born, but I did know
Fischer Black (who, sadly, died of throat cancer in his 50s, shortly after
completing his masterwork). Black contributed pathbreaking papers
to almost every area of finance and was one of the people most
responsible for two of the most important models in finance: the
Capital Asset Pricing Model and the Black-Scholes-Merton option
pricing model. Black was the only common denominator (William

Sharpe, Jack Treynor, and John Lintner were the other three CAPM originators).

In addition to his academic successes, Black ran the Quantitative Research group at the investment bank Goldman Sachs. When you met him, you quickly realized that he was either crazy or a genius, perhaps both. He would talk to you only as long as he was interested, then, in the words of a friend of mine, "He could hang up the phone on you while speaking in person." Black spent all his time writing short notes on ideas that occurred to him, then inserting them carefully into his massive filing system. His book *Exploring General Equilibrium* is deeply eccentric: He states his case in a few pages, then devotes the rest of the book to two- and three-paragraph refutations of professional economists, in alphabetical order by economist last name, straight from the filing cabinet. Law's book also is clearly written in refutation of other ideas. Both men grasped simple truths and explained them clearly, without embellishment. The reason they had to write books instead of pamphlets or manifestos was to separate their ideas from superficially similar popular misconceptions.

I am not antieconomist. Some of my best friends are economists. Professional economists are often very smart people who ask interesting questions and can come up with good answers. Studying economics might help train their minds for that, if you think of the field as a disciplined approach to investigating history and current events. Like astrologers of centuries past, they have to be smart and disciplined enough to master the science and mathematics required for their craft, and they have to be shrewd analysts to make a living, because their fundamental theory is wrong. If you look in economics for theoretical clarity that will help you get rich, or manage a nation's economy, or predict the outcomes of various actions, I think you will be as disappointed as if you had consulted a horoscope. Anyway, I was.

LAW AND MONEY

John Law lived from 1671 to 1729. He was an interesting guy. He was born in Scotland and for most of his life made his living as a professional gambler. As a young man, he moved to England to get more gambling action. In 1694 he was sentenced to death for killing a noted young dandy of the times, Edward Wilson, in a duel. The nature of the quarrel has been lost to history, but the men were rivals for fashionable attention, and Wilson's sister had lived in the same rooming house as Law. Law escaped from prison and fled to the continent, where he began developing his ideas on economics.

He had a great reputation as a philanderer, but in Paris he formed a lifelong partnership with Elizabeth Knowles, an intelligent and outspoken woman who may share credit for many of his ideas. Certainly his work reached full flower after he met her; his practical successes occurred when she was by his side and ended when he was forcibly separated from her. Elizabeth was a descendent of the Tudor royal family and was married to someone else when she met Law (and afterward—she never divorced her husband). It may not be much of a distinction today for a commoner and professional gambler to play house with a member of the British royal family or to be accepted socially while living in open adultery, but these things mattered more in 1700.

When reading about Law, it's impossible to overlook how much people liked him. That's not surprising when things were going well, but even when imprisoned under sentence of death and much later, after financial disaster, he had no trouble attracting and retaining friends in all walks of life, despite barriers of class, religion, nationality, and profession.

In stark contrast, the twice-divorced Fischer Black appeared to be cold and friendless, although a masterful biography by Barnard economics professor Perry Mehrling demonstrates that Black had many quietly intense deep friendships (the highest praise for a biographer is that even if you knew the subject, you didn't really know him until you read the book). Black resembled Law in sexual habits, but differed in having an aversion to all forms of gambling.

Law's modus operandi was to arrive in a new city and be seen in the most fashionable spots. He was witty, charming, athletic, handsome, informed about the world, and beautifully dressed. He would hook up with a fashionable actress or courtesan and give gambling parties in her apartments. Law acted as bank, accepting all bets from guests. He always had large bags jingling with gold coins to reassure players. Call me suspicious, but I've always assumed Law's relationship with the hostesses was commercial, not sexual, and that the jingling bags contained a lot less gold than was suggested by their size and weight.

Although Law played all the popular games of the time, he was most famous for faro. In the modern form of this game, players place their bets on a board with pictures of the 13 different card ranks. In Law's day, players actually took up to three cards and placed bets on each. The dealer, who acted as bank, would then take a second deck with all 52 cards in it, shuffle, and burn the top card (show it and place it face up on the bottom of the deck).

The next 48 cards of the deck were dealt two at a time. The first card was the dealer's, and he won all bets placed on cards of that rank (suits do not matter in faro). The second card was the player's, and the dealer paid on all bets placed on cards of that rank. The entire advantage to the bank arises when both cards have the same rank. In that case, the stakes bet on those cards were "held." They remained in play, but if they later won for the player, he received only his stake back; the bank did not have to match it. If the bank won, it would take the stake as usual. This gives the bank a 0.5 percent edge. Three things have to happen for the dealer to save a stake: 1 time in 17 a pair is dealt, 1 time in 3 this happens before another card of that rank is dealt (actually 36 percent due to the burn card and the fact that the last three cards are not dealt), and 1 time in 2 the player wins the held stake. Because $17 \times 3 \times 2 = 102$, 1 percent of the time the dealer doesn't have to pay a winning player. The player wins 49 percent of the time, 1 percent of the time he gets his stake back, and 50 percent of the time the dealer wins. Players would also bet on the order of the last three cards. There are six possible orders (the first card can be any of three, the next can be either of the remaining two, then the last card is determined—$3 \times 2 = 6$).

Law won consistently at a game that is closest to fair—something few could do. While the bank has a small edge, it requires a great many bets of roughly equal size for that to overwhelm the variability in outcome. That's why faro did not succeed in casinos, even though they usually doubled the bank's advantage by taking the stake when a pair was dealt. It is extremely easy for the dealer to cheat in faro by dealing seconds (looking at the top card and dealing the second-to-top card instead, if that is favorable). Although it's certainly possible that Law cheated, my guess, based on his personality and talents, is that he made his real living on proposition bets (bets on specific propositions made up at the time). This is where his shrewdness and mathematical talents would give him the advantage, and this is how most honest professional gamblers win.

Cheater or not, Law would soon win enough that people stopped playing against him, so he would move on to the next city. Before doing that, however, he would discuss economics with the leading local experts and political authorities. This led him to become the most sought-after economic advisor in Europe. Eventually he was entrusted with running the economy of France. He did this so successfully that the word *millionaire* was invented to describe all the people he had made rich. Before Law, there were not enough of them to require a word. The boom was followed by a stunning crash. Law was blamed for this, as well as for the contemporaneous South Sea Bubble in England. However, his ideas continued to be studied and emerged a half century later embedded in much more elaborate frameworks of political and moral reasoning that developed into modern economics. Twenty years ago he was thought of more as a con man than an economic genius, but his reputation has improved remarkably. He is now considered an important early influence on economic thought, with ideas that might have worked except for the corruption and despotism in France at the time.

I think even more of him. I think his ideas did work and led to both the invention of poker and the economic growth of the United States. Law discovered the secret to getting rich, but it threatened established political institutions. His revolutionary idea could flower only far away from governments. It gained enormous power when combined with another secret—the network economy. This was developed by the American Indians living near the Mississippi River and its tributaries. It was not the system of a single tribe or family of tribes but covered intertribal exchange throughout the entire area drained by the Mississippi River and had influence beyond, west of the Rockies and in the Great Lakes region. It was the most sophisticated economy in the world in the sixteenth century, and it functioned entirely without money. By the eighteenth century, disease (primarily smallpox brought from Europe) had wiped out three-fourths of the Indian population, but memory of network economy principles remained, stimulated both by Law's innovations and by the importation of West Africans who had developed their own river-based exchange systems.

DUTCH TREAT

Law's reasoning began with the question of why Scotland was so poor and Holland was so rich. Scotch poverty meant prices of land, labor, and other economic inputs were low in Scotland, so the country should be able to produce outputs more cheaply than Holland. Yet Dutch traders consistently undersold Scottish ones, and Scots wanted to buy lots of things from Holland, while the Dutch found nothing they wanted in Scotland. This is one of the basic questions of economics: Why does regional poverty—and personal poverty, for that matter—not self-correct?

His first answer was that there was not enough money in Scotland. Most trading was done by barter, meaning that goods were exchanged directly for other goods rather than bought and sold for money. Law wrote (I have modernized the language in this and subsequent quotes):

> The state of barter was inconvenient, and disadvantageous. He who desired to barter would not always find people who wanted the goods he had, and had such goods as he desired in exchange. Contracts taken payable in goods were uncertain, for goods of the same kind differed in value. There was no measure by which the proportion of value goods had to one another could be known.

Many other writers made these same points, but Law inverted the usual meaning. Economists generally assume that people want to trade in order to raise their overall level of consumption, so the lack of money frustrates them because it makes exchange inefficient. Law would be more at home in a modern business school, where students learn to "sell the sizzle, not the steak," and that the customer purchase experience can be more important than the product. Starbucks is not taking over the world because people always wanted to drink more coffee but it wasn't available. People trade when it's fun, and they don't trade when it isn't. Trade induces economic activity, so people have more things to trade.

Empirically, it is clear that when more money is available, more economic activity results. It could be that people want to trade in order to raise their level of consumption and that more money makes it easier to trade. But it makes more sense to Law and me the other way around. Money makes people want to trade. President Franklin Roosevelt observed that "a full pocketbook often groans more loudly than an empty stomach." I know why someone with money jingling in his pocket will want to spend it, and when it's gone why he will want to earn some more. Without the money in the first place, he might well have been content to produce goods for himself, to go fishing or pick berries rather than produce goods for market. He might have been happier that way, although he would consume a lower money value of goods. Or he might be less happy. But I don't think people choose whether to participate in market economies based on whether it makes them happier. I don't know if a tribe of self-sufficient nomads is better or worse off than commuters hurrying to work in a modern economy—I'm not sure the question even makes sense. I do know that it takes shiny, jingly things, or psychic equivalents, to turn one society into the other.

From a financial point of view, the jingle of the money is important. Coins are made to be pretty and fun to handle. Paper money is elaborately engraved with patriotic and mystic symbols. Poker players know that people play differently depending on whether cash or chips are used to make the bets. Spending patterns with credit cards are different than with cash, and checks are different from either. Home stock trading first caught on not when the financial and communications technology became available for efficient execution, but when user interfaces borrowed from video games were added in the late 1980s (it was called "Nintendo trading" at the time). To understand a market, it is not enough to know its economic effect, the real goods that are transferred. The mechanism of transfer is important as well.

Consider medieval market fairs. Economists tend to see them as an agreed place where people will show up with goods at the same time. This makes barter more convenient because a wide range of products are available. It also allows faster circulation of the small supply of silver money. Increasing the velocity of money has the same effect as increasing the supply. In later development, commercial paper further augmented the money supply. Of course, when a bunch of people from far away get together, they're going to want to have some fun, too. Entertainers will take advantage of the gathering to show up; there will be gambling and contests, flirting and drinking, and purchase of luxury goods. The economist's view emphasizes the market; the fair is a sideshow.

People who study finance, and businesspeople as well, usually emphasize the fair instead. If there's a place where people can have fun, they will come. Of course, when a bunch of people from far away get together, they'll bring some goods along to trade.

These are not competing views. No doubt there is truth to each. But they raise the question, if you want to stimulate the economy, should you create more markets or more fairs? Do you explain the explosion of retail sales in the Christmas season as businesses responding to demand created by religious celebrations or as consumers responding to an altered shopping experience created as successful merchandizing ploy? Or consider the value of a stock. Economics sees the value as arising from the ownership of the net assets of an underlying company. In finance class, we teach students to compute the value by looking only at the stock's trading characteristics—when and how much the price moves up and down. Again, both views can be true, but the question is, which one is a more reliable guide to successful investing?

Economics and finance take different views of gambling. In economics, gambling seems to have little point. Money is transferred from one person to another, but no productive activity takes place. Standard utility theory claims that the bet makes both parties worse off when it is made. In finance, gambling is an exchange like any other. All exchange stimulates productive activity, whether exchange by gift, gambling, barter, or money transaction. Even involuntary exchange—theft and piracy—are stimulants and have an important part in financial history, but not in conventional economic history (the largest involuntary exchange of all—taxes—does interest economists).

It's easy to underestimate the importance of exchanges other than buying and selling for money, or to regard them as relics of primitive societies. We can measure exchanges only when they involve money. The tips of the gifts and gambling icebergs with dollar amounts attached each total over a trillion dollars a year in the United States, compared to a $12 trillion money exchange economy. We can only guess how much of each is hidden. Some of the most important things in life are supposed to be bartered, but not bought or sold. We can earn respect, repay loyalty, and reciprocate affection, but not with or for money. Other things, such as love, friendship, and sex, can be given freely as gifts, but trading is socially discouraged. We admire someone who gambles her life for an important goal, but not someone who kills herself for the life insurance money.

To see the relative value of these two spheres, consider the following choice. You could be transferred with all your friends and family, but no material goods, to an earthlike planet somewhere in the galaxy, or you could remain behind as the last person on earth, owner of all the material goods in the world. Although both are hard choices—the emigrants will have trouble surviving without skills or tools in their new environment and most of the stay-at-home's assets will be useless without other people to run them—I think most people would immediately opt to leave rather than stay.

Most people refuse to exchange the most important things in life for money. An ironic consequence of this is that we get less of these important things. Money exchange is more efficient than gift, gambling, barter, and theft. Because we refuse to put a dollar value on human life, society spends hundreds of millions of dollars to prevent some deaths and little or nothing to prevent others. A rational market would quickly find a market clearing price of a human life, and we would have both fewer deaths and more resources to devote to other tasks. I don't know if that would be a better or a worse world.

THE TROUBLE IN SCOTLAND . . . AND NEW ORLEANS

Without an adequate supply of money, trade in Scotland was often done by barter. Law wrote:

> In this state of barter, there was little trade, and few artisans. The people depended on the landowners. The landowners worked only so much of the land as served the occasions of their families, to barter for such necessities as their land did not produce; and to lay up for seed and bad years. What remained was unworked, or gifted on condition of vassalage and other services. The losses and difficulties that attended barter, would force the landowners to a greater consumption of the goods they produced themselves, and a lesser consumption of other goods. To supply themselves, they would use the land to produce the several goods they had occasion for, although it was best suited for goods of one kind. So much of the land was unworked, what was worked was not employed to that by which it would have turned to most advantage, nor the people to the labor they were most fit for.

Paper money backed by land was Law's proposed solution for Scotland. Paper money backed by a combination of gold, government debt, and shares in operating companies was his solution for France. Law is distinguished from other early advocates of paper money by his emphasis on showmanship. He understood that getting people to work harder was a marketing challenge. There were no mathematical laws of economics to be discovered and exploited by precise engineering. Instead, you had to persuade people to play a game. As a professional gambler, he naturally combined careful calculation with a cultivated air of play.

But paper money was not Law's one-size-fits-all answer to stimulating economies. His unique genius is demonstrated by a less well known idea, which he called "so much greater [than paper money] that it will shake the foundations of the world." In 1715 he wrote to Philippe, Duc d'Orléans, regent of France:

> But the bank is not the only nor the greatest of my ideas. I will produce a work that will surprise Europe by the changes it will bring . . . greater changes than those brought by the discovery of the Indies or by the introduction of credit. By this work Your Royal Highness will be in a position to relieve the Kingdom of the sad condition into which it has fallen, and to make it more powerful than it has ever been . . ."

He was right about everything except helping France.

When Law was running the French economy, he noticed the same problem in France's Mississippi possessions as he had documented in Scotland. The natives were not interested in accumulating great wealth, and the French colonists were only marginally better. When times got tough, the French moved in with the Indians. Spain had been much more successful with its New World possessions: It basically took what it needed and motivated the natives with slavery or the somewhat gentler mission plantation system. England had been successful in inducing the natives to trade. The French colonists wanted to try one or the other of those approaches; they kept asking for more slaves and more trade goods.

Unfortunately, the Mississippi Indians refused to trade, except for small deals between individuals. They insisted on gift exchange for large transactions. A delegation of Indians would visit New Orleans. The French would entertain them and lavish them with gifts. The delegation would reciprocate and, after a couple of weeks, leave. When the colonists toted up the bill, they discovered the food and deerskins they got from the Indians cost a lot more metal knives and gunpowder than the exchange rate enjoyed by England. Simply put, the Indians were better at gift exchange than the French; the English were better at trading than the Indians. The French also tried enslaving Indians, but that did not work well, either. They would escape or die trying. It was often more work to force them to work than to do the job directly. It was much harder for African slaves to escape because they did not have relatives living in nearby woods, nor were they as experienced at surviving in the American wilderness.

It's obvious why the Indians would reject slavery, but trade was disadvantageous as well. The issue remains important. Ethnographer Chris Gregory's brilliant *Savage Money* lays out the effect of trade exchange on traditional cultures today. Everywhere Indians accepted trade, they soon found themselves in abject dependence. In contrast, the Indians of the area drained by the Mississippi River maintained political control over an area larger than France and Germany combined until almost 1900 and were a significant military power during that period. In all other parts of the Western Hemisphere, the natives were killed or dispossessed much earlier, and either assimilated or restricted to areas of marginal economic value. After 1600, their military power was significant only for local raids or in combination with European troops. The great empires of the Incas and Aztecs collapsed quickly, while the dispersed network societies of the Mississippi endured.

SAVAGE MONEY

Consider an American Indian living a traditional life who is offered a gun and ammunition enough to kill 20 deer, in return for 10 deerskins. This seems like a great trade. Hunting with a gun is far easier than with a bow. He can feed his entire village for a winter with the deer meat, and the 10 deerskins left over from the trade can be used to buy metal knives, blankets, and other goods that are laborious or impossible to produce by hand. The trouble is that the price of ammunition will keep going up in terms of deerskins. Pretty soon he finds he has to work all the time just to get enough goods to survive. He's no longer feeding a village; he cannot even support a family. He is entirely at the mercy of his ammunition provider—he must accept any indignity or starve.

Going back to his original life is not easy. In the first place, the traditional production cycle is complex: Things must be collected, planted, dried, seasoned, or otherwise processed over long periods. If he has neglected these things, it's hard to start fresh. Also, skills are forgotten and specialists are dispersed. Game is much harder to get because intensive gun hunting has made deer scarce and shy. Perhaps most important, his neighbors now have guns. If he doesn't, he cannot defend himself. The only practical option is to move to a more marginal economic area, which delays, but does not halt, the process. Or he can assimilate.

You might ask why the Europeans got to set the exchange rates, instead of the Indians. The answer is that it worked both ways. Some early English colonies failed as the result of uncontrolled exchange rates. A metal knife that originally bought a winter's ration of corn would later fetch only one-tenth that amount. If the European didn't like that price, the Indians only had to wait until he got hungry. In other areas, such as French Canada, relatively equal trading terms persisted for centuries, mainly because the French were content with moderate profits and did not want to invest the resources necessary to build an empire. The trouble is that where the Indians had the upper hand, the colonies died out and the egalitarian settlements were taken over by the more aggressive ones. Moreover, the European colonists themselves were similarly exploited by people across the Atlantic. This pattern only began to fade at the end of the eighteenth century, when North America developed domestic manufacturing capabilities and independent trade, not to mention political independence.

Gift exchange makes it much harder for the Europeans to cut the price of deerskins. If they give less ammunition and fewer trade goods, the Indians bring fewer skins. The Europeans can respond by cutting off tribes who deliver the fewest skins, but this prevents those tribes from becoming dependent. The inefficiency and imprecision of gift exchange prevents Europeans from setting the exchange rate exactly at the subsistence point.

Gambling exchange is even better. The exchange rate has to result in a subsistence wage to the losers, or they'll stop hunting for you. The average hunter therefore gets a surplus over bare necessities. Everyone knows this intuitively; you don't need an economic example. In a money transaction, the person receiving the money experiences some social inferiority. The customer is always right, the boss is always right, and you're always on the wrong end. There is an inherent dependence in making a living from selling your goods or your labor. But in gambling, the winner feels superior. Gift exchange is more complex: Either the giver or the recipient can feel inferior, or gifts can be between equals. Both gambling and gifts create a mutual bond much deeper than customer/clerk or employer/employee. There is a pride in things we win and sentimental value in gifts we receive that are absent from most purely market transactions. In fact, it's hard to find many purely market transactions—most human exchanges contain some elements of gambling and gifts (and, for that matter, theft).

John Law understood these differences, as far as I can tell, alone among contemporary thinkers. He knew that neither slavery nor more money would solve the Louisiana problem. The one method that worked even a little was selling the Indians brandy. Once introduced to it, they would sometimes be willing to go into money exchange to get more. (The English used this ploy extensively in the American colonies, and later did the same thing with opium when China refused to trade.) But Law knew this course was ultimately destructive. He wanted to create a dynamic economy of hardworking risk takers.

The first thing Law did was round up a shipload of prostitutes and send them to New Orleans. After all, the world's oldest profession consists of taking something that is supposed to be only gift-exchanged and persuading men to make a money exchange instead. French women were held to be particularly skilled in this art (although, at the time, it was Vienna that was known as "the brothel of Europe"). Also, the colonists had been consorting with native women who were, shall we say, undemanding. A French coquette has motivated many a man to earn more money. Your Indian girlfriend is happy for the two of you to move in with her folks when the weather is cold or food is short. Law figured French women would insist on a house in town and other luxuries.

To everyone's surprise, when the ship landed in New Orleans, men crowded on board, seized the first woman they could find, defended or lost their prize in fistfights, and—married them. Law had counted on one prostitute motivating a dozen or more men; one to one was not as efficient. However, it did work to some extent, since the married couples showed at least some glimmerings of ambition.

If you can't beat 'em, join 'em. Law decided to send over married couples instead. Of course, no one wanted to go, so he came up with an offer. Any single man in prison could get a pardon and a free sea voyage by agreeing to marry. Any single woman could get a small dowry from Law and a husband by agreeing to go to New Orleans. To make sure he didn't get cheated, Law insisted the newlyweds be chained together until the ship set sail. When this caused public outcry, Law had flowers threaded through the chains and told people it was a rural wedding custom.

Law had some other ideas, such as sending over a colony of Germans who had a better reputation for hard work than the French. But his most important idea was to round up a shipload of faro dealers, complete with cards. These men established trading post casinos up and down the Mississippi. The dealer would take all the cards of one suit from one deck and place them face up on the ground. By each card, he would place a pile of goods. Bettors would see a pile they liked and would place their own pile next to the same card. The dealer would negotiate until both parties agreed the piles were of equal value (this system is similar to silent barter, which was widely practiced in Africa and may be where Law got the idea).

Next, the dealer would take a fresh deck of cards (that is, one with all 52 cards) and deal faro. As you can imagine, after a few days of playing this, the dealer would have lost all the trade goods he brought and be loaded down with the goods he wanted from the Indians. There was almost no risk to him. Some Indians would be lucky and have two or three times the value for their goods; others would be unlucky and leave with nothing.

There we have two of the crucial elements of poker: cards and gambling. We also have two of the elements of futures trading: gambling and exchange. To get the rest of the pieces, we have to go backward in time to one of the great mysteries of economic history.

NETWORKS

The first extensive contact between Europeans and natives of the lower Mississippi was the expedition led by Hernando de Soto. De Soto discovered the most sophisticated and successful preindustrial economy in the world. Raw materials were shipped thousands of miles, combined with other goods and processing over a region larger than Europe, and the finished goods distributed just as widely. All this was done without money, writing, long-distance communication, or a common language or culture. Unfortunately, de Soto brought along diseases that wiped out three-quarters of the native population. That disrupted the economy (think of the devastation caused by the Black Death wiping out only a quarter of the European population). Without written records, the secret of the economy died as well.

In Europe at the time, long-distance exchange took place at fairs. Everyone would bring their goods to a central place, where buyers and sellers could search among all goods for the best bargain. Information was exchanged about what was valuable where, so individuals could plan complex processing involving raw materials and skills from different places, with the finished goods sold in other places. A mountainous region might have plenty of sheep. The sheared wool could be processed in an agricultural region using surplus labor in the winter. Chemicals for dyes could be harvested in other regions and brought to cities with the specialized processing skills to refine them. A larger urban area might have high-knowledge fashion workers to design the finished product, choosing among materials from all of Europe. This is fairly easy to accomplish if everyone involved gets together in one place, and you have writing, a uniform commercial code, and universally accepted money to help arrange things.

The other common system for long-distance exchange is the caravan. You bundle up a lot of goods and move on to the next trading place. There you make whatever exchanges are profitable, and move on. War and banditry (or piracy if it happens on the water) are variants of this—both very important forces in the development of long-distance and complex trade.

Now consider the problem of long-distance trade in a river network, in a region where mountains, deserts, and swamps make long-distance land transportation prohibitively expensive and dangerous. River transportation is cheap, but it's seasonal. Generally, you go downstream in the spring and upstream in the fall. But there are many exceptions to the rule, patches of the river that are too turbulent in the spring even for downstream travel, and other places where the water is too low in the fall for any transportation at all. Moreover, secure transportation requires microknowledge of various sections of the river. Everyone sticks to relatively short travel up and down the river from their home. These obstacles rule out fairs and caravans, and reduce the effectiveness of wars and banditry.

Trade between neighboring villages on a single river is simple enough. In spring the upstream folks bring down some goods they have accumulated during the winter, and in fall the downstream folks return the visit with surplus from their harvest. Without a convenient store of value, like silver, you need to do this by gift exchange. Different tribes have surplus goods available at different times of year, and the river imposes transportation constraints on bulk goods.

If there is steadily increasing demand for a good over a stretch of river, we could imagine that good changing hands in gift exchange from village to village over a long distance. But that's very slow if we work on an annual cycle for each exchange. European goods brought by de Soto were distributed throughout the entire drainage basin of the Mississippi and integrated into the economy within five years. Local trade cannot explain that.

The bigger problem is that demand does not always increase steadily. Suppose the nomadic hunters of tribe A live near the source of river A, in northern mountains. They collect a lot of fur pelts, because they kill animals mainly for food. Their nomadic lifestyle discourages carrying around a lot of heavy stuff, and also developing the sort of fixed technologies needed for efficient boatbuilding and food storage.

A downriver tribe lives to the south and at lower elevation. It does enough hunting to supply its own needs for pelts. The farther south you go and the lower the elevation, the warmer it gets, and therefore the less demand there is for furs. But at some point, river A combines with river B. If we go upstream to the headwaters of river B, we find tribe B. It lives in a cold climate, but survives by fishing and gathering. It would pay a lot for furs. Its environment is very cold, and its domestic economy does not naturally produce enough things to keep it warm. However, because it is not nomadic, it does have technology for making canoes and preserving food, things that tribe A would love.

With long-distance communication, tribe A and tribe B could strike a profitable deal. But how are they going to even know of each other's existence, much less explore mutually profitable exchange? How can any tribe in between see the opportunity to act as an intermediary? This is particularly important because in realistic examples it isn't simply raw materials or finished goods that are shipped. Goods are combined with other goods and processing at different stages along the journey. Organizing all of this is a challenge with full information and a computer. How did the Native Americans do it with only local information?

I don't know the answer; I don't think anyone does. But I'm willing to bet it involved gambling exchange. Gambling results in some random movement of goods, allowing them to jump over stretches of river where no residents want them. This explains the otherwise mysterious fact that people often gamble for things they don't want. Accumulation of gambling wealth encourages people to broaden the scope of their gift giving, since you get diminishing returns in gift exchange by saturating your nearby neighbors with the same items. A robust gambling culture throughout the river network creates a pool of liquid trade goods that allows experimentation and innovation.

Now for a short digression into geography. The longest rivers in the world are the Nile and the Amazon, but the navigable parts of them run through desert and jungle, respectively—regions that support only sparse populations. Next is the Yangtze, which is similar in many ways to the Mississippi, but drains only half as large an area. Moreover, population is not dispersed evenly throughout the Yangtze network; since ancient times there have been dense urban agglomerations and virtually uninhabited regions (much like the Mississippi network today).

The only river system comparable to the premodern Mississippi, the fourth-longest river in the world, is the Congo river system in Africa. Both it and the Mississippi provide navigable access to a million square miles that contain about two-thirds of the natural resources of their respective continents. In both places, land transportation is difficult and populations were distributed fairly evenly before modern times.

We know more about the premodern economy of West Africa than we do about central North America. Although the area encompasses hundreds of different cultural groups with different languages and customs, there were some constants. Women did the food marketing in neighboring villages and kept track of complicated multigenerational kinship ties. This allowed information to flow over kin networks for long distances, with gossip and economic data passed along from village to village. We have some hints of this in the Mississippi region. For example, when French explorers Jacques Marquette and Louis Joliet met the Illinois Indians, the chief gave them his 10-year-old son to take with them on their travels. U.S. explorers Meriwether Lewis and William Clark found a Shoshone from Idaho, Sacagawea, living 1,000 miles away and across the Rocky Mountains in South Dakota. Both examples of long-distance travel were out of network. They linked tribes of the Mississippi river system to tribes outside it.

This gets interesting because the French imported West African slaves, primarily from the Congo and Senegal river systems. The Senegalese quickly adapted to herding horses and cattle along rivers from Texas (where they had been liberated from the Spanish by the local Caddo Indians) to Louisiana. The Congo River African women found it more natural to join in network trade with the local Indians. So we've got John Law's faro dealers mixing with network traders from the two great economic river networks in the world. It would be surprising if this creative mix hadn't generated spectacular economic innovation.

ADVENTURERS AND PLANTERS

Unfortunately, we don't know much about the next century. By 1850, poker and futures markets had developed most of their modern features and were spread widely throughout the Mississippi region. It's easy to pick out features that clearly link both to John Law's ideas and to West African and Mississippi Indian cultural elements. But we can only speculate about when and where they were mixed.

Historians are not much help. The leading historian of the American South in the early twentieth century was Ulrich Bonnell Phillips. He famously dismissed the history of the Mississippi region before it became part of the United States in 1803 as concerning only "redskins and Latins." In the later twentieth century, Harvard professor Bernard Bailyn was the most celebrated historian of the Colonial period. He referred to the people living in the Gulf of Mexico region as "exotic," "strange," and "bizarre." Daniel Usner has written the only useful economic history of eighteenth-century Louisiana and calls the attitude of mainstream historians "the geographical trivialization of the Gulf South in colonial American historiography." In shorter words, he added:

> Its people have been largely ignored or casually dismissed as mere bit-players in the drama of American development—colorful, no doubt, but peripheral and unimportant. Before falling under the sovereignty of the United States, lands along the Mississippi River appear to be an amorphous area sojourned by French woodsmen and Indian warriors while waiting to be occupied by Anglo-American settlers and their African-American slaves.

Those Anglo-American settlers worked on the basis of an old economic system of Adventurers and Planters. The words are confusing. Planters had the adventure, while Adventurers stayed planted at home. Adventurers—from the same linguistic root that gives us the modern *venture* capitalist—put up the money for a new colony or town. Planters were the people who actually settled the new place. They were led by professional town founders, who had to be skilled at administration and dealing with natives.

This is a hierarchical system of settlement. The original colonies are funded by European investors. As colonies mature and have more capital than high-return investment opportunities, they give birth to new towns. These new towns are beholden to their parent colony and send their economic products through them. Every frontier town, however remote, was connected through such a hierarchy to a port, for shipping goods to Europe.

This system was impossibly slow and rigid for the spectacular economic opportunities of central North America, especially after steam travel made upriver shipment of bulk goods practical and offered reliable year-round transportation. A very limited pool of capital had to move quickly over unknown and dangerous terrain to service literal and figurative gold rushes. Opportunity raced far ahead of legal systems that would protect conventional investments (or the lives of conventional investors and their agents, if they traveled out west to inquire in person). Moreover, the Planters were not peaceable town folk, the surplus population of a settled town with social and blood ties to their investors. Some were renegades and outlaws; all were tough and independent, with few ties outside the region. In modern terms, the West needed a dynamic self-organizing network of economic relations.

Of all the ways this need was met, the soft money bank is the one most recognizable today as a financial institution. Consider a group of people who arrive together at some place in the West. It could be a mining camp or a place suitable for farming, ranching, lumber production, or some other activity. These people show up with a diverse collection of assets: tools, provisions, livestock, and other items. Somehow the people and assets have to be organized into efficient production teams.

With developed financial markets, this is easy. Some people organize companies, or the companies can be organized back in a city. The companies raise capital by borrowing money and issuing stock, then use it to buy whatever assets and hire whatever people are needed. The profit from the business activity is used to repay the borrowings plus interest and pay dividends to the equity investors.

But our hypothetical camp is far from cities, and there is little money available. No outsiders are offering to invest. A common solution was for one person with a small amount of gold or silver to set up a bank. It's called *soft money* because it issues banknotes far in excess of its hard capital. If anyone tries to redeem any significant amount of notes, the bank will fail.

The bank makes loans to people, who use the money to buy assets and hire labor. People take the banknotes because there is no alternative except to try to eke out a living with whatever assets they brought with them. The notes are accepted within the town, although not outside it. Of course, no one holds much in banknotes at any time; you get them only to spend them quickly. This liquidity allows people to organize pools of assets appropriate for various economic projects, an impractical exercise using barter.

If the projects are successful, goods of real value will be produced and shipped to outside markets. There they can be sold for hard money—gold, silver, or notes from sound banks. The soft money bank will gradually evolve into a hard money bank. If the projects are unsuccessful, the bank will fail. While everyone involved understands this risk, taking banknotes is much less risky than extending credit to individual entrepreneurs. A person running a logging camp, for example, might promise to pay his workers when he sells his logs. If his business fails, the workers do not get paid. But if he pays his workers in notes borrowed from the soft money bank, they will collect as long as the overall town is successful, even if this one business fails. Moreover, a business based on personal credit will liquidate if it fails. A business funded by a soft money bank loan will be taken over by the bank if it does not meet interest payments. Often it can be reorganized and succeed under new management; if not, the assets can be usefully dispersed to other bank borrowers. When everyone in town has a stake in the town's success, that success is much more likely.

POKERBANK

It's easy to see that a town poker game fulfills many of the same functions. If people convert their assets into poker chips and play, the winners can acquire enough assets to start businesses. Poker chips take the place of banknotes. Like the notes, no one holds significant wealth in them for long—you buy them only to play poker, and exchange them for real assets at the conclusion of the game. The losers can work for the winners to get enough chips to try to win the businesses.

One apparent disadvantage of a poker game versus a soft money bank is the randomness of the allocations. The businesses are run by the best, or luckiest, poker players. In contrast, a banker will decide who gets loans based on honesty, ability, and experience. However, in the context of the American frontier, this may actually be an advantage. There weren't experienced bankers to make these decisions, and the documentation or references needed to base them on didn't exist. Skill at poker was arguably as good a qualification as any. More important, it was accepted. Poker losers generally delivered their assets, whereas people rejected for bank loans might refuse to accept banknotes, causing the whole system to fail.

A clear advantage of the poker game is that it does not require anyone to be accepted as banker. In modern poker games, one player or the house generally acts as banker. The bank sells chips to players and redeems them at the end of the game. On the early frontier, poker was played with a check system instead. Each player had his own chips, which were identifiable. At the end of the game, players bought back their own chips. Winners would have some of the losers' chips left over. It was the winners' responsibility to collect from the losers. Something similar is sometimes done in private games today. Each player is given a fixed number of chips, which they return at the end of play. Those players with fewer chips than they started with write checks to the players with excess. That means no one has to act as bank, and no one has to bring large amounts of cash to the game. If a loser cannot or will not pay, it's a winner's problem, not the whole table's.

This last point is critical. Unless you gamble or work in finance, it's easy to forget that financial rights and obligations represent relations among people, not numbers in a theory. It's not enough to know who owes you money and how much; the nature of their obligation can make all the difference in the world. Poker writer David Spanier tells the story of Doyle Brunson and Pug Pearson's trip to London. Two tough-looking gentlemen called on the two World

Series of Poker champions in their hotel room with the message that 25 percent of their poker winnings should be contributed to a local crime boss. Pug preferred not to play under those conditions and went back to the United States. But Brunson asked whether the 25 percent cut paid for collection services as well. When informed that it did, he decided it was a good buy. In finance, wise people always negotiate in advance precisely who has what responsibilities if some parties to an agreement fail to adhere to it.

Another difference between a soft money bank and a poker game concerns the distribution of profit if the town succeeds. With the soft money bank, the bulk of the money will go to the people who were selected for bank loans and who then made successes of their businesses. The biggest cut of all goes to the banker and her investors. The people who were not given loans will do well, earning their wages plus interest, but not as well. With poker as the financial institution, the game will continue until the town is successful enough to attract outside capital. Business owners will have to keep playing to meet their ongoing expenses and capital needs. That means everyone who plays has a chance of coming out on top in the end. In that sense, it's fairer than selecting some people at the beginning to get rich. On the other hand, in the poker game, a lot of people are going to end up with nothing. With the soft money bank, only people who default on their bank loans lose everything. In that sense, poker is less fair.

Which system you prefer depends on your available economic opportunities. If there is a gold rush or land opening or new railhead popping up all the time, it makes sense for the losers to move on and try their luck again. This is an environment for risk takers who will either get rich or bet again. When economic opportunities start to narrow, towns have to cultivate a middle class, people who value security over the chance to get rich. In those circumstances, a bank looks more sensible than a poker game.

A variant of this system was documented in Yukon gold rush camps later in the century. It probably happened elsewhere, but we have no record. Miners would work all season, then play poker all winter. The winners could leave, having accumulated as much gold as they could carry, and as much as they needed to be wealthy for life. The losers would mine for another season and try their luck again. This is much more efficient than everyone working until he gets a required stake. By concentrating assets, some people got to leave early, which opened places for newcomers.

The poker game is a more dynamic institution than a bank. If the opportunity expands, the game can easily accommodate newcomers; if the opportunity turns out to be less than expected, losers can find themselves frozen out. The bank is more of a cooperative effort in which everyone will succeed or fail together. That is attractive to many more hardworking people than the poker deal, so the bank will attract more useful settlers. However, it can lead to disaster if the town is successful, but not successful enough to support everyone who came. If the opportunity is larger than expected, the successful soft money bank can attract capital in the form of money from outside investors, while the poker game attracts nearby adventurers with skills and physical assets on location. Depending on the circumstances, one of those things may be needed and the other useless.

The biggest advantage of the bank is that it leads to a stable evolution to a permanent settlement. As it becomes more successful, its notes will be accepted farther away. It will facilitate transactions at transshipment points and processing centers. Outsiders who want to invest capital will find businesses run with money accounting and a history of loan repayments. Lenders like that more than a business founded in a poker game and recently taken over in another poker game by an inexperienced manager, with no written records except some IOUs and a framed full house. Stability is important for activities like farming and ranching, where there is a large immovable investment. It is less important in mining, hunting, and lumbering, where people stay only until the local resources are exhausted.

It did happen, however, that poker games evolved into permanent settlements. The next step was an outside gambler who arrived with significant capital. Professional gamblers were typically excluded from poker games: You had to participate in local economic activity to play. But at a certain point of development, a professional offering faro, chuck-a-luck, and roulette was welcome. This person would provide safe-deposit services and import luxury goods and necessities. He also provided a degree of rough law enforcement, since he had to defend his own property. As the town grew, it could attract a professional gunman in exchange for the faro concession. Wild Bill Hickok, holder of the famous dead man's hand of aces and eights, did this for a living. Finally, the town could get to the point of collecting taxes and hiring a sheriff, who might even be directed to shut down the gambling halls and public poker games.

FLASHBACK

MY FIRST HAND OF COMMERCIAL POKER

All six Gardena poker rooms were single-story buildings with the ambiance of airport gate waiting areas. They were clean, with high ceilings and functional furnishings. About two-thirds of the floor was segregated by a rail. Outside the rail was a restaurant, bar, TV room (mostly tuned to games for illegal sports betting), guard desk, cashier, and the all-important board, where all the games and players waiting for seats were listed. Lots of people were hanging around—some waiting for seats, some doing various kinds of business, and some just passing the time. Inside was poker.

The players I wanted would arrive around nine o'clock in the evening. Tom and I had intended to arrive at four o'clock, but getting barred at the Horseshoe had cost us over an hour. From four o'clock to six o'clock there is a switchover from the afternoon to the evening crowds, so you're sure to get a seat. I wanted a few hours to get used to the table. Robert had cautioned against starting at a low-limit game or playing tight at the beginning. I had the advantage: I at least knew the Gardena game vicariously, while the other players didn't know me at all. When you have the advantage, you exploit it; you don't fritter it away to get your bearings or build up your confidence. It's easy to become timid when you don't know what you're doing, but in a competitive situation you have to think about your knowledge relative to what the other players know. My plan was for the good players to arrive to find me well ahead in the game, playing with relaxed confidence. I was probably cocky enough in those days to imagine them reacting with fear, or at least respect. It did not go according to plan.

We were playing Five-Card Draw, jackpots high with a bug (a wild card that can only be used to complete a straight or flush, or as an ace). There was an ante and no blinds. I have been told that lowball was more popular, but I saw more high myself. They say June is a slow month, however, and things may not have been typical. There were five players at the table, none of whom paid the slightest attention when I sat down. They ranged in age from about 25 to 50. As a group, they looked like midlevel office workers after a two-day bus ride, not colorful Damon Runyon characters or dangerous sharpies fresh out of jail. My game collected $10 every half hour from each player, metered by a large clock on the wall with red lights at each half hour point. When the light went on, the chip girls made the rounds for the house money.

The game was fast, but not as fast as Robert had coached me. When you pay by the hour, time is money. I was prepared for a hand a minute. That's fast but not impossible for modern hold 'em with a nonplaying, professional dealer. But Five Card-Draw with six players requires 35 to 40 cards dealt on a typical hand, while six hold 'em players need only 17. Amateur dealers who are playing hands slow things down as well. It's true, there are only half as many betting rounds in draw poker as hold 'em, but 60 seconds is still a very short time to physically manage the chips and cards, much less think about the betting. Anyway, I think we played at only half that rate, about what I was used to at serious private games. No one wasted time, but I had no trouble playing unrushed poker without anyone expressing annoyance. I got two flush draws in the first hour—one, I filled and won a small pot without showing; the other, I didn't fill and bluffed to win another small pot. I got a few pairs worth playing, but none improved on the draw. I was behind a little, but not seriously, and I was playing comfortably. I was getting action—people would open and see some of my raises—but also respect—people would sometimes fold to my raises as well. So far, so good.

One big difference between Gardena card rooms and casinos is the amount of cheating. Casinos invest in the best available security to prevent players from cheating the house, and the same equipment and policies keep players from cheating each other. Professional dealers also act as a safeguard; in Gardena, players dealt the hands. A floorman was available, but only when called. He did not watch every hand at every table. The most important difference is the relationship of the house to the players. Card rooms cater to the regulars, the people who come in every day and pay rent. If a tourist or dabbler walks out mad, that's no great loss.

Casinos, however, tend to regard any dollar that comes in the door as rightfully belonging to the house. They take a limited amount, because if everyone always lost, no one would come back. Every dollar professional poker players win in a casino from tourists and dabblers counts against that limit. Casinos tolerate professionals because their reputations attract business and they fill out tables. They do not tolerate cheaters because they not only take money the house could have won, they drive away business and hurt reputation. Card rooms like regulars; casinos like losers.

Cheating

Robert told me to watch for chip stealing (say what you will about Las Vegas being tacky, you don't have to worry about your chips when you go to the bathroom), signaling, and passing cards. A new player could not expect to get help from the floorman, especially if the other players at the table claimed to have seen nothing. This kind of thing was more common at the lower limits, but at all tables the regulars tended to close ranks against newcomers. The card room could not exist as an economic institution if strangers could walk in and help themselves to money.

Subtle collusion worried me more. There are two things a group of regulars can do to conspire against a newcomer. Neither requires any overt cheating or prior agreement, and players do them naturally, even unconsciously.

The first tactic is to fold all but the strongest hand among the regulars. That means I win the same pots I would anyway, but I collect from only one player instead of from two or more. That's crippling to long-term expected value. It would be overt cheating for the players to compare hands and select the strongest, but if regulars do not try to play deceptively and don't try to win from each other whenever I'm also in the pot, they can figure out pretty quickly who the designated champion should be. Of course, I can try to pick up on this as well, but they've spent hundreds or thousands of hours scrutinizing each other's play and mannerisms—they will have a big edge at this aspect of the game. Whenever I fold, they can revert to their regular game.

Another form of collusion is two regulars raising each other back and forth when I'm in the pot. Although the amounts of the raises are limited, Gardena has no limit on the number of raises. Therefore, two players against me can play effective table stakes poker whenever they choose, while I can only play limit. This tactic is less worrying. Unless the regulars have a formal profit-splitting arrangement, the raiser with the weak hand loses money. Regulars might pass an extra raise or two back and forth as favors, but only overt cheaters would try to get me all-in. Also, the colluders have to bet $2 for every $1 I bet. That's a steep price to pay for the option to evade the limit. Years later, I saw a similar kind of cheating on the Chicago Mercantile Exchange.

I thought I spotted the first kind of collusion in Gardena. When I was in a pot, I usually seemed to be drawing against exactly one other player. Other people won pots before the draw or played in three- and four-way hands. Not me. By watching this carefully, I thought I could get the edge back. If the regulars were not playing deceptively before I folded, I didn't have to worry about being bluffed or about people drawing out straights or flushes. I'd be going up against high pairs, two pairs, and threes—seldom weaker hands. Moreover, I thought I could get a clue to the predraw strength of their hands by the way they played.

In this situation, it doesn't pay to draw to a straight or flush. You don't make enough from one other bettor when you hit to make up for the times you don't hit. Bluffing isn't profitable either, because the designated champion will call much more frequently than a purely profit-maximizing player. On the other hand, a low pair that would normally be folded is a good hand. If you draw two pair or three of a kind, you will usually win against one other bettor who started with a higher pair. If you don't improve, you fold after the draw. However, to disguise the fact that you're throwing away all your straight and flush draws and playing low pairs instead, you have to draw only one card occasionally—say, when you're dealt trips.

Anyway, that's how I was playing, and it seemed to work pretty well. I was up quite a bit when I was dealt an interesting hand that exists only in this kind of poker. I got king, jack, and ten, all of clubs, and the bug. In most kinds of poker, a player who has an incomplete flush (the famous "four flush") or straight has a reasonably low chance of completing it. For example, if you have four cards of the same suit in draw poker without wild cards, there are 9 more of the suit in the deck out of the 47 cards you haven't seen. The chance of drawing one of them is 9/47, or

19 percent. In hold 'em, if you have an open-ended straight draw after the flop, 8 of the remaining 47 cards will fill it; 340 out of the 1,081 two-card combinations you could get on the turn and river, 31 percent, give you the straight.

But in draw poker with a bug, if you get three suited cards in a row, plus the bug, 22 out of the 48 remaining cards in the deck will give you a straight, flush, or straight flush. That's a 46 percent chance. A lot of the poker rules for playing straight and flush draws are based on the assumption that you have a low chance of completing. My hand wasn't quite this good, but there were 12 cards (any ace, queen, or nine) that would give me a straight and 10 cards (any club) that would give me a flush. That double counts the ace, queen, and nine of clubs, any of which would give me a straight flush. So I had 9/48 = 19 percent chance of a straight, 7/48 = 15 percent chance of a flush, and 3/48 = 6 percent chance of a straight flush. Overall, I had a 40 percent chance of filling.

The Betting

Harrison opened the betting, and Jason raised. I knew the first names of the people at the table and they knew mine, but no one had offered, or asked for, any more information. Harrison had a California cowboy look, with a dirty flannel shirt, string tie, and boots; Jason was a younger, red-faced guy in jeans and a blue oxford cloth shirt, wearing his hippie-length hair tied back with a leather braid. Later I learned that Harrison owned racehorses and had a cattle ranch as well, so it wasn't a costume. He treated me very nicely on a subsequent visit to the racetrack. Jason was a student but getting a bit old for not having picked a field of study or enrolled in a degree program. That was his offered opinion about himself, not my judgment. He asked me if I thought he should get into computers. I told him yes, and I hope he took my advice.

In Five-Card Draw, you raise with two pair before the draw. One pair, even aces, is too weak, especially since the opener must have at least jacks. Also, since you will draw three cards, you get a lot of information in the draw. Generally, the more information you expect to get in the future, the more you want to see it cheaply. That may sound counterintuitive, but it's true. With three of a kind or better, you typically want more people in the pot, and you want to disguise your strength. However, two pair is usually strong enough to win, but not strong enough to raise after the draw. If you want to make money with this hand, you have to do it early. And since you draw only one card, you have most of the information you're going to get about this hand. Since you probably know more about your final hand than the other players do about theirs, you want to force them to make decisions now. Of course, these are just general guidelines. Poker requires you to mix up your play so no one can guess your hand from your betting.

At that point, there were three small bets in the pot, plus the antes, and I had to put in two to call. That made calling nearly a break-even proposition. However, if I filled my hand, I could make additional money after the draw. If I didn't, I would just fold it. So it was an easy decision to stay in. Given my theory and experience to date, I expected Harrison to fold if I stayed in the hand. But unlike most straight and flush draw situations, I didn't mind further raises, since I would get two bets from Harrison and Jason for every one I had to put in, and my chances of winning were better than two to one. That logic wouldn't apply to a raise I made myself, since I expected it to be called only by Jason, and I didn't have better than an even chance of filling.

Nevertheless, you always consider raising. In poker, you need a good reason to call. When you're uncertain, you fold or raise. That's one of the essential lessons of the game. The safe, middle-class strategy is to take the intermediate course when you cannot evaluate the extremes; you make a strong decision only when you're confident it's right. To succeed in poker, you must be bold precisely when you're unsure of what's going on. The logic is that if you're uncertain, you should try to throw the other players off balance as well. Also, most money is made and lost in uncertain pots. If you're not going to be bold when the most money is at stake, you should find a different game.

A raise would cost me expected value, but it would represent my hand as three of a kind (the two pair rule applies when you are the first raiser; raising after one player has jacks or better and another has represented two pair requires a stronger hand). When I drew one card afterward, the raise would suggest instead that I had aces up. Of course, I could also have three of a kind with a kicker, or a straight or flush draw, but those are unlikely plays in this situation, especially against two bettors (remember, I was writing Harrison off, but I didn't think Jason knew that—you have to keep in mind what your actions look like to the other players). Bluffs are rarely constructed to be confusing; typically, a bluffer will tell a consistent tale. Four of a kind would cross Jason's mind, but it's too rare a dealt hand to consider. If you play poker to avoid losing to pat quads, you'll lose a lot of money on the other 99.97 percent of the hands. The upshot is that if I raised now and drew one card, Jason would probably think I had two pair, one of which was aces.

The advantage of this deception was that Jason would probably think he had been beaten if he didn't fill a full house on the draw. I could bet and probably win the pot. If he started with three of a kind, or filled a full house, he would check and collect an extra bet from me, in which case the strategy would cost me two bets. But all the other times, either I fill or Jason folds and the raise gets me at least one extra bet, sometimes the whole pot. Another advantage is that if Jason has a very strong hand and I fill, we will do some mutual raising after the draw. If I raise predraw, he'll put me on a full house; if I call, he'll think it is a straight or a flush. This will save me some money if he has a full house and I get the straight or flush; he will be afraid of my aces full. But it could cost me a lot more money if I fill my straight flush and he gets a full house.

These same general principles apply to most drawing hands, although, of course, the details differ. You should raise on some of them, but call on most. You should think about which of your opportunities are the best for this play. This one was cheaper than most because I had 19 chances of filling my hand, but it also had less potential profit. The deciding factor was that a raise hurt my situation if I got the straight flush, which could be a royal flush. If you get a royal flush, you owe it to yourself to get the most you can out of it. So I called.

Now came the first surprise. Harrison raised and Jason reraised. This was the first time two players had even called after I bet, and they both raised. Instantly, I reverted to my backup conspiracy theory. This looked like overt collusion. Either Harrison or Jason had signaled to the other a very strong hand, and they were acting in concert to push up the stakes.

Of course, nothing could have made me happier. I was contributing one-third of the additional chips to the pot, and I felt I had a 40 percent chance to win it. Each $1 that went into the pot was 7¢ in expected value in my pocket. It's true that there was a small chance Harrison or Jason had a straight or better, but even that worked in my favor. If it was true, I could make so much money if I filled my straight flush that it more than made up for the loss if I filled the straight or flush and lost to a full house. I could also make a lot beating a pat straight with a flush, or a pat flush with an ace high flush. Winning money is twice as sweet if the other players think they are cheating you.

The Draw

I called, doing my best to look like a guy who was doggedly pot committed. Now came another shock. Harrison announced that he was splitting his openers and drawing one card. This had not happened at the table yet. I had read the rules and knew the declaration was required, but I noticed a lot of rules were routinely ignored at the table (for example, losers of a showdown routinely threw their cards away without showing them, something that hurts a newcomer more than a regular since he doesn't know playing styles).

The predraw betting was much too strong to justify Harrison's staying in, let alone raising, on an ordinary flush or straight draw. It was too expensive if he didn't make it and might not win if he did. He couldn't have the bug because I did, and anyway I was just calling. But it doesn't make sense to break up a pair and draw one card for anything except a straight or flush draw.

It seemed more likely that Jason had passed Harrison a signal to open and raise, then fold after the draw. My guess was that Harrison didn't have openers and announced the split to divert suspicion. He could angrily muck his hand after the draw. But he had helped Jason suck additional money—my money—into the pot. Or so they thought. They didn't know about my royal flush!

Jason took one card, which was also puzzling. Two pair was far too weak to pass a signal for this kind of trick. I figured him for a high three of a kind. If you draw one card to three of a kind and a kicker, there are only four cards in the deck that can improve your hand (the one that matches your three of a kind and the three that match your kicker). If you draw two cards, you could get your fourth match on the first new card, and if you don't, you're in the same position as if you had kept a kicker. So you have one extra chance to improve. With me calling three raises, Jason would want all the insurance he could get. There was no possible deception value to the play. And there's no point to keeping a kicker because it's a high card—with a full house in draw poker, the rank of the pair is irrelevant (with community cards, as in Omaha or hold 'em, it matters a lot).

The one exception to this logic is holding an ace kicker because there are four cards that can pair it: the three aces plus the bug. In that case, you have exactly the same 5/48 (10 percent) chance of improving by drawing one or two. It's still slightly better to draw two, because you have more chance of getting four of a kind instead of a full house, but that very rarely makes a difference. So I figured Jason for a high three of a kind plus an ace. That was bad in the sense that he had at least 1, and maybe 4, of the 19 cards I needed to fill. But it was good in that I was holding at least 1, and maybe 2, of the 5 cards he needed. On a relative basis, I did him more damage than he did me.

Jason's draw also eliminated almost all the possibilities that he had been dealt a hand that could beat a straight or flush. Four of a kind was the only remaining possibility. It wasn't totally out of the question, but it was unlikely enough to be a minor factor in calculations. I drew one card and got a king. There went my dreams of a royal flush confounding and bankrupting the cheaters with their four of a kind.

Harrison and Jason both checked. This was more confusing, but I didn't care. There was little point to raising, and none to folding. So I checked.

Harrison had three sevens; Jason had a busted flush. Jason looked at my hand and called loudly but calmly for the floorman.

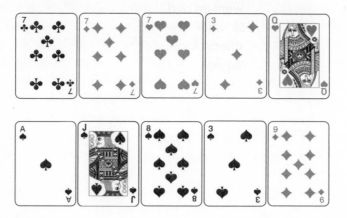

Harrison's declaration of splitting openers had been pure misdirection. He had been dealt three sevens and the queen. When Jason raised and I called, he figured Jason for two pair and me for two pair or three of a kind. He liked his chances enough to raise, but when Jason reraised and I called, he figured he was probably beaten. Since he was planning to take one card anyway, announcing he was splitting openers made it less likely that either Jason or I would bet after the draw, in fear that he had filled his straight or flush and was planning a check-raise. That did in fact occur, although given our draws, Harrison would have chased us out with any bet at all. Jason's two raises were normal poker misdirection; he was betting a flush draw like two pair.

Jason said Harrison's declaration of splitting was illegal. He insisted that Harrison's hand was dead and the pot belonged to me. Harrison argued the poker adage that "talk doesn't matter." After each had stated his case calmly, the floorman asked if I wanted to say anything. I didn't—Jason had put things clearly and I didn't know the house convention on the subject. Harrison turned up his discard (it was a five). The floorman awarded me the pot.

I had a little trouble fitting this into my conspiracy theory, unless Jason was trying to gain my confidence in order to sell me the Brooklyn Bridge. I don't know if the game changed after that, or just my perception of it, but we seemed to be playing normal poker. Jason left about an hour later, with no offer of a bridge nor any attempt to get my last name, and new players sat down. I went up and down for the next few hours, never again reaching the peak after my disputed victory. I left about two o'clock in the morning, ahead for the night. Tom left only reluctantly— maybe he really was a regular.

CHAPTER 6

Son of a Soft Money Bank

The Heyday of American Gamblers and Poker Players from 1830 to 1890, and Why That Era Had to Be Re-created in 1973

The closing of the American frontier meant the end of soft money banks. In the latter part of the nineteenth century, state banking laws began mandating minimum reserves and audits, even in the West and South. The federal government started issuing its own notes, displacing private banknotes. The federal banking reforms of the 1930s were another blow. Cousins of soft money banks survive today in the United States as savings associations among immigrant groups, such as the Korean *gae*, or as Ponzi schemes, which are usually fraudulent, and pyramid or multilevel marketing schemes, which sometimes are. Antigambling laws were not as successful, but they did drive gambling underground. Poker remained an important business networking tool well into the twentieth century, and a source of venture capital as well, but it retained nothing like its nineteenth-century peak. Other gambling games, such as numbers games among urban minorities, retained an important economic function.

It was not changing laws and public attitudes that led to the decline of Wild West financial institutions so much as improved competition from mainstream financiers. Better communications and record-keeping technology allowed capital to flow more freely and efficiently throughout the country, and later the world. The modern corporation could assign professional managers to highly risky businesses, with capital costs far below those of smaller firms, while providing personal financial security to its employees. Only the unreconstructed rebels preferred poker (but there were a lot of us).

But before you consign soft money banks and poker to the economic museum, you should know that they had a child, one that rose to power in the 1970s when those business corporations were floundering and many financial institutions were either failing their customers or falling into bankruptcy, or both. This child shared genes with both parents—it had both gambling and exchange at its core.

THE STORMY, HUSKY, BRAWLING LAUGHTER OF YOUTH

Remember that in the Adventurer/Planter model of the relatively sedate Northeast, each town paired with its parent town. It naturally shipped its goods there, whence they moved to the next town, and so on to a port, unless they were consumed along the way. With such a simple system, and plenty of capital and trust among parties, elaborate financial arrangements were not necessary.

The dynamic self-organized economic network of the West also had centers for consolidation of goods, but they had no chain of natural descendants to feed them. Places like Minneapolis, Chicago, Kansas City, San Francisco, and St. Louis, and hundreds of smaller markets, built processing, storage, and transshipment facilities. Never before in history had such large markets grown up so fast. Between the rapid exploitation of the economic resources of the West and accelerating technological change, facilities had to be built before reliable networks developed to supply the necessary raw materials.

Cities, and city-wannabes, had to compete frantically to keep their facilities operating. Erratic supply of raw materials makes production much more expensive and hinders the development of stable economic relations with larger markets like New Orleans and New York. If Chicago was to realize Carl Sandburg's boast of Hog Butcher to the World, it needed to wrest a steady, predictable supply of pigs from a decidedly unstable region with lots of competition.

With more capital, and better rural law and order, the cities could have sent buyers scouring the hinterlands to purchase crops, livestock, lumber, minerals, and other products. But they didn't have the hard cash for that to work. It would have been suicidal to carry cash outside the city limits, and the only place to spend hard cash was in the cities, anyway. Moreover, owning the goods far away from the cities was less than half the problem. Processing, storage, and transportation were as important as ownership. The cities needed the goods producers to come to them, to drop off their goods and leave with manufactured goods and urban services rather than silver.

This situation is reminiscent of the motley collection of people and assets that showed up at the mining camp or cattle range. One guy wants to buy a boatload of flour in August because he's got a boat and a buyer in New Orleans willing to commit to a firm price today. Another guy has a flour mill, another has a grain-cleaning facility, another one has a railroad, another has a storage silo, and another one knows some farmers willing to commit today to sell wheat at the June harvest. Collectively, they could make a profitable deal, but finding and trusting each other is impractical.

One solution is to imitate the soft money bank by setting up some kind of marketing collective. Each person would sell his asset to the collective, which would apportion the proceeds from the final sale. Without a lot of capital to guarantee payment, however, everyone's economic fate would be linked. If a few members reneged or failed, or the collective was managed badly, all members could be bankrupted. Nevertheless, this solution was tried in many places. It often worked on a relatively small scale, and some of these cooperatives and marketing associations survive today, but the soft money bank remained a secondary economic model for commodity exchange.

I know of no record that anyone ever suggested playing a session of freeze-out poker so that one person would end up with all the assets necessary to commit to the delivery of flour, but it might have happened. If so, it was less popular than the collective idea. But the idea of the poker check was instrumental in the dominant solution that did emerge.

The first trick is to express each asset as a spread. Instead of saying the guy with the flour mill wants to be paid to grind wheat, say he wants to buy wheat and sell flour. The guy with the railroad wants to buy wheat at one location along his line and sell wheat at the railhead in the city. The difference between the buying and the selling price is the fee paid for the service. This is one of the essential insights into futures exchanges: Almost everyone is trading spreads. Traders don't bet that the price of wheat will go up or down; they bet on calendar or location or grade or other spreads. This distinguishes these exchanges from stock exchanges, where, until recently, most transactions were single—either a buy or a sell—rather than buying one thing and simultaneously selling another.

The advantage of trading spreads is that the number of possible assets is reduced. If there are five locations, three grades, and four delivery months, a participant could be offering to convert any of $5 \times 3 \times 4 = 60$ different things into any of the 59 other things. That means you need 3,540 different prices. That's an exaggeration, since no one offers to turn flour back into wheat or move grain backward in time. But you do need hundreds of prices to cover all the important combinations. If everything is quoted as a spread, you need only 60 prices. Each person can subtract one price from another to figure out what he's being offered for his service—and let me emphasize this crucial point—*even if no one imagined his service* so no one bothered to compute the proper price. You also need to standardize the locations, grades, delivery dates, contract sizes, and other specifications. The system breaks down if there are too many variations.

The next trick is to designate a central place and time for everyone who wants to trade in any of the 60 items to meet. The guy with the grain silo, for example, can show up and buy 10,000 bushels of June wheat for $0.90/bushel, and sell 10,000 bushels of August wheat for $1.10. These are forward contracts: Neither wheat nor money changes hands until the agreed delivery date. Our silo owner has just rented his facility from June to August for $2,000.

He has a couple problems, however. First, he has to come up with $9,000 in June, which he doesn't have. True, he's been promised $11,000 in August, but that's too late and, anyway, the guy who made that promise doesn't have $11,000. Second, most of the wheat that comes into the city does not meet the precise contract specifications he has to deliver in August and that he is best equipped to store in June.

The reason these things don't matter is that the silo owner has no intention of completing either contract. A few days before the June delivery deadline, he'll offset both contracts by selling 10,000 bushels of June wheat for the going price and buying 10,000 bushels of August wheat. If the harvest is big and there is a shortage of grain storage, the price of August wheat will be more than $0.20 higher than that of June wheat. The silo owner will take a loss on his forward contracts, but that will be offset by the higher rent he can charge on his facility. If the harvest has been small, his profit on the futures contract will have offset his loss in rental income. He doesn't care what happens to the price of wheat—only what happens to the spread between June and August wheat.

But after he offsets his contracts, he's got a new problem. He's bought June wheat from one person and sold it to another, and the same thing with August wheat. If one of those four guys disappears, the silo owner is on the hook. He'd like to treat the contracts like poker checks and make the buyer responsible for collecting from the seller. What makes this possible is that almost no one takes delivery: By the delivery deadline, almost everyone is holding offsetting contracts. That means there is a ring that connects his purchase of June wheat to his sale. It may go through one counterparty or dozens, but if they can all get together, they can all tear up their contracts and settle for any differences in price. This is exactly what happens after a poker game if there is no bank. In the forward markets, it's called *ring clearing*. In practice, most participants dealt with brokers and guaranteed their performance by posting money as margin. Only the brokers ring-cleared among themselves. Eventually this system evolved into the modern futures exchange with a clearinghouse— first at the Minneapolis Grain Exchange in 1886, but the basic elements were in place much earlier. When a forward contract acquires features that make it suitable for public trading, such as the margin and clearing described here, it is called a *futures* contract. A futures contract involves the same basic economics as a forward contract, but the mechanics are more complex.

I lied a little bit—actually, a lot. I wanted to explain why the futures exchanges developed and the essential nature of spread trading. So I made up the part about the silo and mill owners, and all the other guys, trading the futures spreads. Processors and shippers of commodities use futures markets differently, but I'll get to that in a minute. The main point is that thinking of futures exchanges as places where commodity dealers place spread bets to hedge their operations completely misses their main economic function. Hundreds of traders are watching thousands of spreads, looking for any tiny discrepancy that will earn them a few dollars. The most important fact about futures exchanges, and the reason they are close cousins to poker games, is that they exist so people can gamble.

This is quite different from the nineteenth-century stock market. Although superficially similar in economic function, they should not be confused. There were obvious physical differences. The New York Stock Exchange was much more genteel and calm than the vulgar and frantic Chicago Board of Trade. Most of the stock market floor traders were executing orders for customers in return for commissions; they took no risk. The specialists who traded with their own money were given inside information about customer orders that made their activities almost riskless. The stock market existed for efficient execution of stock orders; it was not primarily a gambling establishment.

Of course, some people did use stocks to gamble. There were even some famous high rollers like Daniel Drew, Jay Gould, Jim Fisk, Cornelius Vanderbilt, and Jesse Livermore. All but Livermore made their fortunes in business before getting into stocks, all lost money on their net stock transactions, and all were crooks. They made money in stocks by trading on inside information, manipulating prices, disseminating false information, looting companies, and bribing legislators. Only the last was clearly illegal at the time, but it was so common as to be unremarkable. Some of the lying and looting may have crossed the legal line, but there were no insider trading or manipulation laws, nor any Securities and Exchange Commission to enforce them. But even when it was legal, it was not honest. People who call a market like this a casino are insulting casinos.

In contrast, the futures exchanges were the source of many fortunes. There was plenty of sharp dealing, notably corners. But corners are open economic bets, and the attempts resulted in losses at least as often as gains. No bribery or breach of fiduciary trust was involved—just an attempt to extract a monopoly profit by owning all the available supply of something. Few successful corners involved a commodity, especially later in the nineteenth century as the supplies got too large for even the wealthiest and boldest traders. Most reported attempted commodity corners were simply large bets that the price of the commodity would go up. In a typical real corner, a group of traders would buy particular location, calendar, or processing spreads greater than the total supply of transportation, storage, or processing available to service them (think Enron's "Fat Boy" trades in the California electricity market—*plus ça change, plus c'est la méme chose*). This was a smaller total value than the entire stock of a commodity, and the purchases could be spread among different commodity exchanges, which made them less obvious. The sellers of these contracts would be forced to buy them back at high prices because the alternative was to deliver on them in roundabout and expensive ways. While this is now illegal, it was part of the game at the time. If you bought Kansas City June wheat and sold Chicago June wheat, you either had arranged for rail transportation between the cities or knew you were making a bet. In any case, cornering the market is quite different from fraud, theft, and bribery.

In standard economic history, futures contracts are said to have evolved from *to-arrive* contracts, which have been known since ancient times in the Near East and China, and exist at least in rudimentary form wherever you have both private enterprise agriculture and money. It's hard for me to believe that anyone who accepts this history has ever traded commodity futures. Trading to-arrive contracts is like old-fashioned stock exchange trading. You buy or you sell, and there's very little evidence that anyone can do better than random chance, except by cheating. It's like betting red or black at roulette. It's relatively calm, with total trading volume proportionate to actual business exchanges. Most people trade one-sided, there is no spread betting, and they hold positions for extended periods of time. Professional traders make their money charging commissions to customers or taking positions with low risk exposure.

In to-arrive contracts, the seller promises to deliver agricultural commodities for a fixed price to a buyer when the commodities arrive in town. Note the implicit assumption that the commodities will arrive in town. The harvest may be early or late, ice may block an important river route, but the seller is making no commitment about when the commodity will arrive. In a typical contract, the seller has to deliver within two weeks of when the first shipment actually does arrive. This is a crucial distinction: The seller is providing a price guarantee, not a delivery guarantee. The buyer cannot use the contract to ensure a steady supply for his processing facility; he can use it only to modify his exposure to price movements.

Such a contract makes sense in the Adventurer/Planter model. The crops come in from known areas; only the time and quantity are uncertain. Some people like to lock in a price ahead of time; others like to wait. To-arrive contracts were never big business, never had a large economic effect. The largest to-arrive market in the United States was Buffalo. From the opening of the Erie Canal until the development of western railroads, Buffalo was the only practical transshipment point for Great Lakes agricultural products for most of the year. Unlike Chicago and other cities that relied on railroad and river transportation, Buffalo didn't have to compete for its crops. Buffalo's futures exchange attracted quiet commission clerks, not the aggressive risk takers of the western exchanges. No one got rich trading futures in Buffalo, but not too many people went broke, either. There is no poker game named Buffalo, although there is a Chicago, an Omaha, and Texas Hold 'Em.

The main economic purpose of the Chicago Board of Trade was to allow traders to gamble in such a manner that the winnings would be invested in infrastructure to enhance the city's regional importance. Like the soft money bank and the poker game, capital had to be concentrated. The obvious approach, tried earlier in the century, was for the government to underwrite projects by guaranteeing bonds or funding them directly with taxes. This led to disaster because the economy was far too dynamic for effective government investment decisions. The one conspicuous success was "Clinton's Folly," the Erie Canal—the nickname coming from the New York governor who championed the state spending. But the New York situation was different. The Erie Canal created a convenient transportation route to producers who had none before; there was no question of competition. Illinois was trying to offer cheaper transportation to producers who had alternatives. This always leads to price wars and usually the bankruptcy of one or both transportation systems. The West was wilder than the East—too wild for gigantic, government-funded development projects.

Infrastructure design was also too complex for bank loan officers or good poker players to be trusted to make the correct decisions. Outside capital from the Northeast came at a high price (especially after Jay Gould et al. finished playing games with it) and only after the markets had already been established. The futures exchanges provided ideal training grounds for learning about infrastructure and funneling concentrations of capital to anyone who noticed an exploitable inefficiency. Every successful corner funded the development of infrastructure to remove a bottleneck; every unsuccessful one prevented overinvestment in an already robust part of the network. New trails were blazed by traders seeking unconventional ways to break attempted corners. The volatility of exchange prices constantly tested all links of the network and sent the scarce capital rapidly to points of greatest need. Fortunes were made and lost on the futures exchanges, to the point that exchange gambles shaped the pattern of development, and the very fabric, of most Mississippi region cities. Indeed, it takes only a little imagination to read commodity price trails in the skylines of all the great cities of the American West.

TRIAGE

I'm now going to engage in a burst of literary triage. I know from experience that most people do not accept that trading futures is the same as playing poker but totally different from trading stocks or to-arrive contracts. Many of them stopped reading a ways back, but if you're still here, you can skip this section. There's another group that knew all along in their bones that poker and futures are inseparable. You don't need this section, either. For those in the middle, I'm going to try an emotional argument. The first group won't accept it, and the second group was born knowing it.

Futures trading is tremendously exciting—emotionally identical to playing poker. It cannot be compared to the routine buying and selling of securities in the hope that the price will go up or down, any more than playing poker can be compared to playing roulette. When you do trade, it lights you up; you know you are alive. You're plugged into a network that lifts you up to the sky or plunges you down to the depths. You never want the market to close; you can't imagine what to do after the bell. You jump out of bed in the morning filled with purpose. It's hard to explain to other people—especially loved ones—but the purpose is to gamble. As Bob Feduniak (a top tournament player and extremely successful trader, whose wife Maureen Feduniak is one of the top women players) told me, the thrill of poker is

> . . . shared in a way that every poker player knows, that every other poker player understands (even if they often don't want to hear the details of the bad beats). Maureen and I certainly have a connection with poker friends that is different. We (and many others) sometimes find it trying to be around even family and close non-poker friends during World Series of Poker and other big events because we're not quite in the same sector of the galaxy at those times.

John Aglialoro, another top player with a successful financial career, told me much the same thing. There is a special bond, he said, between anyone you have sat with at a final table of a major tournament. There is nothing else comparable.

I am often asked why I stopped trading, and sometimes but much less often, why I don't become a professional poker player. The answer is the same in both cases. I love the feeling that comes with these activities, but I don't want to feel it all the time. I like to drink, and some of the best times in my life have come when, and because, I was drunk. But I don't drink every day, and I certainly don't want to be drunk all the time. Few people trade for more than a decade, and the happiest serious poker players I know play relatively infrequently and have another source of income. It's hard to find long-term successful traders or full-time professional poker players with happy marriages—or, indeed, any surviving marriages at all.

Different people experience different physical manifestations of this excitement. For me, it's dreams. After I play poker—even the most casual or low-stakes game—my sleep is broken by restless, creative dreams. The only other time I get them is when I'm trading. All my best (okay, and worst) ideas, and most of the fabric of my personality, come from these dreams. There is a deep, ancient connection between gambling and divination. Some people are plugged into it, and others are not. I'm sure there are other ways of finding meaning in life; this is mine. This is why I know in my soul that futures trading and poker spring from the same mystic source. Paradoxically, they both unleash and harness creativity. It's like pushing in the clutch of a car to start the engine, then releasing it to engage the wheels, and it's got the same feeling of power smoothly controlled by your skill (I abhor automatic transmissions). In the introduction, I described how many billionaires got their start from poker winnings and that writers and artists created their greatest works under pressure from gambling losses. If the winner from your weekly poker game is going to parlay the winnings into the next Microsoft, and the loser is going to use it as inspiration for the next *The Gambler,* who the hell cares about the money? You want to be in that game.

It is not, however, megalomania. It often seems that way to outsiders, but megalomaniacs and other neurotics go broke quickly in either trading or poker. The same is true for excitement junkies. I don't have to think for a minute to tell you the best time of my life. My son was four and my daughter had just been born. My wife and I rented a house on the Oregon coast for three weeks in August. I spoke to almost no one outside my family. I woke up at 3:00 A.M. to feed my daughter, while watching reruns of *Sea Hunt* and *Miami Vice* on television. Then I'd put her back to sleep and take a long walk on the beach to look at the stars and the sunrise, then go back to bed. There was no excitement. I had no interest in playing cards or in what the markets were doing. Toss in a good library and a fireplace for winter, stock the place with good food and wine, and I could happily live my entire life that way. But I'd never write or come up with new ideas. I would gradually lose any connection to other people. I'd forget how to talk. Poker and trading keep me plugged into society, and to a cosmic muse. I don't need them to be happy, but I do need them to be productive and social.

I also don't need poker or trading for excitement. I've had more exciting times in real life than at card tables or on trading floors. When hiking in the Andes, I washed my face at a waterfall, then discovered the ground was covered with moss that was completely slippery. I had absolutely zero traction. I could move my feet in a walking motion, but it didn't change my position one bit. I was on a wide, flat ledge with about two inches of water from the fall slowly pushing me toward a sheer, 2,000-foot drop (okay, I didn't measure it, I didn't even have the guts to look down afterward, but it was high enough) a few dozen yards away. That was exciting. I sure felt alive then, even if I didn't expect to be for much longer. In case you're interested (and I hope you are), I finally got down on my belly and swam to shore. It took nerve, because the force of the water was much greater when I lay down and you don't generate much forward force swimming in two inches of water. I remember wondering whether I should get on my back instead, so my last seconds of life would have a good view. No poker hand or trade compares to that gamble. At the height of the dot-com boom, I founded an Internet company that ran a public mutual fund. I bought 5 percent stakes in public companies, announced them live on CNN from the floor of the New York Stock Exchange, and organized other shareholders to improve management performance. That was exciting. I once found out at 4:00 P.M. that the board of directors of another public company had suspended the company's founders and top two officers, and I had to go in at 4:30 to tell employees who had never seen me before and were only vaguely and theoretically aware of what a board of directors was, that they were now taking directions from me instead of the CEO or president while the company was teetering on the edges of several disasters. That's a thrill. If I wanted full-time excitement, I'd still be running a company, or fighting to take over public companies, or taking chances in the Andes. Poker and trading are exciting, but not as exciting as real life. Poker and trading excitement is a by-product of a deeper meaning.

Of the three things I've gotten from poker and trading, the money I made matters the least to me. The people I've met are more important. I'm not being sappy—I've made more money and had more interesting opportunities from contacts and friends I've made in these endeavors than I took out in direct profits. But by far the most valuable thing I took away was the creativity the games inspired. That's why I know poker and trading are the same thing.

A TALL, BOLD SLUGGER SET VIVID AGAINST THE LITTLE, SOFT CITIES

Another piece of evidence that futures exchanges are about gambling rather than the commodity business is the widespread popularity of bucket shops. These are firms that accept bets on commodity prices, but match them among their customers rather than trading them on the floor of the exchange. They are bookies, pure and simple, taking bets on commodity price movements rather than sporting events. They offer the same economic bet as a futures contract, but charge less commission, allow transactions in smaller sizes, stay open later, and offer greater leverage than exchange brokers. They also offer more consumer choice. A popular contract was what we call today a down-and-out call option. The buyer puts up a small amount of money to take a bet on a large amount of commodity. If the price of the commodity falls to a certain level, the buyer loses, even if the price later goes back up (that's the down-and-out feature). But it means a small investment with limited loss can return a huge profit, if the price goes up and keeps going up. An up-and-out put is a similar bet that the commodity price will go down and keep going down. A futures contract also offers the ability to make a large bet with a small amount of money down, but the investor is on the hook for the full loss in that case. Exchanges did offer options trading (called "privileges" at the time) but eventually outlawed them to more clearly distinguish themselves from bucket shops.

By the way, you see a lot of fanciful explanations of the name *bucket shop,* usually involving some disgusting dregs of beverage processing sold to the most desperate alcoholics, or an insidious drug whipped up in street-corner buckets, or a penny-ante scheme to steal price quotations using a bucket and a rope. This is all exchange propaganda. None of those bucket shops ever existed, nor did they give their name to the financial kind. The term *to bucket* orders, meaning to combine or offset customer orders, was common and not pejorative. Exchange brokers did this all the time and ran most of the bucket shops until the exchanges prohibited that practice. Only the exchanges, and the newspapers they advertised in, hated the bucket shops.

Clearly, the bucket shop has no connection to any real economic activity any more than numbers games that pay off based on the last digits of the volume number of the New York Stock Exchange or Treasury auctions. They're just bets on numbers, and it doesn't matter that the numbers are determined in a financial institution instead of a ballpark or racetrack. It's just as clear that there's no real difference between the bucket shop and the futures exchange. Customers used them interchangeably. It's true that small-volume customers preferred the retail-friendly, inexpensive, convenient bucket shops, and larger wholesale customers needed to go to exchange brokers to execute in larger size, but many customers fell in the middle. Also many shops were run by exchange members or used the exchange to lay off bet imbalances. The exchanges finally won a long legal battle to have the bucket shops declared illegal, despite their inability to show any difference between the exchange and the shops. Bucket shops are similar to "curb" exchanges run by nonmembers of the exchange on the streets outside major exchanges, offering street-corner transactions at trading-floor prices and cut-rate commissions. The American Stock Exchange began life as the curb exchange to the New York Stock Exchange. It didn't change its name from "the Curb" until 1953.

The reason the bucket shops eventually lost was that they could not concentrate enough capital to make meaningful infrastructure investments. In the early days, traders learned at bucket shops and acquired a stake to join the exchange. That was how Jesse Livermore, the famous stock trader known as The Great Bear, got his start. But as more capital became available, the nickels and dimes concentrated by bucket shops lost their relative significance.

From the standpoint of people dealing in physical commodities—farmers, transporters, and processors—the futures exchange operated like a bank, but one that accepted deposits in and lent commodities rather than money. It was definitely a soft money bank, since the amount of deliverable physical commodity was always a small fraction of the amount that had been lent out. Then and now, farmers seldom used futures contracts. No one wants to deposit into a soft money bank.

Processors did like to borrow, however. This is done by a transaction called *going short against physical*. The processor would buy whatever he wanted to transport, store, clean, grind, or otherwise process. He would get the exact grade and type he wanted—not necessarily something that met contract specifications for delivery in the futures market. He would then sell the same amount of the commodity (or the closest he could find in a futures contract) at a future date, close to the time he expected to finish his processing.

This combination is sometimes explained as hedging the price risk of inventory. If the price of the commodity goes down during processing, the processor makes a profit on the futures position to offset the loss in value of his inventory; if the price goes up, the processor can afford the futures loss because the value of his inventory went up. This scenario, however, does not correspond with reality. When you look at the larger picture, the processor might be in the opposite position. He may have already sold his output at a fixed price, in which case he has no inventory price risk. He may even be negatively exposed to a rise in price of inventory. That usually means a shortage of the commodity, which reduces the value of processing facilities and more than offsets any gain on inventory.

In practice, most processors stuck to their businesses and were content to pay and receive the average input and output prices. Commodity price fluctuation was a very small part of their overall business risk. Commodities were not even a large part of their costs, compared to labor, fuel, interest, and other inputs. What they did care about was steady, predictable supply of raw material that allowed them to run their facilities at low cost and make long-term commitments to buyers. This—not hedging inventory price risk—led to a successful business.

The desire for stability encouraged the processors to buy large amounts of commodities—perhaps enough for three months of processing. A miller, for example, might buy a three-month supply of cleaned wheat from a grain elevator and sell wheat futures at the exchange. That gives him wheat now and a promise to repay wheat in the future. In other words, he borrowed wheat. That grain elevator might sell much more wheat than it had on hand, secure that deliveries would be made before buyers called for their wheat. The futures traders kept close eyes on virtual demand (the three-months' supply the miller wants to hold for stability) and actual demand (the amounts the miller actually takes from the elevator). They were alert to anything that might interrupt the smooth functioning, crop failures, transportation shortages, problems with preprocessing, or increased milling rates. Careful backup plans were laid for every eventuality. Of course, each trader was looking at only a small part of the picture, and was doing it to make money rather than help anyone, but it worked far better than any centrally planned system.

If the infrastructure projects had been small or continuous, the exchanges would not have needed their essential gambling nature. They could have been sedate places of price discovery and planning. But either you build a rail line between two points or you don't. Whether or not you do it affects everyone in the network—every other rail line and every processor of every kind in every city. With a large, secure supply of capital, you could plan out the whole system and build it in logical stages. Without that, you've got to accumulate the available capital in one person's hands, and let him use it for the move that makes most sense to him. Everyone else will react, weather and other forms of luck will have their input, and someone else will get rich enough to make the next move. This system is brutal and unfair, ruthless and irrational, but it works with matchless efficiency. To a financially trained poker player, it's the most beautiful organization in history. This—rather than anything that happened in New York or Washington—is the source of the American economic miracle.

FLASHBACK

THE EDUCATION OF A POKER PLAYER

I learned poker at age seven, playing for edible stakes. I learned about playing poker for money from a friend's father, who was a traveling salesman. He had had a good traditional poker education and taught me the disciplined principles of no-limit Five-Card Stud. He had learned from people who thought that was the only serious poker game (a common belief at the time, akin to today's preference among some purists for no-limit Texas Hold 'Em).

My friends preferred games with lots of wild cards and made-up-as-you-go rules. One hand might be to deal nine cards—three down, three up, and three down; jokers, twos, and one-eyed jacks are wild; whoever has the most cards matching the suit of their lowest-ranking hole card splits the pot. The dealer could even specify "changies," meaning she (this was predominantly a choice of females) could change the rules at any time during the hand. As you might imagine, there were a lot of arguments about pots turning on differing memories or interpretations of the rules; a changies hand guaranteed a fight. It was a childhood version of the "sign now, sue later" contract.

My mentor was, of course, appalled by such games, but with a child's plasticity, I found no trouble applying his strict principles to the anarchy. "No rules" is a rule, and good poker players can still find an edge. I repaid my tutor by helping him work out the effect of exotic games and rules on the play. It seems that his customers and salesmen buddies were fond of variants like draw poker, wild cards, community cards, even games like Anaconda and Night Baseball. They liked limit games. He had learned a simple poker creed well, but it was all rote, and he couldn't easily apply it to new games. I had a good head for math and cards, and we dealt a lot of hands back and forth to figure out how hand values changed and what situations different games presented.

I later discovered that old-style professional poker players almost invariably had similarly dealt hands to absorb probabilities and taught themselves how to calculate, in either early teen or preteen years. These were people who made a living in technically illegal private games, not tournament players or poker writers. It used to be said that professionals at either pool or poker had to start by their early teens and generally drop out of school to have enough time to really learn the game when the mind and body were young enough to absorb it. Like classical music, chess, and mathematical genius, either you had it or you didn't—and if you did, you had to develop it early. Lord Chesterfield famously admonished his son that playing the flute well was the sign of a well-rounded education, but playing it too well was the sign of a misspent youth.

That many modern poker champions have come to the game late is a result, I think, of the advent of better poker theory and computer simulators as well as the differences between tournament and private play. Tournaments emphasize short-term survival rather than long-term thriving. It's easier to learn short-term skills. Tournaments also remove many of the social aspects of play, like getting invited to good games and collecting from losers. These were much more important than actual card play to older professionals. The narrower focus on card play and betting skills is easier to learn as an adult.

Frank's Grandma

I moved from this laboratory work to a literal penny-ante game. My friend Frank was being raised by his grandparents. Granddad was a retired railroad engineer who had played serious poker before marrying a woman whose religious convictions forbade card play, let alone gambling. In an inspiring story of the triumph of love over dogma, Grandma agreed that playing for pennies wasn't really gambling, and it was okay to have cards as long as there were no pictures of people on them. (You could buy such decks from German manufacturers.) So Granddad got to have his fun with friends at low stakes, and Grandma held the line against sin.

Granddad was a steady, serious poker player, who learned to defend his paycheck against railroad workers, who have a lot of time to perfect their game. His friends were cut from the same cloth. Grandma learned the game only after getting married. She was a brilliant player whose only flaw was letting her hyperaggressive style spin out of control. I will remember to my dying day having a heart four flush after five cards had been dealt in Seven-Card Stud (high only) against Grandma's open pair of aces. This is not a promising hand to play, but one other ace and no other hearts had been exposed, and some first-round action had put about 30¢ in the pot, a moderately large amount for our game. Any thought I had of drawing it out was crushed by the look in Grandma's eyes when she pushed 2,000 pennies into the pot, more money than my stack and certainly more than I could raise in pennies, the only legal tender. This was not the civilized table stakes game preferred by modern players. We enforced the old rules: You had 24 hours to match a bet (hands and deck sealed and held by a third party), or forfeit your stake.

Frank later showed me a wall in the basement that held Grandma's poker winnings from 40 years of marriage—jars with over $1,000 worth of pennies. She was willing to bet it all with anyone on any hand. She was good, and she taught me a lot, but I've always felt I could have used her aggressiveness against her if I could have raised a big enough stake in pennies. The male players in the game often discussed pooling our pennies or even buying rolls from the bank (something forbidden by the spirit of the rules) to mount a challenge, but Granddad's harrowing tales of previous failures dissuaded us.

John Aglialoro is a national poker champion who did well on Wall Street and, later, running businesses. He's currently the CEO and half owner of Cybex, the gym equipment company. He also learned poker from his grandmother. He recalls losing the first time he played her, and expecting her to give the money back. She didn't. He credits that with teaching him a lifelong lesson in reality.

Aglialoro thinks it is very important for young people to play poker because it teaches objectivity. Most people are unreasonably optimistic some of the time and unreasonably pessimistic other times. Good poker players learn how to make the tough folds and when to pay to see more cards. I asked him if he thought gambling led to problems like petty theft to cover losses. He replied, "The stress just brought out a character flaw that would have surfaced anyway. It's better to find that out young. The vast majority learn an important lesson that's not in the textbooks: If you do something stupid, you suffer for it."

More Games and the People Who Play Them

In high school, I played in a regular game with the debate club/chess club/calculus class crowd. National bridge champion and hedge fund manager Josh Parker explained the nuances of serious high school games players to me. The chess player did well in school, had no friends, got 800s on his SATs, and did well at a top college, followed up by acquiring a top PhD. The poker and backgammon set (one crowd in the 1970s) did badly in school, had tons of friends, aced their SATs, and were stars at good colleges. The bridge players flunked out of high school, had no friends, aced their SATs, and went on to drop out of top colleges. In the 1980s, we all ended up trading options together.

Playing poker with champions from other games is very instructive. A bridge champion effortlessly remembers every card and knows the probabilities cold. She's got a pretty shrewd idea of what you're holding, and she's got excellent nerve for taking calculated risks. If you're going to beat her, it's got to be with a well-honed strategic sense: Bridge does not teach game theory.

World-class chess and backgammon players have incredible short-term memories and know combinations. But both are complete information games where nothing is hidden from either player. Chess also lacks randomness. More important, in both games you're playing against the board, not directly with another person. You concentrate on the playing tokens, not on a table full of people. If you're going to beat these people, it will be by paying attention, and by understanding that poker is not one-on-one. Poker rewards attention, while chess and backgammon reward concentration.

We played a lot of poker on debate trips, and the same crowd played regularly at home. The level of card play was pretty high—these were smart kids with good memories and mathematical minds. Everyone in the game went on to some kind of distinction as a top professor, lawyer, or scientist. Only one gained the wrong kind of fame: He decided his elderly neighbors were international poisoners and killed them both with an axe. He got away with it until he walked into a police station and confessed.

However, the strategic thinking required for good poker was missing in these debate games. People played straightforwardly. Instead of bluffing, people overbet on marginal hands. Bluffing is raising with a hand that should fold, not calling with a borderline hand. I had better teachers than other players and was able to make a comfortable profit without much effort in this game.

A question that comes up a lot in online poker discussions is how should a novice learn poker? I think you're best with a good, basic book. I like *Poker for Dummies* by Richard D. Harroch and Lou Krieger. When you've mastered that, pick up a good theory book— David Sklansky's *The Theory of Poker* is the best—and a computer simulator. You don't need books on how to play specific games; you get that much better from a computer program. You can pick up 100,000 hands' worth of experience in a few months. Of course, you don't get the emotion, psychology, or tells, but that's an advantage at the beginning. You need the card play situations and strategy to become second nature, you need a feel for the probabilities, before you can exploit the human elements of the game. Once you've done this kind of homework, you shouldn't have trouble finding serious players to help you along. Most experts hate to be asked for advice by people who haven't put in the effort to learn the basics, but it's a joy to teach a diligent pupil.

Harvard

In contrast to most poker players, I had a coddled poker education. I learned from good players in friendly games. The games were primarily social (maybe not for Frank's grandmother), but we took the poker seriously. It wasn't until I got to Harvard that I found games in which the money was the main thing. At first, I had no trouble adapting. I found some congenial games in which I liked the people, enjoyed the play, and could take out enough money to make a difference.

I didn't exactly need the money from poker, but I did need to earn money either by playing cards or by working part-time jobs as a lab assistant or computer programmer. The poker was more fun, and over my four years at Harvard, I averaged three times the hourly wage of those other jobs. I could have won at an even better rate, but at the cost of killing games more quickly. It also seemed like a sign from God that the money to construct my freshman-year dorm, Stoughton Hall, had

been raised in a lottery. How could future generations of students not follow that example?

You had a few choices for serious poker games at Harvard. Bill
Gates—this was before he dropped out—ran one in Currier House. I
played there once in my freshman year, but didn't like it. It was tight,
tense, and unfriendly—boring for most of the night and when a big
hand came up you always felt that someone had lost more than he could
afford. The law school had great games, but they discouraged undergraduates. I played in one with Scott Turow, who went on to write successful legal thrillers. He's one of the people who got me thinking about
the connection between poker and writing. I also played some at the
business school. I learned later from some of the people I played with
that George W. Bush was a regular at those games, and one of the better players, but I have no recollection of playing with him. At the time,
he would have been just another ambassador's son. Maybe when I pick
up my Presidential Medal of Freedom he'll ask me if I really had the full
house he folded a flush to in 1975.

My favorite places to play were the finals clubs. These are private
clubs for wealthy and socially prominent students. None "punched" me
to join, nor could I have afforded the dues if they had. But if there is a
heaven for poker players, no doubt a safe, physically pleasant place to
play cards with rich Harvard students is part of it. The difficulty was in
getting invited to the games.

Pangs of Conscience

By my sophomore year, I began having qualms about my poker play. I'd
always tried to make a profit playing, but originally I played mainly for
the fun of the game. As the winnings became larger and the games were
selected for the size of the stakes rather than the quality of the conversation, I began to wonder whether I was hustling suckers, doing for
money what I pretended to do for pleasure. Some of the games were
what you might call semiprofessional: You had to be recognized as a
good player to get in. That never bothered me, but it wasn't all that profitable. Also, I didn't have the nerve at the time to play with nonstudents,
and the semiprofessional games tended to merge with serious, high-
stakes, grown-up poker in the Boston area. The real money came from

loose social games, where any moderately careful player could expect to win.

I noticed that I had unconsciously adopted a style to maximize my income. I collected jokes and gossip to make cheerful conversation, and I was nice to everyone whether I liked them or not. I would show up at 11 P.M. (most of the easy money came after midnight) with a pizza, just as people were getting hungry and the shops were closing. I tried to take my money in quiet small pots, leaving the bragging value of big pot wins to others. I kept track of who won how much, and when possible tried to steer money from the better players (who were competition) to the losers (who might quit the game if they lost too much). I lent money freely (apparently freely—I kept careful track to be sure it was a rake-back, not a gift) and never asked for it back. I raised no objection to the occasional clumsy cheating. Cheaters are the easiest players to beat, and allegations break up games.

This kind of behavior isn't murder, but it was hard to justify. Why be false for money you don't need? It also scared me how naturally I had slipped into this pattern. I don't think anyone had ever taught me to do it, and I don't think I learned from anyone's example. I worried that my nature was to be a dishonest parasite.

This came to a head when a player I will call Dixie accused me of cheating at a game in one of the finals clubs. I've never cheated at poker (but there's little pride in that, since I've never had to), and this particular charge was absurd. It was Seven-Card Stud (high only). I was dealing and had a flush with only two exposed cards. This is a powerful hand for its rank and deception. But it's also a hard hand to deal yourself. It requires five cards, and you can have no idea at the beginning of the hand how many people will stay in to take cards. The only practical way to cheat your way to this flush is to gather five suited cards unobtrusively while collecting the cards, put them on the bottom, false shuffle and reverse the cut, then bottom deal five times. That's a lot of work compared to, say, giving yourself pocket aces. Any amateur can do that.

But the really silly thing is that Dixie had only a pair of jacks (exposed). I could have had lots of hands to beat him. Only a pure bluff hand would have lost, since I could see his jacks. To cheat at poker, it doesn't help much to give yourself good cards; you can get the same effect just by folding more often. Everyone is dealt a certain number of good hands. If you throw away all the bad ones, you'll end up playing only good ones. Cheating will save you some antes because you don't have to throw away as many hands, but that's not likely to be worth the risk. To gain an advantage cheating, you have to give one or more victims slightly less good cards. On top of it all, it wasn't a big pot. Even Dixie didn't bet the ranch on exposed jacks.

A true accusation does not cut deeply, because you know you're guilty. A false one usually doesn't cut, either, because you know you're innocent. But an accusation that is false in fact, but which your conscience insists is morally true, can be devastating. I didn't rig the deck, but I won as consistently as if I had. What's the real difference?

I don't remember what I said, but I'd like to believe it was something like, "Do you have any reason to say that or are you just having trouble with the concept that two jacks can lose?" It may have been more like "I was not!" Anyway, I remember the upshot was that I suggested he find another game if he didn't like this one and save his accusations until he could back them up.

This was a very tense moment for me. He was a club member; I wasn't. These were his friends; I felt like an outsider. I felt certain they believed Dixie: How could they not when I was a consistent winner and relative stranger? I thought there was an even chance they would ask me to leave, or at least break up the game. But no one moved or said anything, and Dixie soon left. The game resumed, and no one discussed the incident. I felt obliged to stay, since leaving would have seemed to confirm the accusation, but I wasn't having any fun, especially when it was my turn to deal.

I cut back on my play for the next few weeks and did not return to Dixie's club. No one said anything, but I wondered if everyone thought I was cheating. Between this awkwardness and my moral qualms, I considered giving up poker.

Things got even worse when I got a call from a woman with an impossibly syrupy Southern accent. She was a secretary who wanted to set up an appointment for me with a man whose last name was the same as Dixie's. She didn't know what it was about, but he would be in Boston the following week and wanted to see me at his hotel.

Meeting Mr. Dixie

A wiser person would have refused the meeting, or at least insisted on knowing the purpose, but by this point I was thinking like a guilty person. Not showing up, or negotiating the terms of the meeting, would make me seem guilty. As someone who believed he was morally guilty, I had to act like a complete innocent. The complete innocent would be angry at the accusation and expect an apology. He certainly would not be afraid to meet his accuser's relatives. Twisted as this sounds, twisted as this is, it is how I thought. My poker skills had completely deserted me; I was acting like a fish (a bad poker player).

I wondered what was going to happen. I imagined everything from being challenged to a duel to being beaten up by thugs or being threatened with legal action. I admit those things seem absurd, and I knew they were absurd at the time. But what else made sense?

My thinking was colored by the recent experience of my friend Brian, who'd met a friendly young woman at an off-campus party. One minute, he was getting high with her sitting on his lap, her wardrobe in disarray. The next minute, police busted in and hauled Brian into the station house, and he faced possible arraignment in night court for statutory rape. The girl on his lap turned out to be a 15-year-old (Brian was 16 at the time) in the middle of a custody battle. Private detectives seeking evidence of parental unfitness had tailed her to the party and tipped the police. A lawyer from Harvard showed up and asked that Brian be remanded to the custody of the university. A judge so ordered. Brian asked the lawyer what that meant. The lawyer shrugged, "Nothing."

We discussed this unfathomable event endlessly, with many theories—none very convincing. But it clearly showed that mysterious fixes were in place and that adults had strange kinds of power. The only sensible thing was to stay away from adults. (We never considered the alternatives of staying away from wild parties, drugs, or fifteen-year-old girls.)

Reflecting on this, I came up with a theory for my case. Dixie complained to Mr. Dixie that he had been cheated in a poker game. Mr. Dixie couldn't make much of a fuss, since Dixie had no evidence, the game was illegal for everyone, and the amount of money was small. But outraged Southern honor demanded revenge. If Mr. Dixie could draw me away from campus and get me to engage in some kind of illegal behavior, he could enlist the forces of the law to avenge the insult. So I decided he would ask me to play poker or offer me drugs or something of the sort. I resolved to act as if I were on film the entire time, as I expected to be. I know this sounds paranoid, and I'm not sure if I really believed it at the time, but my suspicions were running at a fever pitch.

In keeping with my bravado, I put on my only jacket and tie (I didn't own a suit). That turned out to be a good move. I met Mr. Dixie in the bar of the Ritz Hotel, which encouraged ties, and he took me to Maison Robert, the best French restaurant in Boston in those days, which required them. Mr. Dixie was thoroughly charming, which only heightened my mistrust. I was scanning for private detectives, cameras, thugs, or undercover police, and, of course, I saw plenty of them.

We chatted a little about our lives. He said nothing about poker or cheating or the reason for the meeting, and I was determined to wait him out. I might be frightened and clueless, out of my league, and short on options, but I was going to be relaxed and repay charm for charm. Perhaps it would carry the day, or at least solace my pride during the coming long, dark years in prison.

Eventually, over escargot and sauvignon blanc, Mr. Dixie mentioned that his son Dixie had said I was a good poker player. "Aha," I thought, "a euphemism for cheater." Mr. Dixie went on to explain that he had always considered poker to be a very important business networking tool. If he didn't know people well, he preferred to do business with people whom he had played poker with, or at least people who had played poker with people he had played poker with. It gave insight into character and business sense, strategic ability, and attitudes toward risk. Good poker players, he said, were objective and in control, and it was dangerous to get involved in business with people who fooled themselves or got out of control.

Now I got it. He was going to offer to cut me into some kind of illegal deal. I would either get swindled or get arrested.

He went on to explain that he had raised Dixie to share his views, but his son had been a mild disappointment. His card play was decent, but he couldn't read people. For the first time since Dixie had accused me of cheating, I began to think. As I remember it, I sat openmouthed with a fork in my hand for 10 minutes sifting over the implications. I like to believe that in reality I kept my poker face and made an instant deduction; since I'm telling the story, let's say I did.

I had always considered Dixie a wild player who lost because he took too many chances. Most losing poker players are passive. They call too often, raise and fold too seldom. They are always reacting to other players, never forcing other players to react to them. They will pay far too much money to see whether their hands will improve, far too little money to see my cards. Dixie was a genuinely aggressive player, which put him in the top 20 percent, but he didn't seem to back up his style with the necessary calculation.

Now I could see that I stood between Dixie and making money. His aggressive, wild style encouraged other players to call him. He lost a lot of moderate pots, but could win a really gigantic one. I never won large pots, partly because I preferred quiet winnings, but also because I rarely got caught betting a lot of money on a beatable hand. My tactics imposed too high a tax on Dixie's advertising and induced the other players to be more cautious. Moreover, it wasn't just about the money for Dixie (as I would learn later). He and his father believed that poker was a place to earn an image, and the right image at Harvard would translate into lifetime network benefits. They wanted to be seen as aggressive risk takers who always won when it really mattered. I wanted to win as much money as possible, while being thought of as a regular guy who broke even, or maybe made only a little. However, even for me it wasn't just about the money: I would not have stood still for being thought of as a loser.

This balance between moneymaking and image is very important in serious poker. Players will tell you it's only about the money, then turn around and tip the dealer. If it's only about money, why tip? Some professionals make a living by getting people to want to beat them. They may be abusive to make people want revenge, or they may make winning seem fantastically attractive by putting up an envy-inducing front. Others try to be thought of as lucky, to get people to come after them out of greed.

My strategy of quiet extraction while pretending to be an average player only works for people like Harvard students, who have a wide choice of games. If you play in one place all the time, the statistical evidence of your winning soon outweighs any front you can manage. The tactic is too slow for people who blow into town, bust the game, and leave. It eventually destroys games, and it doesn't generate the next game. If no one knows you win, no one seeks you out to beat you.

Mr. Dixie went on to relate that Dixie had a nice game before someone invited me. He was winning money regularly and establishing an important image among future leaders who would help him in life. He'd worked hard to select the game and mold it to his liking, and he didn't want to find a new one. So he called his wise old dad for advice. "Wait until he is dealing and has a good hand," counseled Dad, "and accuse him of cheating. Those quiet bookkeepers can't handle that. If he's bad, he'll blow his stack and walk out. If he's good, he'll slip away quietly to avoid attention. He can't win if people are watching him, because once they figure out he's winning, he loses his edge."

I wasn't letting my guard down yet, thinking this could still be a setup. But beneath it all, I felt vast relief. I had been feeling guilty, and it was a tremendous thrill to realize that Dixie and his dad had a hundred times more to feel guilty about. Dixie was far more deceptive than I was. His dad could plot lies to destroy a kid, then chat about it casually over escargot. They could do these things, and I couldn't deny I liked them— Mr. Dixie, especially. I couldn't recall having a pleasanter time while being totally honest. If I could like him, I could like myself. It never occurred to me to get angry at the deception; viewed in Mr. Dixie's terms, it was a reasonable strategic move.

Then Mr. Dixie shocked me again. He and his son wanted to surrender. Dixie had been frozen out, not only of the game, but in the club. Everyone took my side, outraged that Dixie had falsely accused the friendliest and most honest guy in the game. They didn't want to play until Dixie apologized and I came back. I had totally misread the situation—and accidentally pulled off a successful bluff.

The Book

Or had I? If the evening had ended there, I would have thought so, but Mr. Dixie gave me a present: a copy of Frank R. Wallace's *A Guaranteed Income for Life by Using the Advanced Concepts of Poker*. I had read many poker books and academic articles, taking advantage of the great libraries I had access to. But I'd never heard of this book. It was totally unlike the rule book/basic strategy guides and cold mathematical abstractions I had seen. The book is a thinly veiled first person account of how Wallace made a living playing poker. He didn't play in casinos or tournaments; he got into many friendly games. The book spends no time on card play; it assumes you have that mastered. It tells you how to gain additional advantages by watching flashed and unintentionally marked cards, keeping the other players playing badly but betting high, and keeping the loose bad players in the game while discouraging the tight good ones.

I had been doing a lot of this stuff without thinking about it. Some of the rest was useful, but a lot were things I wouldn't do. For example, bringing a hero sandwich with mustard to the table, knowing that a few smudges will get on some cards, crosses the line to cheating for me. Taking advantage of things that happen naturally, if the dealer flashes a card or a jack gets a bent corner, is part of poker. If you don't do it, you lose to people who do. But deliberately marking a card is indisputably cheating. Bringing mustard is clearly the second case to me, not the first. It's not that I think cheating is so terrible. But I didn't need the mustard trick, or some of Wallace's other techniques, to beat most players, and they wouldn't work on really good players, anyway.

Wallace's book did blow away my adolescent moral quavering. He wrote in plain words exactly what I did. The quickest road to moral helplessness is to try to reason things out in euphemisms. If your character is any good, you won't go too far wrong as long as you cast your decisions in clear, simple terms. Life's a little complicated sometimes, but nowhere near as complicated as talking about life. Laid out in black-and-white, I had no trouble putting my stake in the ground and saying, "This far and no farther." I didn't have to think about the location—one place felt right. I've always been uncomfortable with making a series of questionable choices; I'm afraid of turning bad by degrees. I think a few questionable choices are part of being human, and I never aspired to sainthood, but I know you can get to some very bad places without making a single truly bad decision.

A lot of things clicked into place after that. A part of my character was formed that has served me well in the 30 years since. This incident is one of the reasons I have great respect for poker as a moral guide, especially for people who choose careers in finance.

CHAPTER 7

The Once-Bold
Mates of Morgan

*How Modern Derivatives Trading Saved
the World in the 1970s*

The exciting era that created poker and futures markets came to an end in the 1890s, to be followed by a period of business and financial consolidation. The huge companies that would dominate twentieth-century business—the Generals Motors, Mills, and Electric—were formed through trust acquisition, directed mostly by J.P. Morgan. Improvements in financial technology meant that much of the gambling could be squeezed out of finance. Investment was still risky, of course, but there was no need to add extra risk to bounce over capital barriers. To use an engineering analogy, the economy went from high-temperature fabrication methods to low temperature. Business management was rationalized and professionalized. Life became duller and safer, more middle-class.

By temperament, I regret the switch. I'm glad I came to adulthood after this peace had broken down. But the 75-year spiritual reign of Morgan saw the final destruction of medieval holdover monarchies and religious tyrannies in most of the world, the integration of a tremendous flow of immigrants, survival through the most brutal and destructive wars in history, and stunning progress in science and technology. I wouldn't have wanted to live through it, but despite the unparalleled horrors, the age can take pride in unparalleled accomplishments.

THE CRASH OF '79

The 1970s was a depressing decade for a lot of reasons. There were the bad clothes and music, of course, but there was worse. The signature genre of the decade was the disaster movie, in which you got introduced to a bunch of characters only to see most of them drowned, crashed, blown up, burned, or otherwise destroyed, while they whined, bickered, and sleazed the whole time.

Another set of popular movies chronicled a very painful end of the world, always brought on by human stupidity. Rent *Silent Running* or the *Omega Man* if you don't know what I mean. *Carnal Knowledge* passed for a sex comedy (and Art Garfunkel passed for an actor). Even the popcorn action flicks managed to be downbeat, like *Death Wish* and *Dirty Harry*. Economics best sellers, from *Limits to Growth* to *The Crash of '79*, all prophesied disaster. The actual economy gave all the support it could, with a race to the bottom between stock and bond returns. We figured it didn't matter anyway, because no currencies seemed likely to retain any value, and the banking system was going to collapse. That is, if the world didn't end first. The economic efficiency and lifetime security of the modern corporation seemed to vanish overnight. The 1960s put a man on the moon; in the 1970s not only didn't we push farther, but budget cuts and technology mistakes meant we couldn't maintain the foothold in space. Brutal, totalitarian, impoverished communist states controlled almost half the people on earth, and there was not a single example of a country emerging from communism back to freedom or prosperity. I'm not even going to mention Vietnam, Afghanistan, the killing fields, rampant terrorism, the oil embargo, polywater, stagflation, or "Ford to City: Drop Dead." You had to be there, and I hope you weren't.

When the call went out for energetic risk takers to save the world, it wasn't clear that anyone would answer. Three-quarters of a century of suppressing risk meant that few people remembered what it was like when dynamic, self-organized financial networks catalyzed economic growth. Plenty of people knew about risk, of course, but how many of them also understood finance? There wasn't much call for smart people in finance before 1970. Interest rates didn't move much, and corporate borrowers seldom defaulted, so there was not much room to distinguish yourself in bond management. Foreign exchange rates were fixed. Stock prices moved, but no one could do better than pick them at random, so that didn't take a genius. Then, suddenly, interest rates were oscillating so much that bonds became riskier than stocks. And stocks weren't so much risky in the 1970s as predictably and safely going down. After a decade of debate over whether corporations should maximize growth or shareholder wealth, boards of directors threw in the towel and embraced stakeholder capitalism, meaning the stock could go down as long as employees and the government got to share in the shrinking pie of shareholder money. President Nixon (the poker player) took the United States off the gold standard in 1971, making all the world's currencies suddenly fiat currencies, worth whatever the government said they were. Since governments had no credibility, some currencies inflated and some hyperinflated. A dollar went from being worth about a gram of gold down to about 40 milligrams, with micrograms seemingly in the near future.

BRIDGE BUMS, CHICAGO SCHOOL, AND THE PIT

Fortunately, although the financial industry did not require smart people, a group of maverick academics had been thinking hard about finance since the mid-1950s. Just as important, the Chicago Board of Trade had not forgotten what made the American economy great. Working with academics from the University of Chicago, the Board of Trade introduced trading in stock options in 1973 at the newly created Chicago Board Option Exchange. Stock trading became fun again. The price of a seat on the New York Stock Exchange had fallen below the cost of a Manhattan taxi medallion, but it would soon rebound to record levels.

Options add spread trading to the stock market. Instead of being able only to buy or sell a stock, you can take a long or short position in puts or calls at a number of different exercise prices and expiry dates. That opens up enormous opportunities for those who can calculate fast on their feet and take controlled amounts of risk with calm judgment.

When the options markets opened in 1973, no one knew how to trade them. Futures traders understood spread trading, but they didn't know options math. Academics knew the math, but didn't know how to trade. The markets called for people who liked risk. The call was answered by the scion of the first family of American bridge.

Since the 1950s, almost all national and international bridge championships have had a Becker competing. Mike Becker is one of the better players in his family—he and his partner, Ron Rubin, have a world and 10 national championships to their credit. Mike played pro bridge, which meant eking out a living playing high-stakes bridge at New York's famed Cavendish Club or being a paid partner for people who really, really wanted to win a bridge tournament. He also hustled some poker and backgammon and was a card-counting blackjack player. Ron had a bit more ambition and thought options trading looked easier than bridge. The first time he tried, he went bust.

Then Ron won $90,000 by coming in second in the world backgammon championship. Wiser this time, he took some options-trading advice from an expert backgammon player, Fred Kolber, and made almost a million dollars the first year of his second attempt. Coincidentally, Mike's investment manager had lost his life savings in an interest rate bet, so Ron staked Mike to trade options on the American Stock Exchange. Mike found it just as easy to be successful. Both he and Ron could figure opportunities in their heads that other traders needed computers for. Just as important, they had years of experience weighing risk and sizing up other players. Others with the right math skills often had no heads for either risk or people.

Mike also had a talent for teaching. He offered his bridge pals a deal: three months of training, supervision when needed, and $50,000 of trading capital. In return he got 50 percent of their profits, which declined by 10 percent every time the trader made $500,000. A trader going to term would make $2.5 million, $750,000 of which would be Mike's. That's pretty good, even compared to his trading income, when you consider he trained about 100 traders over 15 years, with

20 of them going the distance. Mike recruited 50 bridge champions; the rest were poker, backgammon, chess, or go experts. At the peak, 150 of the 400 American Stock Exchange options seats were held by games players trained by Mike or Ron, or the people their trainees brought down to the floor. Only a fraction of the other 250 traders had trained in business schools or math departments. Until the advent of high-quality portable computers in the early 1990s, and some market changes, America's stock option exchanges ran on game-trained brainpower.

The effect was electrifying. Since the stock market had become tolerably honest after federal legislation in the 1930s, investors could not tell the difference between good and bad stocks. Banning insider trading and manipulation made the market fairer, but also a lot more random. Study after study showed that buying every stock was the best strategy. Corporate managers were not slow to pick up that they were on the honor system. Predictably, this brought out the best in the best people and the worst in everyone else. The most common bad reaction was not unrestrained greed, since there were still quaint social sanctions against managers paying themselves hundreds of millions of dollars while the company stock went down. Instead, the bad managers opted for an easy life and comfortable salaries with lots of perks and generous pensions, with shareholder profits allocated to buying off employees, the government, and anyone who protested anything the company did. Companies got lazy, comfortable, and cowardly.

Options trading was more than turning on the light in a roach-infested kitchen; it was like a full-body X-ray. Companies went from investors having no useful information about their stock to having the exact probability of every $5 move over every quarter constantly assessed in public. It took a decade or so, because America's risk takers were rusty at finance, but it whipped things into shape. In 1970, corporations dumped their stock on the market like thousands of farmers flooding a port with grain at the same time, half of it to spoil and the rest to sell at depressed prices due to oversupply, causing a shortage the next month. By the mid-1980s, options traders had transformed it into a smoothly running just-in-time machine, effortlessly adjusting to all types of disruptions, like Chicago in its glory years. This change kicked off the greatest stock market boom in history, along with corporate raiding, leveraged buyouts, demutualization, and other forces of creative destruction. Most of the great American corporations were destroyed or turned inside out in the process, and a generation of workers found that their cradle-to-grave security deal had been converted to a roller coaster. But a new crop of corporations sprang up. Consumers, shareholders, and entrepreneurs won big.

Options are a simple form of derivative (the option value depends mainly on the underlying stock price, while derivatives are securities whose value can be derived from the price of other securities). In the 1980s, and continuing to today, derivative markets sprang up for every imaginable financial variable, and some nonfinancial ones, such as weather derivatives, as well. These markets had the same effect on their underlying assets as stock options on stocks.

WITHERED THESE LATTER-DAYS TO LEAF-SIZE FROM LACK OF ACTION . . .

To see why options mattered so much, consider a simplified example. Super Duper Stores operated no-frills supermarkets in semirural areas outside cities starting after World War II. It used one huge central processing facility to receive, package, process, and ship food to 200 stores in five neighboring states. Over time, the cities and suburbs grew, so that the land occupied by the supermarkets skyrocketed in value. Super Duper acquired a dowdy but comforting brand-name image, store managers were unambitious older white males, groceries were bagged by local high school kids, and checkout was done at a manual register by part-time working wives. Everyone involved—truck drivers, butchers, produce clerks—was a full-time, union employee of the company, with a generous health and defined-benefit retirement plan. No one ever got fired.

The company stopped expanding in the late 1950s because it had reached the distribution limits of its central processing facility, and it could not operate profitably paying market prices for new locations. It used the cash thrown off by its business to pay off all its debt.

When fuel prices jumped, it didn't move to distributed delivery because that would upset the routine. When South and East Asian immigrants moved into Super Duper's service areas, they were not hired—they didn't look the part. Price scanners, modern inventory, gourmet sections, generic goods—none were worth the trouble to investigate. For years, anyone with ambition or new ideas had quit; people who like things quiet and safe stayed.

The stock price stayed in one place, too. When interest rates were low and profits still high, Super Duper paid a nice dividend and was popular among conservative investors. But with higher interest rates, the dividend stream was worth less. One dollar-per-year dividend is worth $50 at a 2 percent interest rate, but only $10 at a 10 percent interest rate. Also, declining profits as a result of increasing inefficiency and competition meant the dividend was first cut, then eliminated.

Why didn't shareholders revolt? I could write a whole book on that, but for now just say that they didn't. Shareholders who got frustrated at the stock going down while management did nothing simply sold their shares to less impatient investors. Why didn't some outsider buy up the company and turn it around? In practice you needed the permission of the board of directors, and the board just said the company was not for sale at any price. Of course, none of the board members owned shares, but they did have generous salaries and pensions guaranteed by Super Duper that could be lost in a takeover.

Let's suppose that the asset value per share of Super Duper was $150. This is what it would be worth either sold to energetic managers or broken up with real estate and other assets sold individually. A rational shareholder might conclude that there was a 10 percent chance of the value being unlocked in any given year. The board or management could discover higher standards; an outsider might make a bid for the company or its assets; even a disaster could be good if it forced change. However, in none of these scenarios do shareholders expect to realize full value. A board or management change will probably be some kind of compromise, a raider will want to make a profit for herself, and a disaster will cut the value of the assets. So perhaps this stock is like a perpetual lottery ticket with a

10 percent chance of paying $100 in any given year. Since there's no cash flow until that happens, if the appropriate discount rate is 10 percent per year, each share of Super Duper has an expected net present value of $50. The only holders of Super Duper stock are people who like this kind of gamble and people who aren't paying attention. Neither of these groups is likely to trade much, so there will be low trading volume in the stock and not much attention paid to small changes in value or probability of unlocking value.

Now suppose options start trading on Super Duper. Only two things can happen to the stock: The price can stay at $50 or double to $100. The probabilities don't matter for the option price. A call option struck at $50 will pay either $0, if the stock stays at $50, or $50, if the stock goes to $100. In either case, it pays the stock price minus $50. Therefore, the option is worth the current stock price minus the present value of $50 at option expiry. Since interest rates are 10 percent per year, a one-year call option is worth $4.55.

This opens Super Duper stock up to more interesting trading. You can buy the stock and sell call options on it to earn a steady, low-risk profit. Or you can buy the options as a pure lottery ticket. If enough people do this, the market will effectively lever up the company. The stockholders are now like bondholders, earning a steady, safe return, and the options holders are like stockholders, participating in increases in the company value. This will inflate stock prices, for the same reason they went up in the 1920s, when it was easy to borrow almost all of the money to buy stocks (both the Federal Reserve and the Securities and Exchange Commission worked to curtail aggressive borrowing to buy stock after the 1929 crash; the options market provided a backdoor way to avoid regulation). Trading volume will increase and far more attention will be paid to the prices. New kinds of traders will be attracted to the market to play these games. Some of those traders will use their profits and market savvy to force actual levering up of companies or other strategies for unlocking value. The increase in stock valuations and the availability of creatively engineered finance will encourage other people to start new companies.

The economist John Kenneth Galbraith famously observed that all financial innovation consists of new ways of disguising leverage.

There's a lot of truth to that, and the public options market—more broadly, increased trading in all forms of derivatives—certainly increased leverage in the economy. But Galbraith's remark is over-cynical in the use of the word *disguise*. True financial innovation provides better ways of managing leverage. Derivatives caused disasters (Warren Buffett called them "weapons of mass destruction"), but creative destruction is still the core driver of economic development.

Going back to Super Duper stock, notice that although the one-year $50 call is worth $4.55, the one-year $50 put is worthless. Until the crash of 1987, stock options traded at close to constant volatilities. That tends to push up the price of both the call and the put. The difference still has to be $4.55, but this trading prejudice might make the call sell at $6.50 and the put at $1.95. This inflated call price makes the stock more valuable, because you can earn a larger income holding it and selling calls. That pushes up the price and further increases the value of the call. When the market crashed, the prejudice disappeared overnight, not just in stock option markets but in all options markets. That dissipated some illusory value in the markets, but it dramatically increased the force and precision of derivatives trading in causing real economic change.

Of course, Super Duper stores and these numbers are highly simplified accounts of a very complex series of events. The point is that options trading mapped the full web of future possibilities, and game-playing traders sent capital zooming to break the bottlenecks. The extra volatility induced by the gambling was essential for two reasons: It tested links in the network, and it concentrated capital by making successful traders wealthy enough to facilitate real economic change.

HISTORY'S BEATEN THE HAZARD

Another games player who switched to finance early was Ed Thorp, the mathematics professor who invented blackjack card counting. In 1961, he wrote *Beat the Dealer* about how he won in casinos. Less well known is his 1967 book, *Beat the Market* (with Sheen Kassouf). Ed did not wait for public options trading in 1973; he began buying and selling warrants (options issued directly by corporations rather than created by exchanges) in the 1960s. He applied the same principles of careful mathematics and controlled risk taking to the market as he had to blackjack and has compiled an unequaled 40-year track record of high-return, low-risk investing.

In coming up with a trading strategy for warrants, Ed discovered a handy formula. A few years later, three finance professors independently came up with their own slight mathematical variant of the same formula. Ed Thorp, Myron Scholes, Robert Merton, and Fischer Black all had almost the same formula, but each had a different reason for believing it was true. Ed showed that it was a way to make money, Scholes that it was required for market efficiency, Merton that it had to be true or there would be arbitrage, and Black that it was required for market equilibrium. Black's insight turned out to be the most important, although it would take him 20 more years to work out its full implications. Merton and Scholes shared a Nobel Prize for their work; Black had died by that time or he certainly would have been included. Thorp missed out on the Nobel, but he got rich using the formula, while Merton and Scholes had disastrous personal financial results. Black's dislike of risk kept him from either extreme.

The four approaches to the option-pricing model led to different interpretations of the events from 1973 to 1987. Most practitioners adopted Ed Thorp's version of the model. Their attitude was that innovations in financial trading open up vast new profit opportunities, so let's get rich as fast as we can. The mainstream academic reaction in finance was in the Myron Scholes school: Options make the market more efficient, and more market efficiency is good for the economy. Underemployed physicists and mathematicians worshiped instead at the Robert Merton altar. They invented something called *financial engineering,* to exploit the kind of mathematical results that underlie options pricing, and structured ever more complex products and deals. For a wonderful account of one of the most prominent financial engineers, pick up *My Life as a Quant* by Emanuel Derman.

There is a lot of truth to all three approaches, but it was Fischer Black, who never attracted a school, who really figured things out. All four of these guys are extraordinary geniuses. Some people think

Black was the smartest, but I suspect that's because he fit the antiso-
cial, half-crazy popular image of a genius. Ed's the most fun to have
dinner with, Scholes is the best lecturer, and Merton's the best if you
want to sit down and work out some math. I think Black succeeded
because he was the least interested in success. He liked a comfortable
salary, which Goldman Sachs more than provided, but he didn't start
a hedge fund like the other three. He didn't publish much in academic journals; he preferred the practitioners' publication *Financial
Analysts Journal,* edited by his friend Jack Treynor. He wrote one
blazingly original paper in an area, then moved on to something else,
unlike some academics who spin every idea into 10 overlapping
papers interlocked in a professional subtopic. He finally put it all
together in a book, which practically nobody read.

AND HE BURNED THEM AS WASTEPAPER

Consider an economic statistic like the quarterly gross domestic
product for the United States, which is periodically announced by
government statisticians. This is an important economic variable; it
and similar statistics fit into many economic theories and models.
Black realized that it was improperly aggregated to the point of being
meaningless.

Most economic decisions have long time horizons. It's easy to overlook that, because most of us participate in only small parts of transactions. If a person cuts down a tree in half an hour and gets paid $20,
he thinks of it as a half-hour transaction. But that tree is going to be
processed in many stages, so it may be months before it is incorpo-
rated into products. Many of those products will be stages in further
production—paper for a company, cross-ties for a railroad, a shelf for
a retail store. There are profit-and-loss statements computed for all
these businesses, which make it appear that end-to-end economic
activity has taken place each quarter. But those are all based on
assumptions that the future will be as planned. That's never true.

Think of all the work you've ever done that was wasted. Maybe
you did something wrong and had to undo it. Maybe your work was
fine, but the project was canceled. Maybe the project went fine, but

it never led anywhere. You might never know that your piece went unused. And don't limit it to short-term work projects. Think of all the training you have received that is no longer useful, or never was. Think of all the time spent waiting or wasted in pointless meetings. Most of what passes for economic activity, that gets assigned a value and added up in those quarterly accounts, turns out in the end to have no value. The things that do have value are often completely unexpected and either undervalued at the time or left out of the accounts entirely. Tiny differences distinguish an iPod that is sold immediately at a premium price and a functionally identical hard-disk MP3 player that is thrown away unsold and unused; a movie that grosses $100 million its first weekend and one that goes straight to the video remainder bin at Kmart; a book that tops the best-seller chart and one that the author's family won't read.

So the quarterly GDP figure combines lots of useless stuff with other undervalued stuff, and it will take years, not months, to figure out the difference. Of course, economists break GDP down into components—sometimes hundreds or thousands—and they study long time series. But, Black observed, none of this gets to the granularity that explains real economic value or the time scale at which important economic events take place.

Suppose, for example, a country decided to build a self-sufficient automobile industry from scratch. It would have to search for iron and coal; build factories to process steel, glass, and rubber; invest in research and design. It would need to build railroads to link these facilities together; those railroads would require more steel and coal or oil, as well as wood and other materials. The cars would need roads and gas stations to be useful. The whole process might take 20 years and involve a million workers at the end. Each year the progress would be valued and added in to the national accounts. People would be paid for their work; companies would be founded and would prosper; schools would be set up to train workers.

But when the first car rolls off the assembly line, it takes only one consumer to say, "I don't like it." The whole 20-year project comes to a crashing halt; all the value created for that period is written off. Maybe some assets can be salvaged. Maybe the car can be redesigned, or bicycles can be built instead. Maybe the steel can be used for buildings. But none of these restructurings are certain, and all involve significant loss in value. Almost all of the million workers will be laid off in the short term, and many of their jobs will not exist in the restructured system.

If you think of the economy as a collection of 20-year speculative projects, many of which will fail completely and none of which will turn out as planned, you see the economic need and the appeal for a gambling rather than a middle-class lifestyle. If you take the safe course, it seems as if you are entering a solid business with a long-term history and stable prospects, but it can evaporate in an instant. It's like a motel on a busy road that suddenly becomes worthless because someone built a bridge 50 miles away that changed all the traffic patterns. Even if your business is one of the successes, the entire economy can crash if too many mistakes are made in other businesses.

As an investor, you can buy a stock with a 20-year history of steadily growing profits and completely honest and transparent accounting without one penny of those profits ever being tested in the sense of contributing to something anyone actually bought. Virtually all of the economic value of things people do buy results from decisions made decades ago. A computer might have been built last week, but the research and development, the training of the workers and users, the building of the infrastructure to supply it with power and communications, the governing law, the business organization of the manufacturer and retailer, and a hundred other essentials were put in motion long before. Without all of those things, the computer either cannot be built or is worthless if built. Given all those things, the additional economic effort to build one more computer is negligible.

Disruption leads to opportunity. That deserted motel might be acquired cheap and converted to a spa resort now that the traffic noise has disappeared. The new traffic patterns from the bridge might change the commute times, hence the relative real estate values, among various suburbs. There's lots of free stuff lying around for anyone who wants it, and lots of unmet needs—unmet because the project that was supposed to meet them failed. Think how much money eBay made just acting as an intermediary to people cleaning out their attics of useless stuff. And think of how Internet search sites, such as Expedia, changed the motel business. Instead of needing a prominent location so guests could find you easily, you could compete by offering the lowest price in town, knowing that guests would find you on the Internet and get directions. What if all the owners of stranded assets bet them in a giant poker tournament? Some winners would walk away with random combinations of otherwise useless assets that just might spark someone's creativity. A lot of successful businesses were founded when someone had to find a use for something they owned.

Fischer Black had a lot more than this to say. My point is that the world he describes is more like the wide open frontier that was organized by commodity futures exchanges than the smooth equations you see in standard economics textbooks. The economic challenges of the future will be met, and the fortunes of the future made, by spread bettors acquiring capital and deploying it dynamically.

FLASHBACK

THE EDUCATION OF A TRADER

As with poker, my trading education began as a child, and with a card game. It was called Pit. Parker Brothers developed it in 1904, to compete with the successful Gavitt's Stock Exchange game (which I have also played, although much later in life) introduced the previous year. Parker Brothers no longer makes Pit, but it has licensed it to Winning Moves, a company that preserves such games for people like me. Winning Moves calls Pit "a timeless classic."

Pit

The game is extremely simple. You need between three and eight players—the more, the better. You use one commodity for each player; each commodity has nine identical cards. Choices are Wheat, Corn, Coffee, Oats, Sugar, Barley, Oranges, and Soybeans. All are real traded commodities except that Oranges are traded as Frozen Orange Juice. When I was a kid, there were Flax, Rye, and Hay instead of Coffee, Sugar, Oranges, and Soybeans. For game purposes, the commodities are identical except for point value. There are nine cards for each commodity, hence nine cards per player. You shuffle the cards together and deal them out.

The object is to be the first to get a hand composed of nine cards for the same commodity, at which point you ring the bell (the stroke of genius that raises Pit above Gavitt's, in which you tried to do the same thing with railroad stocks) and yell "corner the market on" whatever commodity you have (in Gavitt's you yell "Topeka" instead, which is less satisfying). You get the assigned point value for your commodity, from 50 for Oranges to 100 for Wheat, and another round is dealt. The game continues until someone has 500 points.

You get your corner by trading a group of cards for the same number of cards from another player. Players yell numbers such as "trade 1, trade 1" or "trade 3, trade 3." When two players agree on a number, each gives that many cards to the other. All the cards given must be of the same commodity—three Sugars or two Barleys, for example. Of course, the cards you receive will also be the same as each other (hopefully not the same as the ones you gave, but you will get that a lot).

The key to winning Pit is to see a lot of cards flow through your hand. This gives you the opportunity to select the right commodity to corner and change that decision if necessary, and it also provides you with information about what other players have. Obviously, any card they trade you is one that they don't want, and with most players, if they keep the cards in their hand instead of immediately offering them for trade, they want what you gave them. Getting a lot of trading action requires skill at getting attention when everyone is shouting. The game is more fun if cheating is encouraged, because then you can also generate business by revealing what you plan to trade. This puts more premium on calculation. At the same time, you have to keep track of clues about how close other players are getting, to make sure you don't trade someone else their winning cards. If you have the trader gene, the game will cause you to collapse with helpless laughter at the end of every hand, and you will be unable to stop playing long after your friends are sick of it.

Pit captures three aspects of real trading. First is the relatively simple reasoning that goes into each trade, while executing a complex and subtle strategy. Second is the physical high that comes from constant shouting for attention, a combination of lack of oxygen and some kind of brain chemical used for social energy. On an exchange floor, there is jostling (that's a euphemism) as well as shouting. With computer trading, there is a similar feeling—although without a physical outlet, it builds up to unhealthy levels. Many traders avoid this by screaming at everyone and breaking things—not when they lose; just as a general stress reduction (for them) technique.

Finally, Pit captures the melding that occurs whenever a group focuses narrowly on a common object. No doubt ants and bees feel this more strongly than humans—presumably, humans would prefer to relax by thinking for themselves. This feeling is part of the appeal of craps and horse racing, but it's not as strong because the crowd only watches; it does not participate in the play, except by prayer. Some people may get the feeling in team sports or other cooperative activities, but I never have. I don't think I would get pleasure from feeling like a cog in a well-functioning machine, but I love the feeling of being part of a swarm or flock, pursuing my personal goals through affecting the actions of a crowd, but also taking pride in the power and efficiency of that crowd. James Surowiecki wrote a wonderful book, *The Wisdom of Crowds,* that celebrates this phenomenon in more scientific terms.

The Options Floor

With all my experience at Pit and poker, I felt I was ready to tackle the Chicago Board of Trade. Two things dissuaded me. First was the cost. In the early 1980s, it cost about half a million dollars to be a floor trader. Trading stock options was much cheaper. You could rent a seat for only a few hundred dollars in slow summer months when traders wanted to take vacations, and even buy one for an affordable sum. You did have to come up with $50,000 for clearing margin ($25,000 if you closed out your positions every day). This money was deposited with your clearing firm (you had to find one willing to take you). This firm was responsible financially for all your trading. At the end of each session, it canceled out all your offsetting buys and sells, paying or receiving the net cash from the clearinghouse. The $50,000 was to make sure you could meet your losses.

For example, suppose you bought 10 GM June $50 calls at $5.00, later sold 15 of the same contract at $6.00, then bought another 10 at $5.50. At the end of the day, you own 5 of the calls. You owe $5,000 (each contract is for 100 shares) on the first transaction, are owed $9,000 on the second, and owe $5,500 on the third. Net, you owe $1,500 to the clearinghouse. That doesn't mean you lost money—that depends on the closing value of your 5 remaining calls. If they're over $3, you made money for the day on these trades. The clearing firm took care of all these details.

The second reason to prefer options is that I didn't know anything about agricultural commodities—or any commodities. That's not necessarily a disadvantage; you don't need to know much about something to find profitable trading strategies for it. I didn't know much about stocks, either. But because public options trading was so much newer (introduced only in 1973) and so mathematical, I thought there was more chance of succeeding there. The downside was that I would never get to yell "I corner the market on Wheat!"

I don't have any trading records for those days, but to illustrate the game, I'm going to use some recent quotes. These are real quotes, not a made-up example. The options market is much more efficient than it used to be, partly as a result of actions by the Securities and Exchange Commission and partly due to improved trading technology. In the 1980s the opportunities were both larger and more common.

Strike	Call Price	Put Price
Expire September 16, 2005		
45	7.40	0.15
50	2.65	0.35
55	0.25	3.10
60	0.05	
Expire October 21, 2005		
40	13.70	0.05
45	8.30	0.20
50	3.30	1.00
55	0.85	3.50
60	0.15	7.90
65	0.05	12.00
70	0.05	16.30
75	0.05	21.30
80	0.10	26.30
Expire January 20, 2006		
20		0.05
30	23.10	0.05
35	19.30	0.15
40	13.60	0.20
45	9.40	0.70
50	4.50	2.00
55	1.95	4.40
60	0.65	8.20
65	0.15	10.90
70	0.05	16.30

This table shows prices for options on Morgan Stanley stock (MWD), for settlement on August 24, 2005. At the time of these quotes, the underlying stock was selling for $52.29 per share. For example, the upper left of the table tells us that you could buy a call option on MWD at $45 per share that expired on September 16, for $7.40 per share. If you bought that option, you would have the right, but not the obligation, to buy one share of the stock at any time up to September 16, for a price of $45. Normally you would wait until September 16, and if the stock was selling for under $45 per share, you would let the option expire worthless, but if the stock was selling for more than $45 per share, you would exercise the option and buy it. Note that you buy the stock even if the profit is less than the $7.40 you paid for the call. You don't get that money back whatever happens. So if the stock is selling for $46, you buy it for $45. Your $1 profit offsets some of the $7.40 you paid for the option. You're sorry you paid $7.40 for the option, but you still want whatever profit you can get out of it.

A retail customer might buy this option if she was planning to buy MWD but was afraid of some short-term bad news. If she buys the option and then exercises it, she pays a total of $52.40 ($45 to exercise plus $7.40 for the option) per share, $0.11 more than the $52.29 for buying the stock directly. She gets two things for that $0.11. First is the interest she can earn on $45 for a month, because with the option she doesn't have to pay that amount until September 16. That might be about $0.08 of it. Second is the limited loss if something bad happens to MWD over the next month. If the stock dropped to $30 or even zero, she would lose only the $7.40 she paid for the option, not the $22.29 or $52.40 she could lose from owning the stock. Of course, the chance of this occurring is pretty small, which is why she can buy the insurance for only about $0.03.

The put options give the right to sell instead of buy. For $0.15 you can buy the right to sell a share of MWD for $45 anytime before September 21. Instead of buying the call option, our retail customer could buy the stock, then pay $0.15 to buy the put to get the same insurance as the call. Obviously, the call is a better deal. All a retail customer has to do is find the cheapest way to accomplish her strategy. As traders, we're looking for opportunities to guarantee profit.

Playing the Hand

If you've never traded or studied options, the table looks like nothing more than a list of numbers. It's like seeing your first game of Texas Hold 'Em. Three cards get dealt in the middle of the table, and everyone starts talking about different pocket card possibilities and the related strategies. Once you play for a while, you analyze the flop for straight and flush possibilities, and likely pairing combinations, without thinking about it. A poker book might spend 100 pages telling you how to do it, giving you the impression that it takes enormous memory. That's not true—anyone can get the hang of it with a little practice. I'm going to spend a few pages talking about what you do, but remember that this stuff becomes automatic after a short period. Other types of trading involve different calculations, just as you look for different things in Seven-Card Stud as opposed to Texas Hold 'Em. But poker is poker and trading is trading. The same skills are required for all games—you just need to adjust the kinds of things you're looking for and the specific calculations that matter.

The first thing to do is look for a single option arbitrage, an option you could buy or sell for an immediate profit. There are six of them in the preceding table, which shows real data from a more efficient market than I traded (although, then and now, seeing a price on a screen is no guarantee you can execute a trade). If you like that sort of thing, see if you can find them. If you don't, or you already tried, I'll tell you one of them. Look at the January $65 put. You could buy it for $10.90, plus one share of MWD for $52.29. That's a total of $63.19. You can exercise the option immediately, and sell your stock for $65. That's a profit of $1.81. You can do even better. If you don't exercise, you can hope MWD goes above $65 before January 20, 2006. If it does, you can sell it at the higher price and make even more than $65. It's true that you have to pay interest to fund your $63.19 investment—about $0.54 or so—but you get that back because the stock is expected to pay two $0.27 dividends before January 20, 2006.

Before looking for more complex opportunities, I want to talk about how you would actually execute on the floor. Even in my day you wouldn't actually try this one—it's too easy. Even the dullest trader on the floor knew not to sell an option at less than its intrinsic value (what it would be worth if exercised immediately). This price is either stale—quoted when MWD was selling at a higher price and not updated—or an error. The screen prices are less reliable for options that don't trade much, like those far from the current stock price and more distant in the future. But if you were optimistic, you would go over to the post for MWD options. There was a specialist there who quoted bid and ask prices for all MWD options. He would buy at the bid (lower) price and sell at the ask (higher) price. You can't make money if you pay the spread, so you deal with the specialist only to clear out positions. Even if you could make money paying the spread, you need the specialist's goodwill for a number of reasons. Making money from him is not a wise long-term decision.

Instead, you wait by the post, hoping for someone to rush in with a customer order to sell 100 January $65 puts. Many of the traders on the floor are executing orders for customers rather than (or in addition to) trading for their own accounts. These orders are transmitted through brokerage firms to the floor. You bid slightly more than the specialist (a price "inside the spread") to get the order. Of course, you also have to bid more than anyone else standing around the post. You can also make a bid to buy from the traders standing around the post, hoping that someone wants to sell those options but doesn't want to accept the specialist's bid price.

As soon as you get the options, you have to buy the same amount of MWD—100 shares per option contract. If you don't act quickly, you could lose your profit. If you buy the put at $10.90, but the price of MWD goes above $54.10 before you get around to buying the stock, you no longer have a guaranteed profit.

It might occur to you that a computer could look for these profit opportunities better than a human and relay precise instructions in microseconds without error. That's true, and computers do a lot of trading. But they can make big mistakes sometimes. The key to real trading, which I cannot convey with this example, is that while you're looking at the numbers, you're forming opinions about where opportunities are opening up and what kinds of trades are going to work. The numbers are changing constantly. Some apparent opportunities last for months; others for only a fraction of a second. Some types keep recurring; others are one of a kind. Some are right for excited markets; others when there's no action. Only by being there and absorbing all of this can you be a good trader. You have to do the calculations, but market feel is just as important. A computer can tell you the probability of ace-king beating a pair of jacks in Texas Hold 'Em, but it can't predict how another player will react to an all-in raise.

This applies to electronic trading as well as to floor trading. It's more muted, but it's there. You're not just looking at static numbers; the prices are changing all the time. You can see opportunities start to develop. You keep an eye on them until you feel the time is right. Too early, and you may not make enough profit, or you may not be able to execute. Too late, and someone else will beat you to it. You're constantly considering dozens of possible trades, adding a new one when you see some interesting relationship, discarding old ones that didn't develop. Stretch yourself too thin by watching too many opportunities, and you'll make mistakes. Focus too narrowly on your favorite types of trades, and you'll miss out on too many others. If you walk out on a trading floor in a large bank, you will immediately sense the market mood, without even knowing what's being traded. You don't have to be a trader to feel it; everyone knows instinctively.

Most trading today is computer-aided. Your computer searches through prices, looking for specific patterns to call to your attention. You can also let the computer handle the execution, either automatically or after you approve the trade. But that doesn't change the fundamental nature of trading, any more than having an autopilot changes the basic skills a pilot needs. In the early 1980s there were only two computers on the exchange floor, with long lines to use them. Being able to compute opportunities in your head was a key to successful trading. The older traders knew trading but not options math. A lot of the younger guys knew the math but weren't good at doing it in their heads, and they didn't have the trading feel to exploit it.

Parity, Verticals, and Calendars

I'm not going to tell you about all trading strategies. If you want that, you'll have to get a book about it. I highly recommend one written by a top professional poker player, Bob Feduniak (*Futures Trading: Concepts and Strategies,* by Robert Fink and Robert Feduniak). It's out of date in many details, but it's still the best combination of theory and practice available. Another essential is *Dynamic Hedging* by Nassim Taleb, a successful trader who does not play much poker. I discussed this book with both of them, and both have significant disagreements about some of the ideas, but I like their books, anyway. Finally, if you want the mathematics of finance explained with the brilliant clarity of real genius, get *Paul Wilmott on Quantitative Finance.*

However, to get the flavor of the trading game, we have to go beyond spotting obvious mispricings. It's essential to understand that this is a game, that there are strategies and moves. It's not just scanning lists of numbers and running to try to take advantage of them. It's coming up with new ideas. The three I'm going to talk about are old ideas (but still good ones) that give you the flavor.

If you buy a call option and sell a put option with the same underlying, strike, and expiry, you have effectively bought the stock. For example, suppose you buy the September 16 $50 call and sell the corresponding put on MWD. You'll pay $2.65 for the call, but get $0.35 for the put, for a net $2.30. On September 16, if MWD is above $50, the put will be worthless, but you'll exercise your call to buy a share for $50. If MWD is below $50, the call will be worthless, but the holder of the put you sold will execute it to force you to buy a share from her at $50. Either way, you buy a share for $50. Your all-in price is $52.30, a penny more than buying it for $52.29 in the market today (that's still a good deal, because you save a month's interest on $50, which is roughly a nickel).

If you like that sort of thing, see whether you can find some juicy violations of parity in the preceding list. You're looking for a situation where the strike price plus the call price minus the put price is significantly different from $52.29 (you can make money on deviations either way). There are five differences of more than a dollar; one is the January 2006 $45 strike. In this case you would sell the call and buy the put and the stock. You pay $0.70 for the put and get $9.40 for the call, ending up with $8.70. The stock costs $52.29, so you've spent a net $43.59.

You'll collect $0.54 in dividends on the stock, bringing your investment down to $43.04. With interest until January, that's about $43.40. But on January 20, 2006, whatever the price of MWD is, you get $45, for a profit of $1.60.

With this and all the other trades, you don't really expect to hold it until expiry. Prices are out of line and tend to move back. When they do, you take your profit. With luck, they'll overcorrect, and you can make money getting out as well. However, you might get out if they go halfway back, giving up half your potential profit, but freeing up the capital and attention for more profitable trades.

There are some small risks in this trade. MWD might not pay the expected dividends, which reduces your profit but in this case does not cause a loss. The call holder might exercise early, but that doesn't hurt you beyond possibly losing some of the dividends. You get your expected profit early, which is good, and you get to keep the put for nothing (although it's unlikely to have significant value in any scenario in which the call holder would exercise early).

Verticals are buying a call or put, and selling the same kind of option on the same underlying with the same expiry, but at a different strike. For example, you could buy an October $50 call and sell the October $55 call. You would pay $3.30 and get $0.85, for a net price of $2.45. If MWD is above $55 on October 16, you make $5 (both calls are exercised, you buy a share of MWD for $50 with your $50 call, and you are forced to sell it for $55 to the person who holds your $55 call). If MWD is under $50, you get nothing (both calls are worthless). If MWD is between $50 and $55, you get the amount by which it exceeds $50 (the $55 call expires worthless, you exercise your $50 call, and you sell MWD at the market price).

When a stock is selling at the midpoint of a vertical—$52.50 in this case—the vertical has to be worth very close to half the spread—$2.50 in this case, because it's a $5 vertical. I'm not going to prove that—take my word for it. As the stock approaches the upper end of the spread, the call vertical is worth more than half the spread and the put is worth less. The amount more and less depends on the volatility of the underlying and the amount of time to expiry. The $2.45 price for the October

$50/$55 call vertical is reasonable; it should be a little less than $2.50 because MWD is selling for a little under $52.50.

Can you spot any attractive verticals? You should see a lot. One example is the January 2006 $45/$60 call vertical. If we sell the $45 for $9.40 and buy the $60 for $0.65, we get $8.75 in our pockets. Since MWD is slightly below the $52.50 midpoint, this should sell for a little less than $7.50. So we've got our mispricing, but we haven't locked in a profit. We're getting paid $8.75, but we have to pay $15.00 if MWD is above $60 in January 2006. It's a good bet, but it's too risky to hold on its own. Fortunately, the same put vertical is selling exactly at $7.50 (it should be slightly above that level). So we sell the January $45 put and buy the January $60 put. We get $0.70 and pay $8.20, for a net expenditure of $7.50. That comes out of the $8.75 we got for the call vertical. Our net is $1.25.

Now what happens? We have $1.25 in pocket and a bet that pays us $15 if MWD goes below $45, but we have to pay $15 if it goes above $60. So we buy two shares of MWD. If it goes above $60, we make more than $15 profit on two shares of stock, while our payout on the bet is limited to $15. If the stock goes down, our put vertical covers any losses down to $45. We'll unwind the whole position before the stock drops below $45, almost certainly at a profit. We could make this position even safer by fiddling with the proportions of the four options we use, also by adjusting it as the stock price moves and time passes. It will still have some risk, but $1.25 is a significant overpayment to us to take it.

Finally, let's talk about calendar spreads. This means buying one option and selling another of the same type, with the same underlying and strike but a different expiry. Longer-dated options are more valuable than shorter-dated ones. The spread is most valuable near the current stock price and should decline in price for options at higher and lower strikes. Look at the January/October calendar spreads. For each strike price, I've taken the January option price minus the October option price:

As expected, all the numbers are positive (although this is not true for all the options in the table). The $50 and $55 strikes, the nearest to the current stock price of $52.29, are worth between $0.90 and $1.20.

Strike	Call Spread	Put Spread
45	1.10	0.50
50	1.20	1.00
55	1.10	0.90
60	0.50	0.30

The ones $5 further away, at $45 and $60, sell for less, as expected, between $0.30 and $0.50—except the $45 calls. That calendar spread is too big. We should sell the January $45 calls and buy the October $45 calls, getting paid $1.10. As with the vertical spread, we need to offset the risk with another trade. We might be tempted to buy the $60 put spread at $0.30, which looks cheap. That's a good idea, but this position will take even more management than the vertical spread; we can't just hold it to expiry and collect our winnings. As a practical matter, there's not much difference. We're not going to hold many positions longer than a day, and none or almost none to expiry. Most of our profit comes from identifying mispricings and exploiting them before anyone else. We'll cash out when other people come in; in fact, we may be buying from people who were quicker than we were.

Every successful trader finds a niche, depending on taste and capital and skills. Although you're buying and selling with other traders, you all can be making money in theory. Just like in poker, that never happens—there are always losing traders. But you're not trading against anyone, not even some abstract "market." You're playing a game by certain rules. If you play well and have some luck, you win. If you play badly or have bad luck, you lose. Calling it a game, of course, doesn't mean you don't take it seriously. I care very much when it's my money on the line, and even more when it's other people's money—money from people who have trusted me. But it's a game in the sense that there are rules and a score, that you must both think ahead and react immediately to the moment. No one does this because it's useful for society, because no one can know the larger impact of their trades. Some have faith that the market is always right and their trades make it more efficient. Others have different faiths or don't care. No one does this for the money, either, despite what they may tell you (and the money can be very, very good). Everyone who does this does it because they love it.

Bonds

In 1982 I was hired by Prudential Insurance, but not as a trader. My job was to manage a bond portfolio that was used to fund annuity products sold by the company. For example, Prudential would agree to pay the retirement benefits of a pool of 1,000 workers for some company in exchange for a lump-sum payment today. Our actuaries would make projections about how much these payments would amount to every month far out into the future. They would estimate when the workers would retire, what payments they would qualify for, and how long they and their spouses would live. They had a century of experience doing that, and they sent me the results. My job wasn't to worry about that part of it; I started from the cash flows they produced.

The safest way to manage the portfolio would be to go out and buy a collection of U.S. Treasury bonds that would produce exactly the same cash flows as the projections. I could compute those bonds and add up the cost to make my bid for the business. But we'd never win anything that way. To get the price down, we had to use corporate bonds and mortgage securities, which paid higher yields. Also, it was too cumbersome to match every cash flow exactly. It didn't really matter if you had cash coming in a few months early or late 10 years from now. I won business and traded bonds every day; there was no point in balancing things exactly far out in the future.

However, I had to produce a daily report showing that my risk was within acceptable limits. The main risks were credit risk—what happened if some of the bonds I bought didn't pay off as promised—and mismatch risk—what happened if we had an obligation to pay in January and the money to pay it didn't come in until June. There were other risks as well. I had to show what would happen in various stress scenarios, such as a sudden spike in interest rates or a sharp decline in credit quality of all banks.

If I won a bid, I had to go buy bonds for the portfolio. I also had to reinvest cash that built up and occasionally sell some bonds to rebalance.

I had two ways to do this. I could call a big bond dealer, like Merrill Lynch or Salomon Brothers, and talk to a salesperson. These banks had bond traders, but customers like me dealt with salespeople who dealt with the traders. With some smaller banks I dealt with the trader directly, but I was still a customer, not a trader.

Like most investors in high-grade bonds, I didn't ask for specific issues such as the 8 percent coupon Ford Motor Credit bonds due August 2000. Instead, I'd say something like, "I'm looking for about $100 million of A-rated corporates with five- to seven-year maturities, and I can't take any more financial or auto paper." The salesperson would go through the firm's inventory, or bonds she thought could be bought from other shops, and suggest some names. Prudential had a credit department that had opinions on the soundness of different issuers, plus I had reports from public rating agencies like Standard & Poor's, Moody's, and Fitch. Good salespeople earned my business by having other useful information, especially about the trading outlook, such as whether this same bond was likely to be cheaper tomorrow. I could decide on bonds with the highest returns that kept the portfolio within its overall risk parameters and place orders. Or I could wait for the salesperson to call me back when something new came up, especially a new issue her firm was bringing to market.

The other option was to go to Prudential's bond traders. The firm employed two of them for the kinds of things I bought. They worked in a trading room with computer screens showing bonds bid and offered from lots of different brokers. Some portfolio managers used the traders as order takers (traders hate that) standing over their shoulders and pointing out the bonds they wanted. Others would give general instructions at the beginning of the day and trust the trader to find good deals.

It took me only a couple of months to get tired of that. Prudential didn't hire me as a trader, but I still thought of myself as one. The best opportunities could not be constructed one bond at a time. There might be a new issue with a very attractive yield, but not at the right maturity point and from an industry I was already overexposed to. I could buy it, but only if I sold something else and also bought another bond with a complementary maturity. The trouble is that once I made the buy, I was completely committed to doing the other two trades, so I would get bad prices and give away any gain from the initial purchase. I could try to negotiate package swaps with salespeople, but they never gave me good overall prices. I could ask the traders to try to pull it off, but the markets moved too fast and they had too much other work to do it.

Believe it or not, all of this bond management was done by hand. Prudential did buy me some time on a time-share mainframe with a dial-up 128-baud modem, and I programmed some routines in FORTRAN to help. I also had a home computer that I programmed in FORTH for the job. But then Prudential bought a first-generation IBM PC. I never found out who bought it or what it was for, but one day it appeared in an empty office. I immediately typed in my portfolio and wrote a BASIC program to tell me what kinds of bonds would help me the most. I got a list and went up to the trading room, where I picked off several of them from the screen. I went back down to enter the trades, got a new list, and went back up. With the computer to help me, I didn't need to calculate each trade by hand, and I could make some trades that threw me out of balance, knowing I could fix it on the next trip up and downstairs.

I didn't plan it this way, but I couldn't have devised a better way to get permission to trade for myself. I was driving the traders crazy, especially when the market was moving fast. I got my own chair at the desk (the corner, but still on the desk) and screen (only one, while other traders had three, but a screen). The one thing I didn't get was permission to move the PC into the trading room; I still had to run up and down the stairs.

I stayed in fixed-income securities until 1988, eventually becoming the head of mortgage securities at Lepercq, de Neuflize, a small French investment bank active in that business. I never gave up my trading, although I never did it as my only job. This was a slower kind of trading than options on the floor, but the dollar amounts were much larger (my Prudential portfolio had grown to $3 billion by the time I left). The game was pretty much the same: Look for some basic price relationships, pick off the exceptions, balance everything so you didn't care which way the market moved, and wait for things to come back in line to take a profit. The calculations were more complicated and the universe of securities larger, but I had computer power and people working for me instead of being on my own doing things in my head.

Poker at Lepercq

Lepercq did a good business selling mortgage-backed securities to state pension funds. We would buy many home mortgages from banks and other lenders and form them into securities that paid higher yields with less credit risk than corporate bonds. They were more complicated to manage. In some cases we provided educational and advisory services for free, or if you preferred, as part of the profit on the bond deals. In other cases we managed the portfolio for the fund in return for a fee.

To pitch these products and work with customers, I visited over half the state capitals in the United States over four years. Unless you have done this, it may not occur to you how small many state capitals are. In the older states this was done for military protection—the big cities were located on ports and other transportation routes, and thus were too easy to attack. In the newer states rural interests usually prevailed with the argument that having the state capital would make a large city too powerful. Anyway, I had to make the rounds to pitch our bonds to the funds, to lobby for modernized financial management rules, to teach courses, and to deliver performance reports. When I went, I didn't just represent the mortgage department, of course; I was also carrying briefs for Lepercq's other financial products and services.

Many games players find that trading removes the urge to play. Trading and other forms of finance use the same skills as poker and give the same satisfactions. Before I got interested in finance, poker helped me live fully: I often felt dull and slow if I hadn't played recently. A good game charged me up and burned off the accumulated frustrations and minor humiliations of life. I played mostly recreational poker in business school—for the company, not the money. I didn't have the urge to find the best players and the biggest stakes. I didn't feel like staying up all night, even when the game was good. My financial studies and projects were sufficient stimulation. Once I moved to Prudential, and especially when I got to the trading floor, I pretty much stopped playing. Once I started trading, a poker game after work felt like working late. I needed to relax from games, not switch games. The only exception was when an old poker friend would come into town and want a game.

I had played poker for recreation, for money, and for companionship. Now for the first time, I played poker for business. As Mr. Dixie had taught me, I had kept a careful record of opponents, and swapped names and addresses at every opportunity. I didn't have names for most state capitals, but I generally had one for a larger city in the state. That contact could get me invitations to the power games at the capital, where reporters, lobbyists, legislators, and administrators played.

A poker game wasn't directly useful for selling bonds or for getting the rules changed so our products could compete. I never ran into someone directly connected with any matter I was in town to deal with, and if I had, we wouldn't have discussed it at the poker table. In most cases I would have left the game. But in sales and lobbying, knowing someone is much better than knowing no one. It's incredibly valuable to pick up the mood of a place and to schmooze with knowledgeable insiders. If I flew in Saturday, played poker Saturday night, and enjoyed some local activity with one of the players on Sunday, I had a huge edge walking into the meeting on Monday over the banker who flew in that morning. We might both be snake oil salesmen from a dishonest business in the most corrupt city in the world, but I had a few local friends and had demonstrated some skill at something more respectable than finance. Word travels fast in a small town.

There was also a political angle to our activities. Not a large one—Lepercq is a reputable firm selling high-quality products (at a premium price, like most investment banks, but not out of line with anyone else). Still, an in-state bank might feel it should get preference for the business, or a labor leader might argue that state assets should be invested in local businesses that employed union members rather than securities issued in New York, funding who knows what. Someone might feel that legislation helpful to our products would open the door to corruption or excessive risk taking. You always get a better slant from the press if you make yourself available, and you have to know the local ins and outs before you open your mouth. Taking the extra time to learn the nuances makes you more effective with politicians than if you show up with prepackaged boilerplate arguments.

This was a different kind of poker than I had played in the past. My goal was not to make a lot of money, but to pass a test. Part of that test was being a good poker player; part was genuinely enjoying the game rather than using it as a pure sales tool. I wanted to win, but without appearing too deceptively tricky and without hurting anyone. A very loose, hyperaggressive style is good for this. You're in a lot of pots, catching people and getting caught. People know you're in the game. You may be up at the end of the evening, but everyone's won a big pot or two from you.

The other reason to play this way is that you start at a significant disadvantage. The other players know each other, probably have played together for many years. You have to figure out everyone's style starting from scratch. That's a serious disadvantage for a passive player: If you react to other players, you need to know what you're reacting to. An aggressive player cares less about other players' styles—aggressiveness forces them to react to you. That turns your disadvantage into an advantage. Some poker experts advise starting out a new game carefully, playing tight poker until you figure everyone else out. I never understood that; it doesn't sound like poker to me. I recommend the opposite. Maximize your advantage that they don't know you. There's no point letting them nibble away your stack as their price for information about their style. Wait until they call some of your bad hands before you start playing only good ones. At all costs, keep the initiative. Shift your style around suddenly so they're doing the guessing, not you. With some skill and luck, you can do more than your share of the folding and raising, and encourage them into frequent calling.

When I was a finance professor, some students would argue that it was unethical to mix gambling with business, especially with public institutions. Didn't state pensioners have a right to expect that poker didn't influence investment decisions? Of course, the money flowing across the table creates suspicion. It would certainly be inappropriate for a bond salesperson to gamble with the head of the pension fund or the chief investment officer. But the ethics question ignores the very important human aspect of finance. Finance uses a lot of numbers and theory, but at the heart of every good deal is trust. Trust cannot be established by business dealings alone. Conversation, maybe over dinner or on a golf course, can help, but poker is a much better way to learn about someone.

Nevertheless, I wouldn't do this today. The financial and political worlds have changed since 1987, mostly for the better. Fond as I am of poker, it makes sense to avoid any unnecessary private exchanges of money anywhere near figures in positions of public trust. That's sad, but true. Since leaving Lepercq in 1988 (to become a finance professor), I've never played in a game associated in any way with business. I didn't make a rule one day; I just stopped, the way I stopped personal stock trading and giving political campaign contributions to individual candidates. It's not dishonest, but it's not worth the trouble to prove to everyone else that it's honest, and it's certainly not worth risking a firm's reputation over. Broad political organizations and mutual funds and poker with friends are good enough for me, at least until I retire from finance. Anyway, today you can play poker in public—on television even—so there's no need for closed doors.

CHAPTER 8

The Games People Play

How Game Theory Can Make You Lose

The best way to understand certain aspects of poker is a branch of mathematics called game theory. Even if you've never studied it, or even heard of it, game theory underlies a lot of the poker thinking and advice you read or hear. In fact, it's taken over the theory of the game to the point that a lot of people believe poker is all about game theory. But it's not, and understanding the difference is essential to becoming a winning player. It's more important to understand game theory to predict the mistakes of other players who rely on it, directly or indirectly, than it is to use game theory to improve your own play.

Game theory did not infect just poker, it crept into finance as well, where you can also profit from seeing its flaws. Worst of all, it was an important intellectual underpinning of cold war madness. Nominally sane, intelligent, responsible people caused machines to be built to destroy all life on earth. It was not religious fanaticism or pathological hatred that justified their actions, but a game theory doctrine called *mutually assured destruction*. I grew up, like many of my generation, sincerely believing that there was a reasonable chance that a nuclear war would kill everyone on earth. Given that the chance of a healthy young person dying in a year is less than one in a thousand, I really believed that my odds of dying from a bomb before I graduated from college were 20 or 50 times greater than my odds of dying from any other cause. I might well have been right; we'll never know. This kind of logic was caught brilliantly in the movie *Dr. Strangelove*, but it's really not satire: The reality was crazier than the movie.

WHEN LUCK HAS SOMETHING TO DO WITH IT

In games of pure chance, such as craps, you can compute the best strategy using probability theory. That's also true in mixed skill and luck games, if the other players' actions are fixed. For example, probability theory works if you are playing blackjack one-on-one against a casino dealer. But in games like poker and bridge, where all players can make choices, probability theory is not enough.

You:

Board:

Player:

Suppose, for example, you are dealt pocket aces in hold 'em and the board comes down with ace, queen, jack, seven, three with no three cards of the same suit. The only hand that can beat you is king/ten, which gives player A a straight. Looking at it mathematically, there are 45 unknown cards, which can be arranged in 45 × 44/2 = 990 ways. There are 4 × 4 = 16 ways to get king/ten, so the chance of two random cards beating you is 16/990 = 1.62 percent.

Lower Ranking Card

Higher Ranking Card		Ace	King	Queen	Jack	Ten	Nine	Eight	Seven	Six	Five	Four	Three	Two
		1	4	3	3	4	4	4	3	4	4	4	3	4
Ace	1	0	4	3	3	4	4	4	3	4	4	4	3	4
King	4		6	12	12	16	16	16	12	16	16	16	12	16
Queen	3			3	9	12	12	12	9	12	12	12	9	12
Jack	3				3	12	12	12	9	12	12	12	9	12
Ten	4					6	16	16	12	16	16	16	12	16
Nine	4						6	16	12	16	16	16	12	16
Eight	4							6	12	16	16	16	12	16
Seven	3								3	12	12	12	9	12
Six	4									6	16	16	12	16
Five	4										6	16	12	16
Four	4											6	12	16
Three	3												3	12
Two	4													6

This calculation is illustrated in the preceding table. It lists all the card ranks in both the rows and the columns, with the number of that rank available (that is, not in your hand or on the board). There are four of most cards, but only one ace and three each of queen, jack, seven, and three. Each cell shows the number of ways that combination of cards can be made. For example, to see the number of queen/eight combinations, look in the queen row (since queen is the higher card) and the eight column. The 12 you see there is the product of the number of queens (3) and the number of eights (4).

Pairs are slightly different. Although there are four kings available, they cannot be combined in $4 \times 4 = 16$ ways. Once you pick one king, there are only three more available, so it's $4 \times 3 = 12$. That's easy enough, but what can be confusing is that you have to divide that number by 2 to get the 6 you see in the table. The reason you divide by 2 is that the kings are interchangeable. King of hearts/king of spades is the same hand as king of spades/king of hearts (and it's not possible to get king of hearts/king of hearts). But king of hearts/ten of spades is not the same hand as king of spades/ten of hearts. This is the same reason that it is twice as hard to roll four-four with two dice than five-three; any specific double combination is half as likely as any specific nondouble. Craps players call getting four-four "making eight the hard way." With four-four, the first die has to be a four and the second die has to be a four. Since each has probability 1/6, the probability of both is $1/6 \times 1/6 = 1/36$. With five-three, the first die can be either a five or a three—that's 2/6. The second die must be the other number—that's 1/6. But $2/6 \times 1/6 = 2/36$, twice the chance of four-four.

If you add up all the numbers in the table, you get 990. That's 45 (the number of unknown cards) times 44 (the number of unknown cards once you pick the first one) divided by 2 (because the cards are interchangeable). Looking up king/ten shows a 16, so a random two-card hand has 16/990 probability of being king/ten. If you were simply betting on that outcome instead of playing poker, that's all you would need to know.

But you are playing poker; you are not facing two random cards. In a table of 10 players, there's a 14.94 percent chance that one of them was dealt this hand. You have to ask yourself the probability that anyone holding king/ten would have stayed in the hand to this point and bet the way the other player did. You also have to ask what other hands the other player might have to justify his betting to this point. Finally, you have to predict what he will do with this hand, or with other likely hands, after any action you might take. You would feel more confident about winning if another player needed seven/four to beat you instead of king/ten, because this hand would almost certainly have been folded preflop. You would also feel better if the queen and jack were on the turn and river, because king/ten might have folded after a flop of ace/seven/three, but certainly not after ace/queen/jack. The probability of seven/four is the same as the probability of king/ten, and for any given board any order of the cards is equally likely. Yet your betting strategy will be different depending on whether king/ten or seven/four beats you and on what order the board came down. Probability theory is not enough.

One approach is to assume a strategy for your opponents, then compute the best counterstrategy. That's mathematically appealing, because it allows us to view poker like blackjack, where other players' actions are predetermined. A common mistake among people who are good at math is to take an approach that is mathematically convenient, then insist that solution is the only rational one. We'll see how to exploit this mistake later in this chapter.

The key principle of game theory takes the question of strategy one step further. You assume a specific strategy for your opponents. It's the strategy that's best for them, under the assumptions that you know their strategy and will use the best counterstrategy for you. It might seem that this approach cannot be beaten. If your opponents pick their best strategy, you'll have the best counterstrategy. If they pick anything else, you'll do at least as well, and maybe better.

For example, in a baseball game, bottom of the ninth inning, score tied, bases loaded, and full count on the batter, if the pitcher walks the batter or gives up a hit, his team loses. If he can get the batter out, the game goes to extra innings and his team has about an even chance of winning. He has three pitches: fastball, curveball, and slider. He can throw his fastball for a strike 90 percent of the time and his curveball 70 percent, but he's been having control problems with his slider—there's only a 50 percent chance it will end up in the strike zone. The batter can choose to swing or not swing. If he swings at a pitch outside the strike zone, we assume he strikes out and the inning is over. If he swings at a fastball or curveball in the strike zone, assume he has a 50 percent chance of delivering a game-winning hit. But the slider is harder to hit, so even if it's in the strike zone, he'll get a hit only 20 percent of the time.

	Swing	**Lay off**
Fastball	55%	90%
Curveball	65%	70%
Slider	90%	50%

This table shows the probability of getting the batter out for each combination of choices based on these assumptions. If the batter lays off, he will be out if the pitch is a strike, so these percentages are just the probabilities. If he swings, he will be out if the pitch is a ball, and half the time if it is a strike, except for the slider, which gets him out four-fifths of the time if it is a strike.

The pitcher might be tempted to select the pitch with the highest average probability. The fastball has (55 percent + 90 percent)/2 = 72.5 percent, the curveball (65 percent + 70 percent)/2 = 67.5 percent, and the slider (90 percent + 50 percent)/2 = 70 percent. So the fastball is the best pitch, followed by the slider, and the curveball is the worst. This would be correct if the batter chose whether to swing by coin flip. On the other hand, if the pitcher knew what the batter was going to do, he would throw a slider if the batter planned to swing and a fastball if he didn't.

But we'll assume the batter is good enough to spot the pitch type and then choose whether to swing. We're not going to make him so good that he can tell whether it will be a ball or a strike. (He's not Ted Williams or Barry Bonds.) The batter wants to minimize the probability of getting out—employ his ideal strategy—so he'll always pick the column with the smaller number for whatever pitch is thrown. That means he'll swing at a fastball or curveball and lay off a slider. Knowing that, the pitcher will ignore the higher number in each row and choose the pitch with the highest value of the lower number, known as the *minimax* strategy. Under minimax, the best pitch is the curveball, with a 65 percent worst case. That was the worst pitch in the expected value calculation and the one that would never be thrown if the batter's intentions were known. Only game theory identifies the curveball as the best pitch. Of course, in a simple situation like this one, you might see the advantage of the curveball without formal mathematics. But combinations multiply rapidly in real games and even more rapidly in real life. Before game theory was invented, no one had identified minimax as a general strategic principle. Without the machinery of game theory, it's almost impossible to solve games with more than a handful of outcomes.

What if the batter has to make up his mind whether to swing before the pitch? That makes it a different game. The computation is slightly more complicated, but there is a trick that often works. The best game theory strategy often equalizes your opponent's options. Intuitively, if your opponent can benefit from making one decision versus another, you've left something on the table for him to exploit. In game theory poker, you often bet the amount that puts your opponent on the edge, with equal expected value from folding, calling, or raising. That isn't always true, but it works in this example.

Given that the pitcher wants to make it equally attractive for the batter to swing or lay off, he only needs a choice of two pitches to do it. One choice is not enough, since the batter will decide to swing or not based on the probable outcome for that pitch. But if the pitcher mixes two pitches in the right proportions, the batter can swing or not, and the pitcher's team's chance of winning the game is identical. Obviously, it makes sense to choose among the two pitches with the highest expected values regardless of what the batter will do: the fastball and the slider. If the pitcher puts the numbers 1 through 15 in his hat, draws one out, and pitches a fastball if the number is 1 to 8 and a slider if it is 9 to 15, he's got a 71 percent chance of getting the out whether the batter swings or not.

This is another important insight from game theory: It often makes sense to deliberately randomize your strategy, creating artificial risk using gambling devices. People who try to minimize risk, who say gambling is irrational because it creates artificial risk, can miss opportunities. The best nonrandom strategy for the pitcher is to always pitch the curveball, which gives a 65 percent chance of getting the out. The best randomized strategy gives 71 percent, which is better than the curveball, whatever decision the batter makes about swinging. Randomized strategies also have an important place in finance.

GOD GAVE YOU GUTS: DON'T LET HIM DOWN

To dig deeper into game theory, consider the game of guts, sometimes played at poker tables, although it's not poker. You ante and are dealt a five-card poker hand. You look at it, then take one chip of the agreed denomination under the table, and come up with a fist, either with the chip in it or not. When everyone has one fist on the table, the fists are opened. If no one came up with a chip, everyone takes his ante back. If one player came up with a chip, he gets all the antes. If more than one player came up with a chip, all those chips are added to the antes, and the player with the best poker hand among the bettors wins the pot.

I've simplified slightly. In real guts if no one comes up with a chip, everyone antes again and another hand is played, and if only one player comes up with a chip, his hand has to beat a new hand dealt from the deck to collect the pot; otherwise, his chip and the antes are left in for another round. To further simplify, I'm going to consider only two players and assume that the betting chip is the same denomination as the ante chips (usually it would be larger).

If you are dealt a royal flush, you will obviously bet. You cannot lose, and you might win. Game theory tells us to assume your opponent will do the same thing. Now consider a king high straight flush. If you bet and the other player has a royal flush, you are going to lose one chip, the chip you had in your fist. I'm not counting the ante you will also lose. A common way to make a mistake in computing poker strategies is to mix up the accounting. You can measure profit and loss from before or after the ante, or any other point, but you have to be consistent. I prefer to set the zero point after you've put in the ante but before any other bets are made. That's the best way to think about it—that any money already put in the pot is no longer yours. It's not a loss if you lose it; it is a profit if you get it back.

If you bet your king high straight flush, and the other player has any worse hand, you are going to gain at least one extra chip by betting. If the other player bets, you'll win three chips (the antes plus his bet) by betting, when you would have had zero by folding. If the other player doesn't bet, you'll win two chips (the antes) by betting, when you would have won one chip (your ante back) by folding. Since there are four royal flushes that beat you and 2,598,952 hands you can beat, and if you win you get at least as much as the amount you lose when you lose, you should clearly bet.

To be more precise, we should eliminate the hands that are impossible, given your holding. That means comparing three possible royal flushes against 1,533,933 possible hands you can beat, but it's still an easy choice. So we will play king high straight flushes and assume the other player will as well.

We can work our way down, hand by hand, using this logic until we get to a hand that can be beaten by the same number of hands it can beat. There's no hand for which this is exactly true; ace/king/queen/jack/two is as close as we can get. There are 1,304,580 hands this good or better, and 1,294,380 worse hands. Pretend that exactly 50 percent of the hands the other player might have beat it, and exactly 50 percent

lose to it. Obviously, we should play this hand, since 50 percent of the
time it will cost us one chip, and 50 percent of the time it will win us
either one or three chips. You, and by assumption the other player,
should bet on any hand that is ace/king/queen/jack/two or better. This
represents 50.2 percent of the hands you could be dealt. It's over 50
percent because you bet when you hold the median hand.

Now let's start at the other end, with the worst possible poker
hand: Seven/five/four/three/two, not all of the same suit. Most lowball games allow you to count ace as low and ignore straights and
flushes, in which case five/four/three/two/ace is the worst (best) hand.
But guts is a high-card game, so you'd certainly use the ace as high
and insist on your straights and flushes.

Seven/five/four/three/two doesn't beat anything. If you bet, you
will lose one chip if the other player bets and gain one if he doesn't.
But from the preceding analysis, we know he will bet more than half
the time. So we fold this hand. The next-worst hand is seven/six/
four/three/two. This could only beat seven/five/four/three/two, and
we know that will be folded, so we get only one chip. There is no way
for us to win three chips, so we're in the same position as seven/five/
four/three/two, and we fold. We can use this logic all the way up to
ace/king/queen/ten/nine. So the game theory solution is to bet any
pair or better, or ace/king/queen/jack anything, but fold on ace/king/
queen/ten/nine or worse.

GUESSING GAMES

To compute the proper strategy without game theory requires you to
guess the other players' strategies. That doesn't seem so bad, but it's

hard to deal with mathematically. Any game, indeed any interaction with other people, involves incalculable risks. That should make you uncomfortable and discourage you from playing. Always keep in mind the idiot in the horror movie who finds the old scroll with the spell for summoning demons and decides to see whether it works. What's going to happen to him is an important object lesson in incalculable risk. If you do decide to play games anyway, don't invent a fantasy world in which the risks can be calculated.

One problem with game theory is that people don't behave the way it suggests. Extensive experiments have turned up many systematic deviations from optimal game theory behavior, but very few examples where people use it. It's true that under the assumptions of game theory you don't have to worry about that (one telltale danger sign for a theory is that proponents tell you it doesn't matter whether it's true). Your game theory strategy is optimized against the best possible strategy your opponents can choose from their point of view; if they choose anything else, you will do at least as well. But since your opponents often won't choose that strategy, a simpleminded person would say that you are walking around with a shield for a weapon nobody has. Game theorists dismiss that criticism because the simpleminded critic is too dense to follow the math. But you can't ignore dense people—they're not unarmed; they're armed differently. It hurts just as much to be hit by a stupid person as by a smart one. A second problem is that game theory often gives demonstrably wrong answers, even in the simplest games. The most famous example is the prisoner's dilemma. Two criminals are arrested fleeing a failed bank robbery. Unfortunately for the police, none of the witnesses can identify them as the robbers, and there is no other physical evidence. Both of the criminals can be convicted of resisting arrest, which carries a sentence of 1 year in prison. A conviction for attempted bank robbery carries a 10-year sentence. The criminals are separated and each is offered the same deal: Inform on your partner and go free. But if both criminals confess and inform, each will get a 9-year sentence—1 year off for informing.

		Hapless Confederate	
		Confess	Don't Confess
Game Theorist	Confess	Both get 9 years	Game theorist goes free, confederate gets 10 years
	Don't Confess	Game theorist gets 10 years, confederate goes free	Both get 1 year

If one of the criminals is a game theorist who turned to robbing banks after losing all his money playing poker against players too dumb to understand the theory, he will always confess. He'll reason that whatever his partner does, he saves 1 year in prison by confessing. If his partner remains silent, the game theorist goes free instead of serving 1 year. If his partner rats him out, the game theorist gets 9 years instead of 10. So he confesses. His partner, cursing himself for trying to rob a bank with a game theorist, confesses as well. He's not going to get stuck being loyal to a guy who doesn't understand loyalty. So both of them serve 9 years, when less mathematically sophisticated crooks are out in a year. It would be cruel and unusual punishment to put them in the same cell: Imagine 9 years of your cell mate explaining how smart you both are to be there.

There is no problem with the mathematics here; it's entirely self-consistent. The conclusion follows inexorably from the assumptions. I'm also not criticizing the game theorist's decision to confess, since his partner did the same thing for different reasons. The problem is the game theorist's initial characterization of his partner as an opponent. Once that happened, trust, loyalty, and cooperation were meaningless. This was a one-shot game against a faceless opponent, not a step in a human relationship or a business enterprise. The recommended action would be the same if the partner were the game theorist's best friend or worst enemy—in fact, the terms *friend* and *enemy* become meaningless. Everyone is an opponent—not a vindictive opponent; just a decision-making entity maximizing its own utility function without regard for your welfare.

It's easy to see how this kind of thinking poisons international diplomacy. Everyone is an opponent, and you prepare for their most harmful strategies. This applies to friendly and unfriendly countries—for that matter, it applies to domestic politics as well. It is sound military doctrine to "prepare for your enemy's capabilities, not his intentions," but it applies only to enemies. It's crazy to treat everyone as an enemy. Worse, it will cost you money in poker. There is more cooperation than competition at a poker table, but some game theorists can't see that. It applies with even more force in finance.

I am not against game theory; it is a useful tool for understanding some aspects of poker. And I'm not against people who study it; there is brilliant and important work being done in both theoretical and experimental game theory. My criticism is reserved for people who understand the basics, then think they understand everything. I want to play poker with these people, but not rob banks with them.

MASTERS OF THE BLUFF

Game theory does a great job of explaining the concept of bluffing, which cannot be described precisely in any other way. Bluffing is widely misunderstood. When the dastardly villain kidnaps the intrepid gal reporter, she can be counted on to claim she e-mailed her story to her editor, so the villain is exposed already. Killing her will only make things worse. He, of course, will snarl, "You're bluffing."

Sorry, dastardly villain. That was a lie, not a bluff. The intrepid gal reporter didn't bet anything—she didn't have anything to bet. If she says nothing, you kill her. If you believe her lie, you might not. You can't kill her twice for lying. She has nothing to lose by lying, and she gains only if you believe her; both of these conditions disqualify it as a bluff.

Of course, intrepid gal reporter gets away, and dastardly villain gets caught. When he sees her in the courtroom, he may threaten to escape and kill her. Her moronic but good-looking and loyal boyfriend may try to comfort her by saying, "He's only bluffing." Wrong again. Dastardly villain may be betting something; his outburst forfeits his sentence reduction points for sincere contrition. But intrepid gal reporter can't do anything in response. That makes it a threat, not a bluff.

Suppose you tell your boss that you have another job offer and will quit if you don't get a raise. You're betting something; you could lose your job, or at least some pride, if your boss refuses. Your boss has a choice: She can say, "Turn your ID in to Security on the way out" or "Sure, you can have the raise." But it's still not a bluff. Your boss's reaction won't depend on whether she believes you, but on whether she wants you to stay at the higher salary. If she's been trying to get rid of you for months, she'll shake your hand and wish you good luck in your new job, whether she believes you have one or not. If she really needs you, she'll do what it takes to get you to stay. Even if she knows you're lying, calling you on it could cause you to leave out of pride, or at least sow the seeds for future bad will.

A true bluff is not deception, and it's essential to focus on the difference. When you're bluffing, the last thing you want is a confused bluffee. When you're attempting deception, confusion helps you.

BLUFFING MATHEMATICS

To understand the mathematics of bluffing, let's go back to the game of guts and make it into a poker game. Instead of the nonsense with chips under the table and simultaneous bets, you have to either check or bet. If you check, we show hands and the better one takes the antes. If you bet, I can either call or fold. If I call, we each put in a chip, show hands, and the better hand wins four chips. If I fold, you get the antes.

Suppose you start by betting on any pair or better; otherwise, you check. You get a pair or better 49.9 percent of the time—we'll call it 50 percent to keep it simple. In the game theory analysis, you assume I know your strategy. I'm going to call your bet only if I have at least one chance in four of winning, since it costs me one chip if I lose but gains me three chips if I win. If I have a pair of sixes, I beat you one time in four, given that you have at least twos. So half the time you check, and the other half you bet. When you bet, I call you three times in eight; the tables that follow will explain why.

			My Hand		
			Sixes or Better	**Twos to Fives**	**No Pair**
		Action	Call If You Bet	Fold If You Bet	Fold If You Bet
Your Hand	**Sixes or Better**	Bet	You bet, I call, we each have an even chance to win	You bet, I fold, you win	
	Twos to Fives	Bet	You bet, I call, I win		
	No Pair	Check	You check, I win		You check, we each have an even chance to win

The preceding table shows the five possible outcomes. The next table shows their expected values to you. If we both have sixes or better, you bet and I call. Half the time you will win three chips, and half the time you will lose one. Your average profit is shown in the table at +1 chip. If you have any betting hand (twos or better) and I have any folding hand (fives or worse), you bet, I fold, and you win the antes, +2 to you. If you have twos to fives and I have sixes or better, you bet, I call, and I win. You lose one chip.

			My Hand		
			Sixes or Better	**Twos to Fives**	**No Pair**
		Action	Call If You Bet	Fold If You Bet	Fold If You Bet
Your Hand	**Sixes or Better**	Bet	+1	+2	
	Twos to Fives	Bet	−1		
	No Pair	Check	0		+1

If you have no pair, you check. If I have twos or better, I win all the time. You get zero. If I also have no pair, you win the antes half the time, for an expected value of +1.

The following table shows the computed probabilities. We each have sixes or better 3/8 of the time, twos to fives 1/8 of the time, and no pair the other 1/2 the time. The probability of any combination is close to the product of the individual probabilities. So, for example, the probability of you having sixes or better and me having twos to fives is $3/8 \times 1/8 = 3/64$.

			My Hand		
			Sixes or Better	Twos to Fives	No Pair
		Probability	3/8	1/8	1/2
Your Hand	Sixes or Better	3/8	9/64	5/16	
	Twos to Fives	1/8	3/64		
	No Pair	1/2	1/4		1/4

To compute your overall expected value, we multiply the numbers in the preceding two tables cell by cell, then add them up. We get $+1 \times (9/64) + 2 \times (5/16) - 1 \times (3/64) + 0 \times (1/4) + 1 \times (1/4) = 31/32$. Since you have to ante one chip to play, you lose in the long run because you get back less than one chip on average.

In general, if you play your fraction p best hands, you lose $p^2/8$ chips per hand. In this case, with $p = \frac{1}{2}$, you lose $\frac{1}{32}$ chip per hand. The best you can do is set $p = 0$. That means always check, never bet. There is never any betting; the best hand takes the antes. You will win 128 chips on average after 128 hands.

This example illustrates an ancient problem in betting. It doesn't make sense for you to offer a bet, because I will take it only if it's advantageous to me. Accepting a bet can be rational, but offering one cannot. About 200 years ago, some anonymous person discovered the lapse in this logic, which bluffing can exploit. It's possible that some people understood bluffing before this, but there is no record of it. We have plenty of writings about strategy, but none of them has the remotest hint that the author had stumbled onto this concept. Given its importance as a strategy, it's hard to believe no one would have mentioned it had it been known. Moreover, it's such an amazing and counterintuitive idea, it's even harder to believe it was so well-known that no one bothered to write about it.

The stroke of genius is to bet on your worst hands instead of your best ones. Suppose you bet on any hand queen/nine or worse, plus any hand with a pair of sixes or better. You're still betting half the time—one time in eight with queen/nine or worse and three times in eight with sixes or better. I will still call with sixes or better because I have at least one chance in four of winning with those hands.

Notice how the following outcome table has carved out a new box when you check and I have a queen/nine or worse. You move from losing these situations, with an outcome of 0, to winning with an outcome of +2. They represent 1/16 of the table, so they give you an additional expected profit of 1/8. That brings you from 31/32 to 35/32. Since that's greater than 1, you now have a profit playing this game. The trade-off is that you now lose by a lot instead of a little when you have queen/nine or worse and I have sixes or better. But that doesn't cost you any money.

| | | | **My Hand** | | |
			Sixes or Better	Nine or Worse	Queen/Ten to Fives
		Action	Call If You Bet	Fold If You Bet	Fold If You Bet
Your Hand	Sixes or Better	Bet	You bet, I call, we each have an even chance to win	You bet, I fold, you win	
	Queen/Nine or Worse	Bet	You bet, I call, I win		
	Queen/Ten to Fives	Check	You check, I win	You check, you win	I check, we each have an even chance to win

There is nothing I can do about this development. I know you're bluffing one out of four times you bet, but there's nothing I can do to take advantage of that knowledge. You're not fooling me, but you are beating me. Declaring your bet first is not a disadvantage, as it seemed at first, but an advantage—but only if you know how to bluff. Unfortunately, in real poker, other players can bluff in return and take back the advantage. Notice that it's important that you bluff with your weakest hands. This is an essential insight from game theory, which could not be explained clearly without it.

This is the classic poker bluff—acting like you have a very strong hand when you actually have the weakest possible hand. You expect to lose money when you bluff, but you more than make it up on other hands. When you have a strong hand, you're more likely to get called, because people know you might be bluffing. When you call, your hands are stronger on average, because you substituted bluffs for some of the hands you would have raised on and called on those hands instead. Bluffing doesn't depend on fooling people; in fact, it works only if people know you do it. If you can fool people, do that instead, but don't call it a bluff.

There are other deceptive plays in poker, and some people like to call these bluffs. I'm not going to argue semantics, but it's important to understand the classic bluff as a distinct idea. People are naturally deceptive, so your instincts can be a good guide about when to lie and when others are lying to you. But bluffing is completely counter-intuitive; you have to train yourself to do it, and to defend yourself when others do it. Your instincts will betray you and destroy the value of the bluff; in fact, they will make it into a money-losing play. It's easy to think, "Why bluff on the weakest hands; why not use a mediocre hand instead so I have some chance of winning if I'm called?" When you get called, embarrassment might cause you to throw away your worthless hand without showing it. You may naturally pick the absolute worst times to bluff and be just as wrong about when other players might be bluffing you. Any of these things undercut the value of the bluff. Bluffing is the chief reason that people who are good at other card games find themselves big losers in poker to average players.

The classic bluff amounts to pretending to be strong when you are weak. Pretending to be weak when you are strong, also known as *slowplaying,* is a standard deception strategy type. I prefer not to call it a bluff. The classic bluff is to raise on a hand you would normally fold; slowplaying is calling on a hand you would normally raise. The bluff goes from one extreme to the other; slowplaying goes from one extreme to the middle. You should always mix up your poker playing, but unless you're bluffing, you move only one notch: from fold to call or call to raise or vice versa. You would never bluff by folding a hand you should raise—that would be crazy. Another distinction is that you slowplay to make more money on the hand in play; you bluff expecting to lose money on average on the hand, but to increase your expectation on future hands.

A more interesting case is the semibluff. This is one of the few important concepts of poker clearly invented by one person: David Sklansky. I don't mean that no one ever used it before Sklansky wrote about it. I have no way of knowing that. But he was the first to write about it, and he had the idea fully worked out. You semibluff by raising on a hand that's probably bad but has some chance of being very good.

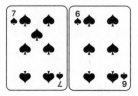

An example is the six and seven of spades in hold 'em. If the board contains three spades, or three cards that form a straight with the six and seven, or two or more sixes and sevens, your hand is strong. Even better, other players will misguess your hand. Your early raise will mark you for a pair or high cards. Suppose, for example, the board contains a pair of sevens, a six, and no ace. If you bet strongly, people will suspect that you started with ace/seven, and play you for three of a kind. Someone with a straight or flush will bet with confidence. You, in fact, have a full house and will beat their hand. Or if the board comes out with some high cards and three spades, people will think you have paired your presumed high cards or gotten three of a kind. You actually have a flush.

I prefer to think of raising with this hand preflop as a randomized bluff. When you make the raise, you don't know whether you're bluffing. I don't like the term *semibluff* because it implies that you're sort of bluffing. You're not. You're either bluffing or you're not—you just don't know which yet. That's an important distinction. Sort of bluffing never works; randomized bluffing can work. Sklansky states that you should expect to make money on your semibluffs—in fact, on all bluffs. To my thinking, if you expect to make money on the hand, it's deception, not bluffing. When you bet for positive expected value, it's no bluff. You may have a weak hand that will win only if the other player folds, but if the odds of her folding are high enough, your play is a lie, not a bluff.

Given Sklansky's refusal to make a negative expected value play, a randomized bluff is the only way to incorporate bluffing into his game. The disadvantage of semibluffs is that you lose control over when you bluff. You need a certain kind of hand for it, so you could go an hour or more without getting one—and even if you get it, it might not turn into a bluff. If you practice classic bluffing, the deal is unlikely to go around the table without giving you some good opportunities. You even have the luxury of choosing your position and which player to bluff, or bluffing after a certain kind of pot.

Semibluffing makes the most sense when two conditions are met. First, the game might not last long enough for you to collect on the investment of a bluff with negative expectation. The extreme case of this is when the winner of a large pot is likely to quit the game. This happens a lot online. Players don't even have to leave physically: If they tighten up enough, they might as well be gone. Second, the bluff is aimed at turning a break-even or better situation into a more profitable one, rather than a money-losing situation into break-even or better. For improving a break-even situation, you can afford to wait as long as it takes for the right bluff. If you're working a losing situation, you should bluff soon or quit the game.

GAME FACT

A game theory analysis of bluffing is just one way of looking at one aspect of poker. Game theory teaches many valuable lessons, but overreliance on it has led to some absurd weaknesses in the standard way the modern game is played.

For one thing, game theory teaches that there is no advantage to concealing your strategy, only your cards. Players are taught to watch intently when other players first pick up their cards and to take great pains to disguise any of their own reactions. Those same players will chatter openly about their playing strategies. "I hate playing small pairs," they'll announce to the world, or "suited jack/ten is the best pocket holding."

Not all of this information is true. The guy who hates small pairs probably does so because he plays too many of them. A guy who swears he'll never touch another drop of alcohol is likely to put away more liquor in the next year than the guy who doesn't talk about his drinking. But rarely in my experience is this talk deliberate misdirection. The important thing is that it tells you how the player thinks about the game. Listen when people tell you stories about their triumphs and frustrations—they're telling you how they play and what matters most to them. Do they crow about successful bluffs or when their great hand beat a good hand? Do they gripe

Game Theory Mistake #1: Focusing on cards instead of strategy.

about people who play bad cards and get lucky or people who play only the strongest hands? Of course, the answer in many cases is both, but you can still pick up some nuances. I don't know whether to be more amazed that players give this kind of information away for free or that other players don't pay attention to it. I learned a more traditional version of poker, in which you have to pay to learn about someone's strategy.

You will learn a lot more useful things studying players before they pick up their hands than after. For one thing, game theory has put them off guard during the shuffle and deal. There's less misdirection and less camouflage. For another, it's hard to learn much that's useful about someone's cards, unless they're wearing reflector sunglasses. You might get a general impression that the hand is pretty good or bad, but you'll figure that out soon enough from the betting. It's hard to read the difference between suited ace/nine and a pair of eights. A really bad player will tip off what he thinks the strength of his hand is, but a really bad player is often mistaken. You can't read in his face what he doesn't know. A really good player is at least as likely to be telling you what she wants you to think, rather than giving away useful information. Anyway, poker decisions rarely come down to small differences in other players' hand strengths. Determining the winner will come down to those small differences, but the way you play the hand doesn't.

However, knowing someone's strategy tells you exactly how to play them. It's often possible to see in someone's manner before the deal that he's going to take any playable hand to the river or that he's looking for an excuse to fold. One guy is patiently waiting for a top hand, smug behind his big pile of chips. Another is desperate for some action to recoup his losses. Knowing this will help you interpret their subsequent bets and tell you how to respond.

If you know their strategies, you don't need to know their cards. Say you decide the dealer has made up his mind to steal the blinds before the cards are dealt. As you expect, he raises. You have only a moderate hand, but you call because you think he was planning to raise on anything. If he turns out to have a good hand by luck, you will probably lose. But you don't care much, since on average you'll win with your knowledge. Knowing his cards would only help you win his money faster—too fast. People will stop playing if every time you put money in the pot, you win. If you did know everyone's cards, you would lose on purpose once in a while to disguise that fact. In the long run, everyone's cards are close to the expected distribution, so you don't have to guess.

The game-theoretic emphasis on secrecy spilled over into cold war diplomacy. A cold war thriller is, almost by definition, an espionage story (usually with the possibility of the world being destroyed if the good guys lose). The obsession with spies looks pretty silly today because almost all major security breaches were by spies selling out their own countries. We would have had far better security with less obsession about spying and counterspying. If you let foreign agents loose among all government documents, they can spend eternity trying to winnow out the few items that are both valuable and accurate. When you segregate all the important stuff in top secret folders, you do your enemies a favor. You double that favor by creating such a huge bureaucracy to manage the secrets that it's a statistical certainty you're hiring some traitors or idiots.

On top of that, making essential public data secret undercuts both freedom of the press and the people's right to choose. When the party in power and entrenched public employees get to decide what's secret, it's even worse. The joke, of course, is that all the cold war disasters were disasters of strategy. It wasn't that either side didn't have good enough cards, it was that they played them foolishly. All the financial and human resources wasted on getting better cards (that is, building more terrible weapons) supported a strategy of risking everything and terrifying everyone, for nothing.

Getting back to poker, another reason for focusing on strategy rather than cards is that you cannot change someone's cards (legally, anyway), but it's easy to change their strategy. Consider the

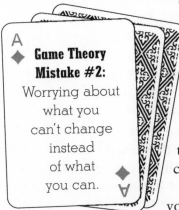

original game of guts discussed previously, in which both players declare at the same time. If the other player follows the game-theoretic optimum strategy of playing the strongest half of his hands, ace/king/queen/jack/two or higher, there's no way for you to win. But if he deviates in either direction, playing more or fewer hands, you can gain an advantage.

If he plays fewer than half his hands, your best strategy is to play all of yours. If

A
◆ **Game Theory Mistake #2:** Worrying about what you can't change instead of what you can. ◆

he plays more than half his hands, your best strategy is also to play loose, but only half as loose as he does. For example, if he plays 70 percent of his hands, you play 60 percent (half the distance from 50 percent). If he plays exactly half his hands, it doesn't matter whether you play anything from 50 percent to 100 percent of yours. This general result applies to many game situations. If another player is too tight, even a little bit, you respond by being very loose. If another player is too loose, you want to be about half as loose. Another general result suggests that you try to make a tight player tighter and a loose player looser. You want to drive other players away from the optimal strategy, and it's easier and more profitable to move them in the direction they want to go anyway.

To a game theorist, this information is irrelevant. You play assuming your opponent does the worst possible thing for you, so you don't care what he actually does. But I do care what he actually does. My guess is that most poker players are going to start out too tight, since they've been trained to wait for good hands. That means I start out playing all my hands. I'll probably make money that way. At worst, I'll have a small negative expectation. If so, I'll find it out very soon, the first time a player bets with a weak hand.

Of course, my playing all my hands and his losing money steadily will encourage him to loosen up. I can judge the degree of looseness very precisely because I see all the hands he bets on. That's another reason to start out loose: I want to learn his strategy. Game theory does not value that, because it starts by assuming that everyone knows everyone else's strategy. Once he loosens up enough to play 50 percent of his hands, I want to pull him looser quickly. As in judo, the trick is to use the other person's momentum against him.

How do I do that? I bet blind. Instead of looking at my hand and squirreling a chip under the table, I pick up a chip and put it in my fist above the table. I don't say anything; I just do it. Betting blind (when it's not required) is an important ploy in poker to change other players' strategies, but it has disappeared from modern books because game theory says it is never correct to ignore information.

If I do things right, I can get him playing much more than 50 percent of his hands. To take advantage of that, I have to play half as loose as he does. That will take some close figuring, but I can do it for a while. When he gets tired of losing showdowns, he'll start to tighten up, and I'll go back to playing all my hands.

Of course, he could be trying to do the same things to me. If he stays one step ahead, or gets me playing by emotion instead of logic, or just keeps me off balance, he's going to win. One of us will win and one will lose, and the luck of the cards has nothing to do with it. There's no neat mathematical way to decide who will win, and there's no way to calculate the risk. That's the essential nature of games—good games, anyway—and it's entirely missing from game theory. Everyone was born knowing this; it took mathematics to confuse people. If you keep your common sense, play a clear strategy, and encourage other players to play a strategy you can beat, you won't find many people playing at your level.

This example reveals another defect of game theory. The optimal strategy often means that all opponents' strategies work equally well. The game-theoretic strategy for Rock Paper Scissors, for example, is

to play each shape at random with equal probability. If you do this, you will win exactly half the games in the long run (actually, you win one-third and tie one-third, but if ties count as half a win, that comes out to winning half the time). You win one-half, no more and no less, if I always play rock, or always play what would have won last time, or always play the shape you played last time. You can't lose, but you also can't win. That's not playing at all. If you want to avoid the game, why waste the effort to pretend to play?

It makes more sense to adopt a strategy that gives other players many opportunities to make costly mistakes rather than one that gives you the same return no matter how they play. Instead of starting from the idea that everyone knows everyone's strategy and plays perfectly given that knowledge, let's make the more reasonable assumption that there is uncertainty about strategies and imperfect play. Now winning comes down to making fewer mistakes than other players. You can accomplish that by reducing your own mistakes or increasing theirs.

If you're the better player, the first course is difficult because you're already good. But the second course is easy: As the better player, you should be able to manipulate the table and keep everyone else off balance. If you are equally as good as the other players, it still makes sense to try the second approach. If you avoid one mistake, that's one mistake in your favor. But if you induce a mistake in other players' play against you, that's one mistake per player in your favor. Only if you are the worst player does it make more sense to improve your own play than to try to disrupt others. In that case, the game theory approach is a good defense. But, as I've said before, an even better approach is to quit the game until you're good enough to compete.

SMALL-MINDEDNESS

The last three errors of game theory come under the general heading of thinking small. In principle, game theory can address many hands of poker against many other players. But the complexity of that quickly overwhelms the most powerful computers. The only exact game theory solutions we have for poker involve single opponents in simplified games. Researchers take cards out of the pack, reduce the number of betting rounds, and change the rules in other ways to get tractable equations. I have nothing against this approach. I employed it myself to use the simple game of guts to explain the concept of bluffing. But it only gives partial illumination of one aspect of poker. If you rely on it more generally, you will lose money. Worse, you won't be able to see your obvious errors because they don't exist in your simplified framework.

Poker advice books that are hopelessly infected by game theory are easy to spot. They will deal with two situations entirely differently. With lots of potential bettors, either preflop or in multiway pots, there will be no mention of game theory ideas. The author will be content to figure the chance that you have the best hand. Given that information, he will play the hand straightforwardly, fold with a poor chance, call with a medium chance, or raise with a good chance. There may be a little deception thrown in—a slowplay or raise to get a free card—but no bluffing. It's all probability theory, not game theory. The author might come right out and say not to bluff more than one other player at a time. That's not poker wisdom based on experience but a convenient assumption because it's too complicated to calculate a multiway game theory bluff. Game theorists avoid them not because they're bad, but because they're incalculable. I think the incalculable risks are the only ones likely to lead to real profit.

Game Theory Mistake #4: Playing against an opponent instead of with the table.

Once the author gets the hand to you against one other player, the rest of the table disappears into the ether. The approach switches to game theoretic. Of course, there's never any discussion of the shift.

There are several problems with this approach. One is that your decisions should take into account everyone at the table, not just the players still contesting the pot. It doesn't make any difference for this hand, but it will for future hands. If you get called on a bluff, the entire table will change the way they play you.

Players who have folded—the good ones, anyway—will be studying just as intently as if they were in the pot themselves. Since they don't have to worry about their own play, they have more attention to spare for yours. I've often found that it's easier to figure people out by watching them play others, either after I've folded or when I'm a spectator, than by playing a hand against them myself. When I'm playing, I know what I have, and it's impossible to forget that when assessing them. When I don't know any of the hands, a lot of things are easy to spot that I would have missed if I were playing. A third situation that is revealing in another way is after I know I am going to fold, but he doesn't. I spot different things in the three situations, and combining them gives me a better picture than any one alone. Of course, since game theorists care only about disguising their cards, not their strategies, they don't think there's anything to be learned by watching. Next hand will have different cards, so there's no carry-over of useful information.

A specific example of carryover and its impact is the question of when to bluff. The traditional poker advice, prior to the existence of game theory, was to bluff every time you won two pots without showing your hand. Of course, this was never meant to be done mechanically. It would be foolishly predictable to bluff every hand after two wins without a showdown. The advice was meant to help you gauge your bluffing frequency, tying it to its goal of getting people to call your strong hands.

Game theory suggests the opposite view. Winning a hand without a showdown is like a half bluff. The other players don't know whether you had good cards or not, so they'll react in the same way as if you were called and had nothing, but less strongly. Two hands won without a showdown equal one bluff, so there's no need for another one. Instead, you should make sure the next hand you play is strong, since you are likely now to be called.

Both these analyses are correct, so we seem to have a dilemma. Do we bluff more often when everyone folds against our strong hands or less often? This is a false dilemma, created by treating everyone at the table as one many-headed opponent. At any given time, there are some players at the table you would like to loosen up with a bluff and others you hope will play even tighter. The trick is to run the bluff, but at the player least likely to call it. There is more than one other player at the table; you can pick your bluffing targets. You would like to do the opposite with your good hands—that is, get them when the loose players also have good cards—but you can't control that.

Not only is the bluff more likely to be profitable when run against a player unlikely to call, but it will have enhanced effect. Even though you probably won't show your cards, the loose players will pick up that you're bluffing the easy target. People hate to see you get away with a bluff. You'll get more action making money from successfully bluffing a conservative player, without showing your cards, than from losing money going to showdown with a player who always calls, then showing the weakest possible hand. And if the easy target does call you, you'll get twice as much effect. So it's cheaper and more effective to bluff the players you are not trying to affect. If the loose players aren't calling you, bluff the tight players. If the tight players fold against a couple of your good hands, wait for the nuts before you take on the loose players, then steal the blinds all night against the tight players. It's the simplest thing in the world, unless game theory makes you forget there's a whole table out there rather than just one opponent.

Another problem with using probability theory for many opponents and game theory for one is the abrupt transition. You pick your starting hands from a table based on their probability of developing into the best hand, but you make your late-round betting decisions from game-theoretic optimal strategies.

This switch prevents you from having a consistent, smooth approach to the game. It makes your bluffs much easier to spot, and your strong hands as well. You may also face the problem of remembering the hand. At the beginning you are focused on one view, so it's hard to pay attention to the things you might need later in the hand if you stay in. It's even harder to pay attention to yourself, to make sure you give the signals that might induce mistakes in other players later.

More important than these considerations is that success requires thinking in terms of both strategy and probability both early and late in the hand. At the beginning, thinking only about how strong your cards are leads to playing hands likely to turn into the second-best hand. You win the most in poker with the best hand, but you lose the most with the second-best. Far better to have the worst hand, fold it, and lose only your share of the antes and blinds. When choosing which cards to play, you should consider the chance of the hand being the best and the difference between its chance of being the best minus the chance of it being second-best. You also have to factor in the chance that you will know you have the best hand, since you will win much more in that situation. However, you might throw away a hand that is probably best if there is even a small probability that another player knows she has the best hand against you.

Of course, it's possible in principle to expand the game theory analysis to a full table of players. Remarkably, it turns out to be simpler to solve this game than the two-person game. If you assume everyone at the table adopts the strategy that is best for them collectively, you should fold every hand. You can't make money playing against a table of people colluding against you. Some theorists argue that this is an unfair approach, that you should instead assume that each person plays independently of the others. That may make an interesting mathematical exercise, but cooperative and competitive interactions among players at the table are a crucially important element of poker. I'm not talking about explicit collusion. That is a consideration, because it happens, but it is against the rules. I'm talking about the natural interactions that develop at any poker table. Exploiting these to your benefit is a key to winning poker; fighting against their current is a recipe for disaster. Game theory strategies often have the effect of isolating you at the table, driving the table to unconsciously close ranks against you.

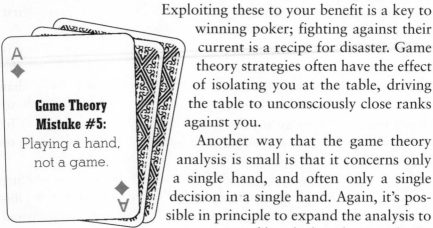

Game Theory Mistake #5:
Playing a hand, not a game.

Another way that the game theory analysis is small is that it concerns only a single hand, and often only a single decision in a single hand. Again, it's possible in principle to expand the analysis to cover a series of hands, but the complexity makes the problem intractable. Your goal is probably a lifetime of winning poker—or at least a session. Playing one hand perfectly is at best a small step toward that goal and may even be a step in the wrong direction. The erudite David Spanier, in *Total Poker,* discusses the strategy of running a complete bluff all the way to showdown in the first hand in London clubs. Complete bluffs of this type are rarer in England than in America—at least they were at the time he was writing. His play attracted enough attention to get his strong hands called all night. Obviously, it's impossible to even discuss a strategy like this in the context of one hand.

Actually, game theory requires doublethink on the question of whether it applies to multiple hands. On one hand, the mathematics work only if only one hand is to be played. On the other hand, the assumption that everyone knows everyone's strategy is sensible to make only in the context of multiple hands. Randomizing your strategy is a mathematical trick to think about playing many hands—all hands you might have multiplied by all the actions you might take—while actually playing only one. If I were going to play only one hand of poker in my life, I would play it to maximize expected value. I wouldn't bluff. I would use probability theory, not game theory, to choose my actions. A game theorist can argue that if the other player guesses this, I'm worse off than if I pick a game-theoretic strategy and my opponent reads my mind about that. But if the other player can read my mind, I don't want to play poker against him in the first place.

There are two problems with expanding the game theory analysis to cover multiple hands. One is that, as with multiple opponents, the complexity mounts rapidly. Another is that the assumption that everyone knows everyone's strategy means there is no learning, so there is no reason to play any one hand differently from any other. To get a meaningful game theory for multiple hands, we would have to assume a theory of learning.

Game theory allows you to set an optimum probability of bluffing when you play a single hand. That computation involves a lot of dubious assumptions, but the result is a reasonable guide to the optimum *frequency* of actual bluffing over many hands. That is, if game theory tells you to bluff with 5 percent probability in a certain situation, it is probably about right to bluff about 1 time out of 20 when that situation occurs. But probabilities are not frequencies and forgetting the difference is a dangerous blind spot for many people who are good at quantitative reasoning. It is a terrible idea in poker to select the time to bluff at random—that is, to use a random-number generator to decide what to do each time you get into the situation. Selecting when to bluff is where game theory leaves off and the game begins.

The final blind spot of game theory is that it fails to ask why people are playing in the first place. The analysis begins with the players seated around the table with their money in front of them. Where did they come from, and where will they go after the game? What is at stake besides money? If it is only money, it doesn't make sense to play, especially if there is a house rake.

Game Theory Mistake #6: Ignoring the world beyond the table.

You might argue that the good players have positive expected value of money and the bad players are misguided, but game theory is based on rational, fully informed players.

This may not matter much if players are forced to play the game, as in prisoner's dilemma, or if the play is purely recreational. Neither of these conditions is typically true of poker, at least when it is played for meaningful stakes.

In the late 1950s, Doyle Brunson, Sailor Roberts, and Amarillo Slim teamed up to drive around Texas playing in local poker games. All three would go on to win the championship event at the World Series of Poker in the 1970s. Brunson won it twice. How would you predict this dream team of professionals would fare against local amateurs in the back rooms of small-town Texas bars?

If you just think of the action at the table, you would predict that they would win a lot of money, and you would be right. But if you take a larger view, you would ask why anyone would let three strangers drive into their town and drive off with its money. The answer, of course, is that people didn't. Sometimes the local sheriff would arrest the three and collect a fine larger than their winnings. Other times they would be robbed as they left town, losing their stake plus their winnings. Bad debts ate up more of the profits. Add it all up, and they lost money on their poker. All they did was transfer money from the town's poker players to its sheriff or gunmen. They were unpaid accessories in armed robbery, providing the robbers with a convenient insulation from their local victims.

So why did the three keep playing? They were actually part of a network that was laying off bets on high school football games among local bookies. They were paid for this service. The poker playing was just an unprofitable sideline.

This theme is repeated in the biographies of almost all the famous poker champions before the 1990s. They win huge amounts of money, yet they are frequently broke. They're obviously very good at winning money at poker, but not so good at keeping it. There appear to be forces outside the table that are important to consider if you want to be consistently successful at poker.

If you think only in terms of the table, the easiest way to be successful is to find a table of rich, bad players. But why should such a table exist? Why would the bad players play? Why wouldn't some other good player compete for the profits? The same situation occurs in business. It's not enough to notice some market where it appears you could sell a product at a profit. You have to ask yourself why no one is doing it already, and also, if you do it successfully, why someone won't copy you and force you to cut prices. There are good answers to these questions—sometimes. That's why there are successful businesses. But if you don't ask the questions, you won't have one of the successful businesses. And if you don't ask the questions at the poker table, you will not win in the long run, even if you're as good as three World Series of Poker champions put together.

Mistake #6 is the closest game theory mistake to the subject of this book, and it is discussed at length elsewhere. But to consider a simple example, how do you make a living playing poker in a casino? Of course, you have to be a good poker player, but that's only the first step.

If you take money out of the game, it has to come from someone else. The three logical possibilities are (1) the winning players, as a group, could win less; (2) the losing players could lose more; (3) or the house could collect a smaller rake. The source of your income could be one of the three, or any combination.

Let's start with the house. Anyone planning to make a living playing poker in a casino should read a book on casino management. I have to admit that none of the successful casino players I know have done this, but most have either worked in a casino or spent enough time getting to know casino employees to absorb the house mind-set. Some of them are just naturally good at figuring out the economics of a situation around them.

The usual casino model, used in almost all games, is that the house wins what the players lose. The constraint on casino revenue is how much its patrons are willing to lose. In poker, the winning players are taking some of the potential revenue away. Why would the house allow this? It could be that poker is cheaper to run than other house games, but that's not true. It requires more floor space and employees per rake dollar than other casino games, and poker also requires more employee skill. The factor that occurs first to most people is that there's less risk for the house, since it takes its cut regardless of the outcome of the hand. But for large casinos, the risk from games like craps and roulette is negligible, given the number of bets made. Another minor point is that poker players are more apt than other customers to play during the casino's nonpeak hours, 2 A.M. to 5 P.M. But that's nowhere near enough to explain casino poker games.

One answer is that poker players are different from other casino gamblers. Or, more precisely, they're often the same people, but they have different budgets for their casino and poker losing. They are willing to lose money in poker that is not available to the house in blackjack or slot machines. The other part of the answer is that poker players do not demand the same services in return for losses as other casino customers. They do not expect generous comps, nor do they ask for credit. Casinos in competitive markets typically have to pay out 75 percent of their gross revenues to induce gamblers to show up. That covers overhead, comps, and bad debt losses. The total is pretty constant, although different customers consume the three items in different proportions. With poker players, the house keeps almost the entire rake. That means that, in principle, the house should be willing to let winning players, as a group, walk off with a total of three times the rake; then it would keep the same 25 percent of customer losses it gets in other games. That covers only consistent winners. People who win one night and lose it all back the next are not counted against this budget.

The first implication of this insight is that it pays to play poker in competitive casino situations. You're the floor show. Las Vegas and

Atlantic City casinos are accustomed to spending more to attract customers than local Indian reservation casinos without competition closer than three hours' drive.

A foolish player will say the house has nothing to do with it. But there are lots of ways for the house to cut itself in for some of the winners' money. A common one is to increase the rake and award some of it back to the losing players. Online casinos rebate 25 percent or more of the losses for consistent losers. In the short run it could make the same amount of money by cutting the rake by about 15 percent and eliminating the rebate. That would mean the consistent winners make more, and consistent winners withdraw their profits, while the consistent losers lose more. Consistent losers never withdraw, so giving them the rebate is as safe for the online casinos as putting that money in the bank. In bricks-and-mortar casinos, bad-beat jackpots are more common. These also take money from every pot and award it to losers.

Another common practice is to employ shills. These players are employed and financed by the house, and the house keeps their winnings. The house can also adjust the betting and seating rules to the disadvantage of players trying to make a living.

I don't claim that these tactics are foolproof. There may be a consistent casino poker winner somewhere who wins in spite of the house. But I've never met one. Think of the Malay proverb "If you row upstream, the crocodiles will laugh at you." Positioning yourself so your winnings also help the casino is rowing downstream. There are some mean crocodiles running casinos, so you want them on your side.

What makes you popular with casinos? Don't annoy the paying customers or the staff, or cause disputes. In fact, it helps if you are actively pleasant and encourage other players to stay cool. Keep the game lively, so losers get their money's worth and the rake isn't as painful. Don't hit and run—that is, don't win your money quickly and leave. Keep a big stack of chips on the table. It's a major bonus if you bring in players through either personal connections or your reputation. The worst sin is to push customers to other casinos or steal them for private games. In a casino, big brother is always watching, a powerful friend and a vicious enemy.

You also have to worry about the other winners. If they conspire against you, it will be hard to be successful. You won't be left alone at good tables, and when more than one of them is against you, you will have a crippling disadvantage. How can you take money from their pockets without encouraging them to gang up on you? First, figure out who they are (especially the ones better than you) and don't sit in when they have a soft game. However, when they come to your game, you have to punish them. It's more important for you that they lose money in the session, or at least have a struggle to eke out a small profit, than that you win. Being personally respectful and pleasant is a good idea, although I know people who successfully practice the opposite strategy.

If you are accepted, you will displace someone else. The game can support only so many winners. The remaining winners will have the same shares as before. Then you can afford to sit in with other winners, with the unspoken understanding that you're all playing against the losers and won't challenge each other. Your other duty is to defend the game against newcomers—especially obnoxious ones who chase losers away or don't respect the established pecking order. You have to sit in on their games and prevent them from making a living, so they will move on and leave your gang in peace.

The losers are important, too. If people enjoy losing money to you, you will be more successful in the long run. Making someone mad will often help you win a hand; putting them on a tilt can help you win for the session. But making a living this way is like selling a shoddy product and ignoring all customer complaints. A lot of people do it, but it's a better life to give real value and have satisfied customers coming back. Knowing who the losers are and why they are willing to lose is essential to keeping them satisfied. Even if you don't know them personally, you can learn to recognize types. Some losers are happy to bleed extra bets all night if they can rake in a big pot or two to brag about tomorrow. Others are impatient and hate to fold too many hands. Pay attention to what people want and give it to them in return for their money.

Thinking about the larger economics is just one reason you cannot analyze poker by considering only one hand. It's not true that success is measured by your profit or loss on one hand. Perfect game theory strategy induces other players and the house to conspire against you, just as game theory diplomacy polarized the world and nearly caused it to blow up.

Game theory is a simplified world, like physics without air resistance, or efficient markets finance. There are deep insights that can be gained this way, but you cannot let the simple models blind you. There is air resistance in the world. If you're dropping cannonballs off the leaning tower of Pisa, you can ignore it. If you are parachuting, particularly into a poker game, you cannot.

FLASHBACK

LIAR'S POKER

Trading has always been a rowdy occupation, and hazing an important part of the apprenticeship. That hazing takes the form of verbal abuse, practical jokes, demeaning tasks, and challenges. In the mid-1980s it reached spectacular heights. For the first time in history, getting a chance at a trading position for a major institution had a high probability of making you wealthy for life in a few years. Traditionally, most traders washed out early, and even successful ones worked for years to achieve moderate wealth. Markets in the mid-1980s showered millions of dollars on people with moderate skills. Most Wall Street firms had not learned how to manage traders, especially those making more than the CEO, so the riotous behavior was unrestrained.

Trading changed during the 1980s, as banks and other financial organizations built huge trading floors on the same architectural principles as casinos. An entire floor of a building would be filled with rows of long tables jammed with computer screens. A single row of offices and conference rooms surrounded the floor and blocked all the windows. While head traders were assigned offices, no trader would be caught dead spending time in an office. All the action was on the desk, moving hundreds of millions of dollars around with keystrokes, hand signals, and brief telephone calls.

How to Succeed in Trading

At the same time, the markets were getting far more complex. Easy opportunities were being snapped up, so it took more precision and calculation to make money. Old-fashioned traders could "read a tape"—make deductions based on the trading at slightly higher and lower prices to guess the next move, and use a few tricks about psychology and economics. Those skills declined in importance compared to advanced mathematics and detailed information. My friends were PhD *quants* (a Wall Street term for mathematically sophisticated financial workers) with the skills to excel in these markets, if they could master basic trading skills. The old-fashioned traders preferred to keep the quants at a distance, providing support to traders rather than doing trading themselves. A good quant might make a $125,000 salary with a $300,000 bonus, which is nice money, but a junior trader could make a million or more, and a successful quant trader much more than that. To climb to that level of income required getting past the senior traders. Not only did they have self-interest in keeping quants off the desk, they tended to prefer shrewd, macho risk takers like themselves over older, married, nerdy PhDs. There were a few exceptions—traditional traders who respected precision and mathematics—and they built some of the most profitable trading desks in history.

Once you got a quant job at a good trading house and watched the action for a few months to figure things out, you had to take another step to get in with the traders. One way was to pal around with them on after-work and weekend binges. This was expensive, and many quants couldn't get comfortable with the drinking, drugs, prostitutes, high-stakes gambling, and general wildness. Traders had lots of opportunities to stick the tagalong little brother with the check or embarrassing aftermaths.

Another problem is that traders only have to work during market trading times, a few hours per day. During that period they can't leave their screens, but the rest of the time they have nothing pressing to do. Many of them work hard in the off-hours on new strategies, but they can still indulge in frequent binging without impairing their job performance. Quants didn't enjoy that luxury. They supported the traders when the market was open, sorted things out after the market closed, then worked on their long-term development tasks. It's a lot easier to trade with a hangover than to debug a complex computer program.

A safer route was to gamble in the office. Traders had a number of games to exploit the wannabes. The most popular was Liar's Poker, made famous by Michael Lewis in his wonderful book of the same name (Penguin, 1990). It is not a poker game in any sense, and as played on Wall Street at that time, it wasn't even much of a game. Liar's Poker was simply ritual hazing with a hefty price tag for those lowest on the totem pole.

Liar's Rules

The game was played with $20 bills, usually for stakes of $100 per person. After blindly drawing bills, the players gathered in a circle and the bidding began. A designated person called out an opening bid—say, "four threes." That meant the person was betting that there were at least 4 threes among the serial numbers of all the bills. The next person to the left could either make a higher bid—four of some number larger than three or five or more of any number—or challenge. The game continued until someone challenged. Say the bid at that point was 12 sevens: The bills were examined and if the challenged bid was correct—that is, if there were at least 12 sevens among the bills—the challenger had to pay each player $100. If the challenged bid was not correct—if there were 11 or fewer sevens among the bills—the bidder had to pay everyone $100. After the events of this chapter, the game was civilized by requiring everyone to challenge before a showdown.

Even more so than in poker, the key was position in circle, and that made it simple to rig the game. Traders bid in hierarchical order: The head of the desk, or biggest moneymaker, always went first. He was followed by the lesser traders, then the junior traders, then the assistant traders or quants and other wannabes. So the top traders couldn't lose. They made lowball bids that no one could challenge, and in any case, traders wouldn't challenge each other. The junior traders did their duty by making the bid high enough that the round would never come back to the seniors, so some assistant or quant would take the loss. If by some miscalculation it did come back to the senior trader, no one would be foolish enough to challenge his bid, no matter how high it was. Some more junior person would fall on his sword instead. If you ever hear someone claim he was a great Liar's Poker player on Wall Street in the 1980s, I'll bet he was on the house side of a rigged game.

The sadistic thing about Liar's Poker is that the top traders could well afford losses, but assistant traders could not. The quants were paid much better than assistants, but even they had trouble when traders would cheerfully call out, "Another hand for a thousand?" Even $10,000 games were not uncommon, although they would be planned for weeks ahead of time and attract a crowd. (Michael Lewis describes a $10 million game that was offered but not accepted; I never saw anything higher than $10,000 myself; but that's $10,000 per player, all lost by one person.)

Since Liar's Poker was a ritual, there was strict protocol for passing this test. You had to do your time in the low end of the circle, paying frequent losses without complaint, and work your way up. You advanced by challenging a lot, which gave you status over the guy ahead of you on the ladder and protected the big traders from losses. As you moved further toward the good end, your financial losses went down, but you had the important task of ensuring that losses stayed at the shallow end of the pool. You stopped challenging and started making aggressive bids that might be challenged. If you were aggressive about protecting your betters, taking losses when necessary, you could move up further. Eventually, if you could get to the best spot held by a nontrader in Liar's Poker, you would be the heir apparent for the next slot that opened up on the trading desk. This game would have made perfect sense to chimps deciding who was alpha male, but it was no way to pick traders.

The most common version of Liar's Poker began by sending an assistant trader down to the cash machine to get twenty-dollar bills. Although the most common stake was $100 per person, twenties were used to play the game because you could get them easily from a machine, with mixed serial numbers. Asking a teller for hundreds often resulted in new bills with ordered serial numbers; it also presented more opportunities for manipulation. Also, the serial numbers for bills higher than $20 have exploitable patterns. The assistant was instructed to get many more bills than would be used for the game—say, 30 for an eight-person game— to lessen the advantage of someone bribing him to record all the serial numbers.

The assistant put the bills in a large envelope; some shops had a ritual hat or pot. Each player drew one bill without looking at it. Bills have eight digits in the serial number, and each digit is equally likely because twenties and smaller bills are printed in full runs of 100 million (then the letters are changed for the next run). With 10 players, the average number of each digit is 8. About half the time (47 percent, to be precise), there will be more than 12 of some digit.

Cooperative Liar's

The interesting strategic point about this game is that you actually cooperate with the players on either side of you. Say there are 10 people in the game. If you challenge and are successful, you make $100. If you challenge and are wrong, you lose $900. So you need to be 90 percent sure you are correct to expect to make money from a challenge.

The same thing is true in reverse with respect to being challenged. If you make a bid that has more than a 10 percent chance of not being correct, you expect to lose money if challenged. So the bidder is trying to make a bid that is 90 percent sure, and the challenger should challenge only if he is 90 percent sure the other way.

What gets hard is when the person to your right makes a bid that has, say, a 50 percent chance of being correct. Any higher bid you make will have less than a 50 percent chance. You don't want to challenge; you're paying off at nine to one on an even shot. Since you make $100 when you're right and lose $900 when you're wrong, your expected value is negative $400 to challenge. But bidding and getting challenged is even worse. Say you think there is only a 40 percent chance that your raised bid is makeable. That makes your expected value negative $500 if you are challenged.

However, if you make the bid and are not challenged, you have a virtually sure $100. It's almost impossible for the bid to go around the circle back to you without being at an absurdly unlikely level—an easy challenge. If you think there are five chances in six your bid will be challenged, it's a break-even decision for you to challenge or bid yourself. Challenging means losing an expected $400. Bidding means losing an expected $500 five times out of six and making an expected $100 one time out of six, for an expected loss of $400. So you look the person to your left in the eye and try to figure out the odds that he will challenge you. What all three of you—the person to your right, you, and the person to your left—really want is to have the bid pass around to the rest of the circle, so you will all be winners. Sticking it to your neighbor by making a high bid that gives him a difficult choice just increases the danger for both of you.

You'll notice that none of this calculation takes into account the serial number on your bill. That can help a little bit. If you have two or three of the digit in question, you're more likely to bid; if you have zero, you're more likely to challenge. But this matters only when the decision is close anyway.

Liar's Poker was also used to defend prejudice. While WASPs dominated top banking jobs, traders were often ethnic Catholics and Jews, and Asians were starting to make inroads. But there were almost no women traders or American-born blacks or foreign-born Asians. Recent immigrants from Central Europe and South Asia were filling U.S. graduate schools in the hard sciences and graduating to quant jobs on trading floors, but they were strongly discouraged from trading.

It wasn't enough that these people had jumped over innumerable government and private hurdles just to have a chance at a decent life. They were some of the toughest and smartest people on earth, and I was angry that they were being played for suckers in this stupid game.

Destroy the Game

I set out to bust Liar's Poker. Not to beat it by winning a lot of money, but to destroy it as an institution. It offended my egalitarian poker principles, and it was being used to repress my friends. Killing it would not only remove an obstacle to advancement for quants, it would prove to traders that mathematicians could beat them at their own game. I put together a computer bulletin board group composed of quants who wanted to be traders—who wrote down all the bids and results of games on their floors—and blackjack and other gamblers I knew from old card-counting and other casino-scheme days.

I suppose I should add a disclaimer at this point. I am known as an anti–Liar's Poker activist. Many people claim that the games were fair and good fun. I have been accused of being puritanically opposed to gambling on the trading floor—also of organizing a cheating ring for Liar's Poker games. Another version credits me with a diabolically clever algorithm for beating the game. All false: I like gambling, the system was not cheating, and it was simple. But you're getting only my side of the story here. It's my book; let those guys write their own books if they like.

The traders had stacked the deck, but cheaters are always the easiest people to beat. Our side started with a few advantages. First, the data we were getting showed that the traders didn't know how to play. Their bids were too low and predictable. They fixed on one digit early and almost never changed it. The first guy would look at his number and bid, say, six plus the number of his most common digit. If he had 2 sevens, for example, and didn't have 3 of anything, he might bid 8 sevens. This is an entirely pointless bid. Without looking at his bill, there is a 55 percent chance of at least 8 sevens being out there. Given his 2 sevens, the chance rises to 74 percent. If he's completely bluffing and has no sevens, there's still a 43 percent chance that there are at least 8 sevens among the remaining bills. Given that the next player needs 90 percent certainty to challenge, you might as well bid 1 zero and not give away any information at all.

The next guy would use a similar rule. If he had 3 or more of anything, or 2 of a digit higher than seven, he would bid 6 plus that, otherwise he would bid 9 sevens. Pretty soon, it would go around the circle, keeping the digit the same, raising by 1 every time. Given our data on people's strategies, it was pretty easy to figure out when to challenge. Basically, if only 1 digit had been named, it probably had been overbid by the time it got to 12. However, if someone had come in with a new digit at a reasonably high level, it could often be a good bet, even at 14 or more.

The secret, we found, is that there are two kinds of games. In one, a digit gets picked up early, often because it is a high digit and none of the first few players have more than 2 of anything on their bills. In that case, the chance is less than 3 percent of getting 14 or more of the digit. So traders got used to thinking that 14 was almost impossible. But in other games, someone had 3 or 4 of a digit early and would change digits at a 10 or 11 bid. There is better than a 25 percent chance that there are more than 14 of some digit. Another underappreciated fact is that there is an 18 percent chance that the other 9 bills have 10 or more of a randomly picked digit. So if you have 3 or 4 of something in your hand, you can jump in with a new digit at the 13 or 14 level, without giving the next player a positive expectation of challenging you.

The system we came up with involved no cheating. You took the same action whether you were next to another system player or one of the traders. But it was quite different from the way people had been playing. The first system player would often challenge, at much lower levels than people were accustomed to. If he didn't challenge, the other system players would throw out bids in different digits, which kept the level from getting too high and usually meant that the bid came back around to the head trader. No one had seen the game played this way before, and no one knew how to react.

Another advantage we had was preparation and training. I wrote a computer simulator to let people practice thousands of hands. Even avid Liar's Poker players didn't have this kind of experience. The computer tracked actions and gave advice. This is commonplace in poker programs today, but it was a secret weapon in the early 1980s. We also arranged some in-person practice sessions, without money. I encouraged people to play fast—this was even more disconcerting than the unusual bids. The last trader would say "eleven threes" and five system players would put it back to the head trader at 13 eights in five seconds. Not only did this make it hard to figure out what people had, it created the impression that the system players knew exactly what they were doing. No one had the nerve to challenge such rapid-fire confidence, and the head trader certainly couldn't lose to a quant.

This led to our last advantage. There were cracks in the establishment. The second trader wanted to beat his boss, and the third trader wanted to beat the second. As long as it was traders against quants, traders cooperated. But when it became clear that some trader would take the fall, they reverted to wild type. They could have adopted similar tactics to the quants, and it would have been a fair game, but they were too competitive among themselves. They weren't trying to maximize expected value; they were trying to beat and not get beaten.

I went along to watch the first time we tried the system. About two in the afternoon, a trader called for a Liar's Poker game. Six traders said they would be in, and all the quants came over. Some of them were invited into games but had been reluctant in the past, knowing it was rigged against them. When they all volunteered, the traders let them in, but, of course, made them sit together to the right of the head trader. The six traders got the bid to 11 twos, and the five quants machine-gunned it to 13 nines in no more time than it takes to shout out the bids. There was a minute of stunned silence, then the head trader challenged. Fifteen nines showed up in the bills. He accused the quants of cheating and refused to pay.

I had expected this. In the next stage, the quants laughed and started playing among themselves. They played just as quickly and with what seemed, to the traditional players, like reckless abandon. It was clear they had a system and knew better than the traders which bids were safe and which should be challenged. The traders had never seen the game played with lots of different final totals—traditional games tended to get up to 12 or maybe 13, seldom more or less. Moreover, in the quants' game the actual count was usually near the total, which often wasn't true in traditional games. It was clear to everyone that the quants had taken the game to a new level, and the traders had welshed. That particular floor stopped playing Liar's Poker. The traders didn't want to lose to the quants, but if they played without inviting them, they'd look scared.

If you think this was a pivotal event, you don't know trading floors. Revolts like this are common, part of moving up the ladder. You have to take a lot of abuse, but you also have to pick your time to stand up for yourself. If you pick right, you move up a rung. If not, you get slapped down. It's a long game, and the quants took a point, but it was only one point.

Other floors tried alternating the quants with traders, which would have destroyed a cheating system, but made good, honest play even stronger. The traders had given up their positional advantage, and spared the quants the difficulty of having a good player to the right or left. Eventually, attitudes toward the game changed. It had been considered a pure test of trading skill, but now it was clearly a geek game. Liar's Poker disappeared from trading floors. I don't know how much the quant victory had to do with that—games go in and out of fashion, anyway, and trading floors calmed down quite a bit in the 1990s. But an impressive proportion of our Beat Liar's Poker crowd went on to successful trading careers.

I'm proud of the group that did this. We were part of a movement that tamed the wild excesses of the 1980s without getting in the way of the valuable creative chaos. We proved you could have mathematical skills and the nerve to use them. We also demonstrated that in finance, poker, and Liar's Poker, you can always find a new way to look at an old game.

The message board stayed alive and tackled several other hazing/ gambling games that came along. I had only a peripheral involvement at that point. The biggest one was a football betting scheme in which you paid $1,000 and picked one team to win every week, with no spread. One loss and you were out. The twist was that you could use a team only once. It was easy to win the first few weeks by picking the biggest mismatches, but by then you had no good teams left and had to pick even games. It was played winner-take-all, and the pot got close to $750,000 the peak year.

This was a happier story. Most people played it casually at the beginning, like the NCAA or Wimbledon pools that pop up in every office. But by the fourth or fifth week, there might be only one guy on your floor who was still in the hunt. The whole office would get behind him, and the quants would be expected to come up with some football handicapping programs and strategic simulators. This was a game that required precision analysis, but also football knowledge and trading skill. Modern trading is a team effort and works best when everyone respects the essential talents of everyone else.

CHAPTER 9

Who Got Game

*How Real Game Theory
Can Make You Win*

Located 14 miles northeast of Los Angeles, Santa Anita is one of the great tracks of American horse racing. It opened in the midst of the Great Depression, and grabbed attention by offering the first $100,000 purse ever in its Big 'Cap race. Seabiscuit won the 1940 Big 'Cap in his last race. Legendary jockeys Johnny Longden and Bill Shoemaker also chose to end their careers here. Santa Anita hosted the equestrian events in the 1984 Olympics.

On a pleasant southern California weekend between Christmas and mid-April, you can enjoy the pageantry of racing with 40,000 or so other fans. The track also hosts live races in October. But on a Wednesday afternoon in the summer, you will find instead 1,000 hard-core bettors. LA's movers and shakers are far away, plotting next weekend's gross wars or doing lunch with venture capitalists. There aren't even any horses here. The races are simulcast from other tracks.

THIS GUY SAYS THE HORSE NEEDS RACE

People show up mainly to bet: The handle per person on these afternoons is significantly higher than when the rich folk come to see and be seen. Some of the patrons look like they're betting the rent money; others appear too disheveled to have a place to live at all. One guy is dressed no better than the rest, but appears to have bathed more recently than the median.

If you haven't been to a racetrack in the last quarter century, they still have the betting windows you see in movies, but most betting is done by machine. You can use either cash, winning tickets from previous bets, or voucher cards. Our clean bettor is putting his voucher card into the machine repeatedly, in-bet-out, in-bet-out. That's unusual enough that Bertie, the guy behind him in line, peeks over his shoulder. Mr. Clean is putting $100 bets on horse number 9 in the next race. The machines don't allow bets of more than $100 at a time, so he has to do it 10 times to bet $1,000.

Bertie owns and runs a flower shop, but likes to take the occasional weekday afternoon at the track. He's a careful bettor, studying the racing form and placing a few well-chosen $20 bets. He's curious enough to look up horse number 9. The horse is named Epitaph, and he finished last by 36 lengths in his last race. He's predicted to go off at 50 to 1. Suddenly Mr. Clean appears to be something of a high roller.

Bertie is curious enough to seek him out in front of the simulcast screen. "Big race for you, huh?" he ventures. "Could make fifty grand." Mr. Clean looks bemused, then remembers Bertie from the machine. "Yeah," he answers without interest.

The starter's gun goes off, and who should jump into the lead but Epitaph? Bertie literally leaps with excitement, but much to his surprise, Mr. Clean isn't even looking at the race. "He's ahead!" Bertie screams, and high roller looks up and comes out with a forced-sounding, "Yay! Go for it." Epitaph keeps his lead into the turn, then hits a wall. He's got "cheap speed." He matches his last-by-36-length expectation. Bertie is devastated, and high roller finally seems to notice. "Darn," he swears mildly, "I thought I had it there for a minute." But even someone without Bertie's long racetrack experience would know that isn't how you act when $50,000 is dangled in front of you, only to be snatched away. Something's wrong here.

I've always been fascinated by horse race betting myself—the numbers, that is, not the animals or humans involved in the actual sport.

The tantalizing thing is how easy it is to find ways to erase the track percentage and get a fair bet, yet how hard it is to find a profitable system. Before I got out of grade school, I had figured out that the second favorite is the best bet—the public overvalues favorites and long shots. The effect is strong enough in some odds ranges that you can get a mathematically fair bet, overcoming the track percentage. Another rich area for exploitation is exactas and trifectas (picking the first two, or first three, horses in order). These tend to get priced as if the results were more independent than they actually are. This discrepancy is harder to exploit than the second-favorite rule, because you have to buy dozens or hundreds of tickets for it to make much difference. The odds are not static; they're changing all the time you're trying to get your position on. This will be important later.

None of these schemes make up for the smart money that quickly wipes out any actual advantage to the bettor—at least any bettor without knowledge of horses or inside information. While there's an incentive for smart money to exploit, and hence eliminate, any positive expected value, there's no incentive to equalize the negative expectations of other bets. When I was a kid, Washington state tracks took a 15 percent cut. If you bet at random, you gave up something like an edge roughly equally distributed between 0 percent and 30 percent. It took only a little work to get near 0 percent, but I never found a way of getting positive expectation. I haven't checked things recently, but I suspect Internet betting has made things even more efficient than that.

I still like racetracks, but only the beautiful ones like Saratoga, Aqueduct, and Santa Anita, on those weekend days at the heights of their respective seasons. The great thrill of racing is that moment just before the finish of a race, when every eye, brain, and heart of the crowd is focused on one thing, and everyone is a winner for an instant. This is followed by a mass exhalation, and people remember whether they won or lost, and what they have to do tomorrow, and what their name is. But that psychic melding is real, a transitory high that reminds you what being human means, as opposed to being rich or poor, smart or stupid, cool or geek, religious or atheist. You can get the same thing with an all-night dance around a large fire with a primal drumbeat, but that's more trouble to locate.

ROCKET SCIENTIST

Mr. Clean is an economics professor at the California Institute of Technology and one of the leading researchers in experimental game theory. For the first 20 years of its existence, game theory was a branch of mathematics; no experimentation was required. In the late 1960s, a few scattered academics started studying its predictions. The general conclusion is that none of them were true; people did not behave the way game theory suggested they should. The work really took off after the 1987 stock market crash, when orthodox theories of how people evaluate gambles seemed helpless to explain reality. The 1970s disproved conventional macroeconomics and left that field in disarray. The 1980s did the same thing for microeconomics. Daniel Kahneman and Vernon Smith later shared a Nobel Prize for what is now called "behavioral finance."

Colin Camerer, a.k.a. Mr. Clean, is a buddy of mine from graduate school. He was quirky back then, so it's no surprise that he studies economics at the racetrack today. He graduated from Johns Hopkins at 19 and had his PhD by age 23. He started a record label, Fever Records, as an economics experiment. Unless you were part of the punk scene in Chicago at the time, or are a music historian, you probably haven't heard of the Bonemen of Baruma, Big Black, or the Dead Milkmen, but you can take my word that they were exciting and important local bands of the period.

Colin is a horse racing fan who once tried to talk the Cal Tech endowment into taking advantage of an arbitrage (riskless profit opportunity) he had discovered on some Texas tracks (the fund passed on the idea). I asked him whether he was tempted to throw up his professorship and turn his considerable intellect to beating the horse races. His "yes" came so fast that I can imagine one too many students whining about an exam score or idiotic administrator proposing some new indignity depriving Cal Tech of one of its stars. He'd already told me that he fled Chicago to escape "cold winters and MBAs," so he's got a trigger faster than most of the horses he bets.

Colin waxes enthusiastically, "I'd become a tremendous expert in one small niche. I'd follow the bad horses at small tracks and state fairs, with small purses. I'd bet the maiden races where average bettors have no information." To find real value, he continued, sounding like the economics professor he is, "You have to figure out what real fans overvalue. When fans are disappointed, they yell at the jockey, not the trainer. That says to me they overvalue the jockey, so I bet based on trainer. The jockey is the movie star, the face the public sees. But a good movie is more often determined by the director."

One day at the track, Colin accidentally stuck a bet ticket into a machine before the race had been run. After the race is run, you insert your winning tickets to get credit for future bets or cash. The machine flashed a message: "Do you want to cancel?" Colin, like most horse bettors in an informal survey I conducted, did not know you could cancel bets. The mistake started some inventive wheels turning in his head.

He had been studying "information mirages," a conjectural game theory explanation for stock market bubbles and consumer taste changes. Suppose one day, by chance, more than the usual number of people decide to buy a certain stock. The price goes up a little as a result, and, of course, the volume goes up as well. Investors look for this kind of activity as a signal that a stock is about to make a move, so the next day a few more people buy. This trend could become self-reinforcing: the more people who buy, the more people who figure there must be some information out there and buy as well. The same thing could happen if you happened to see two guys on the same day looking stylish and wearing straw hats. You might decide that straw hats are in fashion, and the next time you see one in a shop window, you think about how good those two guys looked. So you buy the hat, and that causes someone else to buy one, and before you know it, straw hats are the rage.

Game theory can explain this phenomenon rationally, but it's hard to test these explanations with stock prices or fashion trends. For example, it's true that stock prices exhibit short-term trends with longer-term reversals, exactly what the information mirage theory would predict. But there are lots of other explanations for those effects, and there is a lot of noise in the data. Perhaps most important, you never really know whether there was true information in the price movement or just a mirage.

Colin wanted to see whether he could induce this behavior in a laboratory, where he could control all the variables. He got some volunteers to play a game. I've simplified it a bit, but you still have to pay careful attention to the rules. Each volunteer was given a "security," a distinctive piece of paper. Everyone was told that a coin had already been flipped, and in 10 minutes, based on that flip, either all of the securities would be redeemed for $20 or all securities would be worthless. Each person was also given an information card. In 50 percent of the rounds, all the cards were blank. In 25 percent of the rounds, half the cards were blank and the other half had $20 written on them. In the final 25 percent of the rounds, half the cards were blank and the other half had $0 written on them. In the last two cases, the cards were always truthful—that is, they always told the correct redemption amount of the security. The rules were explained to all participants, and several practice rounds were held.

When there was real information in the market, as you would expect, the securities moved pretty quickly to their redemption price. If half the cards said $20, for example, there would be a few tentative transactions around $10, but there were always more buyers than sellers, so the price inched up. Once it got to a certain point, everyone figured out that the securities were worth $20. There might be a few transactions at $18 or $19 by people who didn't want to take a chance. When half the people knew the securities were worthless, the price headed down to zero in the same manner.

When there was no information, the trading seldom got beyond the few $9, $10, or $11 trades. Because the price moved so quickly when there was information, people also quickly figured out when there was no information.

But once in a while, an information mirage would occur. There would be a few too many transactions at $11, and someone with a blank card would bid $12. Someone else would shout out $13, not wanting to miss the opportunity, and the security would go to $20 for no good reason. The same thing happened in the down direction as well.

Controlled experiments are nice, but there is always the question of whether undergraduates playing a game for $20 act the same way as professional stock investors managing millions of dollars or fashion-conscious consumers deciding what to buy. You would really have faith in the model if it could be demonstrated in both the laboratory and the real world, by people who didn't know they were in an experiment, playing for stakes that really mattered to them. Horse race bet cancellation was just the ticket for that second step, without it costing him $1,000 per test.

Betting at the horse track is done on the pari-mutuel system. All the bets of a certain type—win bets in this case—for a specific race are put into a pool. The track takes its percentage (15 percent for win/place/show bets in California), and the remainder is split among the bettors who picked the winning horse. Suppose, for example, that $4,000 is bet to win on Paul Revere, $8,000 to win on Valentine, $12,000 to win on Epitaph, and $16,000 to win on Equipoise. The total pool is $40,000; the track takes $6,000, leaving $34,000 to pay off the winners. If Paul Revere wins, the payout is $34,000/$4,000 = $8.50 per each $1.00 bet. This is stated as 7.5:1 payout, since you get your $1 back plus $7.50 profit. If Valentine wins, the payout for those tickets is 3.25:1, Epitaph pays 1.84:1, and Equipoise pays 1.13:1.

When placing a pari-mutuel bet, you do not know exactly what payout odds you will receive if you win. You can look at estimates from experts made before the race. You can see the bets as they come in. Every minute, the bets to date are shown on the tote board. But you don't know actual payouts until the race is run.

Colin picked races with small expected handles (total betting pools) and two long shots (horses unlikely to win) that seemed closely matched in terms of prior record and projected odds. If he put $1,000 on one of them, the odds on that horse would drop suddenly. The combination of the small handle and the long shot, plus the early bet before most of the money is down, would create an observable effect. One of three things could happen:

1. Everyone could ignore the bet and place the same wagers they would anyway. In that case, the odds on the horse Colin bet on would drop and stay shorter than the odds on the matched horse, solely due to his bet.
2. Smart bettors could exactly offset Colin's bet, by refraining from betting on his horse and increasing bets on other horses. In this case, the odds would correct to the proper level, the same level as the matched horse.
3. Bettors could see that money was coming in unexpectedly on Colin's horse and decide someone must know something. This would be an induced information mirage. More money would follow Colin's, and the odds on the horse would drop even more than the $1,000 could explain.

Colin canceled the bet immediately before post time, so the effect would not be shown until after it was too late to change bets.

In the end, Bertie, the betting machine peeker, held the answer to the study. Seeing an apparently sane bettor plunking down $1,000 on a long shot did not induce Bertie to take even a $2 flyer on the same horse. He gave generously of his emotion to Colin and rooted for him strongly, but he didn't risk a nickel on the information mirage. All the other race fans agreed. Although there was some noise in the data, it was pretty clear that the other bettors ignored Colin's attempt at market manipulation (that's what this would be in the stock market, and the Securities and Exchange Commission would come after you for it). The odds were pretty much what they would have been irrespective of Colin's betting.

CHAIRMAN OF THE BOARD

I was worried about putting this story in the book because I wasn't sure about the legality of what Colin did. He had checked it with Cal

Tech lawyers, who concluded that if Colin didn't make a profit from the scheme, it couldn't be fraud (fraud, loosely defined, is lying for profit). That led to some tense moments when Colin was in line behind slow bettors as post time approached. You can't cancel after the race starts. Losing $1,000 would have been a small disaster, but winning $50,000 might have been worse. Someone tracking his betting patterns might argue that the previous bet/cancel was an attempt to manipulate the odds and extract this unfair $50,000 payout. In any case, it would have to be reported to the lawyers with all the unpleasantness that entails.

I decided to contact the California Horse Racing Board to get a quote like "that guy's a crook, tampering with honest bettors," or "if anyone tries this we'll have them in jail before the horses cross the finish line." Then I couldn't be accused of contributing to anyone's delinquency.

John Harris is the chairman of the California Horse Racing Board. For the last 40 years he has been one of the most successful horse owners and breeders in the state. I thought I would have to explain the scheme very carefully, but he came right up with, "Another scheme would be to overbet on everyone but a favorite to see if wagerers back off on an obvious choice due to its not getting much public support." Um, what about the "it's terrible" quote?

John did qualify his responses as first observations without having seen the study or thought about the details. But he didn't think it would work because "most betting comes in late and early attempts to manipulate odds may not have much impact unless one is dealing with relatively small pools to start with." He thought there might have been a better chance in the past. "With so much satellite wagering going on, many players don't really focus on a given race until five minutes to post. In the old days there were more people that tracked every click of the odds, but they are a vanishing breed."

But did Colin break the rules? "I like studies of human behavior such as this one was, but for racing there are safeguards in place to prevent excessive manipulation of odds due to schemes such as those described." John went on to observe that there are standard operating procedures in place at the tracks to prevent manipulations. He thought that large bet cancellations were not guaranteed.

Mike Marten, who runs public relations for the board, had some details for me. Sounding lawyerlike, he wrote, "My preliminary response is that there is no specific prohibition in the Horse Racing Law or in California Horse Racing Board regulations that prohibits this type of activity. However, the individual racing associations, as private property owners, have the right to exclude patrons who engage in improper behavior." He knew of cases in which tracks had "warned certain bettors against this practice." But then the mask cracked, as he offered a tip to "pull it off" (go to the window clerk, don't use the machine).

This is just a guess, of course, but I doubt I would have had such helpful and honest responses in other states, like New York and Illinois, that prohibit anyone with a financial interest in racing from the oversight functions. I've never understood why people volunteer to monitor things they aren't willing to risk their money on. That goes for people who are elected to represent shareholders on corporate boards but own no stock in the company (Wendy Gramm, a director of Enron, bizarrely claimed it would have been a conflict of interest for her to have held stock in the company—you see how well that kind of oversight works) as well as public oversight groups. I think you get more knowledge and attention from someone who does invest, and that person has more moral authority to make tough decisions as a consequence of having skin in the game. Of course, it can create conflicts of interest, but honest people can act properly even in the face of conflicts, while dishonest people won't act properly in any case. At least with an open conflict, you know the situation; the reputation of someone who abuses a position will suffer. With a hidden conflict, you don't even have that consolation.

I think Colin might have had a better chance with creating an information mirage at the track on a February weekend. That's when the well-dressed folks are there, and what is dressing well except trying to create an information mirage? No one bothers to try that at a weekday racetrack. It's eager go-getters who fall for mirages—survivors among the more depressing weekday crowd lost their illusions long ago. The fact that Colin couldn't affect the odds in this milieu doesn't mean it can't happen in the stock market, or among venture capitalists, or in academics and politics.

LEARN BY EXPERIMENT WHAT ARGUMENT TAUGHT

Experimental game theory commonly gives similarly inconclusive results. Generally, investigators find that people do not act the way game theory says they should. Instead, they use more robust algorithms that are more difficult to manipulate. But it's pretty hard to make money exploiting people's deviations from mathematically optimal strategies. There are exceptions on both sides. There are times when knowing the game theory can make you a winner and times when you can win only by ignoring the game-theoretic answer and studying how people actually play.

The Renaissance philosopher of science Francis Bacon told a fable about a conference of philosophers, at which they argued for weeks about how many teeth a horse had. A young stable boy, tiring of the interminable debate, suggested looking in a horse's mouth and counting. The enraged philosophers beat him for his stupidity. Whenever anyone gives you poker advice based on game theory, ask whether they've counted the teeth. The medieval philosopher of science Roger Bacon (no relation) acknowledged that theory was the only conclusive guide to truth, but it could not remove doubt in people's minds:

> For if any man who never saw fire, proved by satisfactory arguments that fire burns, his hearer's mind would never be satisfied, nor would he avoid the fire, until he put his hand in it that he might learn by experiment what argument taught.

Mathematical theory, tested in practice and constantly retested, is a valuable aid to play. Mathematics alone will blind you and let others rob you.

The first recorded poker experiment was done a century and a quarter ago at a Cincinnati poker club. Instead of rotating the blind around the table, a selected member would post the blind all night. The rules were different then; you could not call the blind. The minimum bet was twice the blind—in other words, a raise of the blind amount. That makes the blind less of a disadvantage. While you have to act first, and act blind, you get to act last on the raise. Under today's rule without a required following raise, it's clear that posting the blind is a disadvantage, a negative expectation of about half the posted amount. But in the nineteenth century there was a vociferous debate about whether posting the blind was an advantage or a disadvantage. Experts were about equally arrayed on either side. The Cincinnati experiment was conclusive: The player posting the blind was almost always a winner for the night and, more often than not, the big winner. Posting that kind of blind is a big advantage. Sadly, people continued to debate the issue, not by doing other experiments or criticizing the one known experiment—they just ignored the evidence and insisted that mathematics or other theory proved them right.

The next important step in empirical poker research was taken by Ethel Riddle, a young PhD student in psychology at Columbia University in 1921. Her full study is not easy to find. The psychology department librarian at Columbia managed to dig out for me a badly typewritten, extremely brittle copy with handwritten addenda. All the paper edges had crumbled, and the pages were hard to separate. The binding had long since ceased to hold the pages together. I love documents like this, with their smell of ancient, forgotten wisdom. Someone should put this one in a museum before it is lost forever.

Once you find it, it's not easy to read. Ethel was a behaviorist, and she was addicted to tedious statistical overanalysis. Or maybe it wasn't her fault; maybe that's what it took to get a degree in those days. David Spanier, author of *Total Poker* and other poker works, had the same copy I did, I was delighted to discover. He figured out from it that Ethel fell in love with one of her subjects, but I couldn't trace the source of that deduction. He has either a keener eye or a better imagination than I do (or maybe he stole something from the document). Frank Wallace, who wrote *A Guaranteed Income for Life by Using the Advanced Concepts of Poker,* also came across the study, but he had only a summary copy from the Library of Congress.

Ethel invited experienced poker players into her basement laboratory and had them play while hooked up to polygraphs, machines that measured heart rate, respiration, hand sweat, and other indicators of emotion—the same type used as lie detectors. She paid them $2.00 per hour, but they played with their own money for higher stakes. She recorded every hand and bet, correlated with the players' physical reactions and subjective notes.

What she found would have turned game theory on its head, except that game theory wouldn't be invented for another quarter century. Sadly, the early game theory researchers, who used poker as an important model, didn't bother to see whether what they wrote was true. But even in Ethel's day, theorists for 50 years had been analyzing poker like a card game, hand by hand. Ethel's data clearly showed that money flows were influenced much more by whole-table, session-long interactions than by individual bets or hands. Pre-Ethel, 50 years of calculating probabilities and figuring strategies, and no one had noticed that this didn't matter as much as the table interactions; post-Ethel, we've had 85 more years of the same.

Of course, it's possible that her results don't generalize. Maybe the Columbia fraternity guys she recruited were not typical poker players. They were older than most undergraduates today—mid-20s with 6 to 10 years of serious poker experience—but they weren't Vegas pros (gambling would not be legalized in Nevada for another decade). They might have played differently knowing their actions were being recorded and the game would appear in a dissertation. But when you get good, carefully gathered evidence that your theories are wrong, you should question the theory or gather more data, not invent reasons why the data might be wrong.

THOSE WHO HAVE KNOWLEDGE DON'T PREDICT— THOSE WHO PREDICT DON'T HAVE KNOWLEDGE

One interesting result is that players had almost no ability to predict the strength of other players' hands before they are revealed at showdown. The game in Ethel's basement was Five-Card Draw, the form of poker that gives the least information on that subject. All you can do is guess from the betting and the number of cards drawn. Still, it's surprising to learn that the weakest third of players actually guessed worse than random, and even the best players did not guess significantly better. In other words, if immediately before showdown you ask the average player what he thinks another player's hand is, the answer is only slightly more reliable than guessing based on the long-term frequencies. In this game, anyway, it didn't pay to search for tells or engage in elaborate analyses of the other players' strategies. About the best you could do was note how often each player bet and drew on various hands.

I was mildly surprised at this result, since my experience at the poker table is that average players have some ability to put other players on hands. I've never believed, as some poker books seem to suggest, that anyone can narrow it down to two or three choices before the first round of betting ends, but I do spend mental effort trying to guess what the other hands are likely to be, and I do think it helps. On the other hand, I know from finance that professional stock analysts and managers charged fees for many years, with clear evidence that their picks were worse than random. I'm not debating efficient markets here—the question of whether anyone can pick stocks better than randomly. Regardless of that issue, there are a lot of people treated as experts with consistent 20-year track records that the stocks they bought did worse than the ones they passed up, or that the ones they rated "strong buy" did worse than the ones they rated "strong sell." I've also heard traders explain after the fact exactly why they knew a winning trade was going to win, when their trading log shows clearly that they had guessed wrong but got lucky. So I'm professionally disposed to accept that things are a lot more random than people like to admit. Nasim Taleb wrote a great book, *Fooled by Randomness*, on this subject.

I remember one hand of Five-Card Draw, more or less at random, in which another player raised before the draw, then took one card. This represents two pair. I saw a flicker of disappointment when he got his draw, which was odd. There are only 4 out of 47 cards that make two pair into a full house—you don't expect one when you draw. And there was little reason to think a full house would be needed to win the pot. On the other hand, someone drawing to a flush has 9 out of 47 cards to complete; with an open-ended straight, there are 8. Disappointment makes more sense with these hands. When he raised after the draw, I figured the predraw raise was a bluff on a flush or straight draw, and his postdraw raise was a bluff on nothing. With a straight or better, he would be more likely to let someone bet into him, and two pair is too weak to raise after the draw. This still strikes me as a reasonable inference from the observations.

He turned out to have three queens. Looking back, that was a simpler and more likely explanation of his hand, except for that flash of disappointment. When you have a theory and see it confirmed, it's easy (but expensive) to ignore all subsequent evidence. The flicker of disappointment led me to suspect he had missed a flush or a straight, and the raise after the draw seemed to confirm that. But maybe I had imagined or misinterpreted the flicker. Even if it had happened, perhaps he had just remembered an unpleasant meeting the next day, or that he had forgotten his mother's birthday, or regretted having that second crab cake at dinner.

The point of this story? That it's pointless. That this kind of thing happens all the time at the poker table and no one—no good player I know, anyway—gives it a moment's thought. Sometimes an idiot will wail, "I can't believe you had that," but anyone who's played for more than a few hands knows you are often surprised. There are two kinds of poker hands people remember for a long time and tell stories about: unlikely losses and perfect reads. The rest—the likely losses, the wins, and the completely wrong reads—slip from your mind and conversation before the next hand is dealt.

There's a reason for that. A bad read doesn't really hurt you in poker, unless the other players figure out how to induce it. You only pay attention to reads on close calls anyway, when the decision is balanced and you hope the read gives you a slight edge. If it's only random, that doesn't cost anything. In fact, random is good because you might otherwise get predictable. However, a good read is money in the bank.

In this case, I had a pair of aces, which hadn't improved on the draw. But I was getting almost four to one pot odds to call the last bet (all the other players had dropped out; I was last to act). The guy's shown a good hand by two raises, and he bluffed with slightly less than average frequency. But I'd never seen him hold kickers of any sort, nor had I seen him raise with two pair after the draw against multiple other bettors. I didn't believe he would have raised before the draw with four of a kind, and that's so unlikely, anyway, it doesn't figure in much.

My choices were that he was running a semibluff (admittedly, not something I'd expect, but it did seem to be confirmed by the disappointment flicker), started with two pair and made a full house (maybe it wasn't disappointment I saw), or had acted against his usual play. I'm not only weighing the likelihood of him acting these ways, I'm thinking about the card probabilities as well. On balance, I thought I had maybe one chance in three that he was holding nothing. It helped that my aces would win even if he had picked up a pair on a flush or a straight draw. So it seemed like a good bet, but I was not stunned to see it lose.

Traders do the same thing. We'll tell everyone who wants to listen, and everyone who doesn't, about the trades we figured right from the beginning. The other trades slip from memory and conversation, whether they won or lost, not because we're ashamed of them but because they are too routine. If you're interviewing a trader for a job or backing, the danger sign is whether he seems to be making up rationales for past trades. If the explanations are inconsistent or too pat, you worry. Not because he's lying, but because making up reads after the fact is a deadly disease. You make a winning trade by chance, convince yourself that it was smart, then spend the rest of the day (or career, in some cases) trying to duplicate it. You get too much faith in reads and forget about weighing probabilities and sticking to strategy. Traders and poker players remember and boast about good reads in order to maintain faith that reads have any value at all. Talking about bad reads is like talking about all the old friends you didn't run into during the day.

Unlikely losses—"bad beats" of poker literature and lore—are also important because they remind you to keep an open mind. The guy drawing three to a pair might get four of a kind; the guy who never bluffs might have gone all-in on nothing; that unbelievably clumsy attempt to represent pocket queens, bristling with inconsistencies, might, in fact, represent pocket queens. In trading you can have a perfect position with no way to lose . . . *except*. Except an unexpected takeover bid, or an earthquake, or fraud from the last place you would expect it. If you trade long enough, all of these things will happen to you. If you forget that they might happen, they'll blow you up when they do. Sure, they're extreme bad luck, but sooner or later that happens. Hedge fund manager and risk expert Kent Osband wrote *Iceberg Risk* about how to survive unexpected risk in trading. It's a great poker book as well.

You have to remind yourself that it's not enough to calculate; you must also consider what happens if all your calculations are overthrown. It's not modesty that makes traders and poker players recite their losses; it's self-protection. Talking about wins is unnecessary— your mind is already focused on the ways you might make money. If you need help with that part, you will never be a good risk taker.

IF I HAVE TO FALL, MAY IT BE FROM A HIGH PLACE

If the players couldn't make money by guessing about each other's hands, winning and losing must have been determined by strategy— that is, by type of play. The most easily identified type in Ethel's study was what she called *risker*. (Although she was a behaviorist, her terminology sounds more like Freudian archetypes than Skinnerian positivism; of course, psychological camps were not as well-defined in 1921 as they would become later.) When sociologists discovered California poker rooms in the 1960s, they named riskers *action players,* a term you also hear poker players use and that I used in the Gardena chapter. Traders are apt to talk about *gamblers* or *gunslingers*. I'll give Ethel priority on the discovery and use her term. Whatever your chosen arena of risk, early in your career you learn to identify riskers. They are the easiest source of profits, but are also dangerous until you figure out how to handle them. They represent a small minority of players, but their influence outweighs their numbers.

Riskers play the most hands, make the largest raises, and lose the most money. They are often good players, however, evaluated one hand at a time. They may know probabilities and tactics; they are often very good at card games other than poker. If you want to make a table of guys happy, announce as you're sitting down that you're (a) rich and (b) an expert at bridge/gin rummy/backgammon/sports betting/blackjack—that's a classic risker's resume. If you claim expertise in casino games instead, you will appear to be a stupid risker. Risker strategy guarantees long-term failure, even if it works most of the time. Riskers lose more money than even the bad players. Game theorists in poker sometimes degenerate into recommending being a risker because they consider only one hand at a time.

Riskers are riskers all the time. Most players Ethel studied move among two or more types depending on circumstance. Not riskers. In a sense, riskers aren't playing poker; they're gambling. One explanation for why people become riskers is that they cannot adapt their strategies, they cannot read other players or the mood of the table. No one-size-fits-all strategy can win in poker, but being a risker stirs things up enough that a short-term run of luck might overcome your long-term negative expectation. If you place $1,000 on number 7 at roulette, you have the same negative expectation as if you play 100 spins with $10 on red or black. But you have one chance in 38 of making a $35,000 profit. With the 100 smaller, safer bets, if you have that same degree of luck you'll make an average of only $170. If your goal is to gamble rather than simply hand the casino its expected $52.63, riskers' play makes sense.

Ethel's polygraph got inside a risker's head (or as close as gross physiological changes can take us, which is pretty close) for the first time in history. Her amazing discovery? Riskers don't care. They flat-line on their emotional indicators. Win or lose, the game is not exciting to them; they're not focusing. Moving from her observation to my interpretation, the wild betting is the only thing that keeps them from falling asleep. They're not agonizing over what cards you hold or whether they'll fill their straight—their heart is beating to the march of a different drummer, one who's not watching the game. It's easy for them to be smart cardplayers because they aren't distracted by fear or greed or any emotion whatsoever. It will surprise no one that the riskers were the most financially comfortable of the players, the ones to whom the stake meant the least. The biggest bets of the session meant the least, economically and psychologically, to the people who made them.

What else do we know about riskers? Why do they play? Who are they? In a heartbreaking loss to science, no one did a follow-up study on Ethel's subjects. It would be fascinating to have reconvened them every decade for another game, to see how different poker strategies played out in life, and to see how play changed over the years. But from work done much later, in the 1960s and 1970s, we know that riskers are the poker players who are most successful outside the game. They are successful in business, politics, and the military. They have social success as well: the happiest marriages and families, the best reputations. In fact, when most people think of the kind of poker player they want to vote for or work for, they're really thinking of a risker. Riskers are cool because they don't care. They can be shrewd because they're not blinded by emotion. Winning poker players are untrustworthy, by definition. President John F. Kennedy's handling of the Cuban missile crisis is often held up as an example of masterful poker play. It has risker written all over it. Nixon's duplicity, paranoia, and ruthlessness were more characteristic of a winning poker player. But when people say they want a good poker player as president, they are thinking of Kennedy, who played badly (and some of his relatives were among the worst players, and biggest riskers, at Harvard), not Nixon, who played well.

Nixon is often said to have lost the 1960 election against Kennedy because he sweated during the televised debates, while Kennedy was imperturbably cool. Perhaps that was because Nixon really cared—his heart raced and palms sweated as he mentally planned move and countermove—while Kennedy was thinking about his next daiquiri and assignation. Of course, good poker players learn to disguise their reactions, but Nixon can be forgiven for using techniques appropriate to debates in front of large crowds, not realizing that the television cameras of the first ever televised presidential debates would be so revealing. By 1968 and 1972, he had learned to look as cool as Kennedy when the cameras were on (but not to sound cool when he thought he was in private).

Another example from the 1960s is the most successful espionage-based American television show in history, *Mission: Impossible*. In the pilot and first season, the team was led by Dan Briggs, played by the wonderful actor Steven Hill. He was short, badly shaven, and indifferently dressed. His signature fighting move was to strike first with a knee to the crotch. He had no plan—his team went in, created mayhem, grabbed the target microfilm or agent or weapon, and ran away. The show only took off the next season when Briggs was replaced by the cooler and impeccably tailored Jim Phelps (played by the handsome and inoffensive Peter Graves). On the rare occasions when Phelps had to fight, he would deliver a light karate chop to the shoulder that apparently caused his opponent to fall asleep. Phelps had a clockwork plan that worked flawlessly until just before the last commercial break, when there would be a slight hitch, quickly overcome after the commercial by smooth improvisation. Briggs was a poker player, who sweated because he cared; Phelps was a risker, who didn't because he didn't. A slower and less dramatic transition took place in the James Bond movie franchise. Although even the first movie (*Dr. No* in 1962) would not be described by anyone as "gritty," Sean Connery at his most flippant appears to care more about what's going on than subsequent James Bond portrayers at their most anguished. For secret agents, we love riskers.

An intriguing question is whether riskers are still successful in life. The world changed in the 1970s, as discussed elsewhere in this book, and winning poker skills became more valuable. People are more suspicious of the imperturbable risk taker. We still want our presidents to be more transparently honorable than any winning poker player can be, but we tolerate, even expect, his top aides to be sneaky, ruthless calculators.

You may detect a reluctant admiration for riskers, struggling with my aversion to uncompensated risk that lives deep in my poker players', risk managers', financial quants' souls. There's a risker behind the greatest triumphs as well as the greatest disasters. The world would be a safer, more boring place without them. Michael Mauboussin is among the most respected financial strategists in the world and has thought a lot about the relationship of games playing to finance. He told me that the top financial managers are "wired differently from you and me. They suffer less from losses. They're harder to divert from a mission." Does that make them riskers? "They care about losses, as deeply or more deeply than anyone else. But it's in their heads, not their emotions. A great general puts nothing above the welfare of his troops, then sacrifices them ruthlessly in battle." I asked him to name people he knew who fit this description, and he came up with three: Bill Gross (among the best bond investors in the world, who runs funds for PIMCO and plays a mean blackjack hand), Bill Miller (among the best stock investors, and a coemployee of Mauboussin's firm Legg Mason), and George Soros (superstar hedge fund investor, philanthropist, and activist, who works for George Soros). I think this rises above the level of garden-variety risker you're likely to run into at a poker table. I would say these people have melded the best aspects of riskers with the best aspects of poker players, and, yes, there has to be some unusual wiring to do that. I'm a hardwired poker player—it would take brain surgery for me to be able to toss chips in the pot without physiological reaction or to make ruthless decisions even when they're the right thing to do.

IVORY TOWER RISK

Jonathan Schaeffer is a leading researcher of game theory poker. He collaborated on a computer program that is the closest to date at playing optimal game-theoretic poker (although it does not win against either humans or less theoretically sound computer programs). He criticized an article of mine in which I said that one stereotype of a good poker player is having nerve: "To strong players, nerves are not an issue; the correct play is the correct play. . . ." I think that comes from thinking one hand at a time, like a risker or his computer program.

It's true that good players expect lots of ups and downs, although it still hurts when you get a bad beat. What's hard on the nerves isn't waiting to see the river card, but uncertainty about whether you have things figured out. You never know whether you are playing winning

or losing poker at any given time. The cards are too random to measure that by fluctuations in your bankroll. Unlike a partnership or
team competition, you have no one to offer objective advice. In fact,
everyone around you is trying to conceal the truth from you. If you're
a winner, their every thought is how to change that; if you're a loser,
they're all trying to keep it that way. It takes strong nerve to have
faith in yourself, and stronger nerve to know when to change tactics
or walk away from the table. I think Jonathan, like many game theorists, is chasing a cold war dream of a Kennedy or a Phelps who
never loses, who has courage but doesn't need nerve, because he's sure
he's right, and that his side will triumph, and he doesn't care deeply,
anyway. That was never real, and any hope that it someday would be
died in the 1970s.

Jonathan called my statement a "factual error," rather than a difference of opinion. He's a smart guy who does good work and takes
the trouble to correct people he thinks are wrong. I don't mean to
beat up on him. But that phrase strikes me as typical of the dogmatic
blindness game theory can induce. He doesn't need to look at Ethel's
polygraphs or actually talk to the best poker players—his equations
have shown him the truth, and everything else is error. As an expert
in the field, he's entitled to some dogmatism, but there are thousands
of lesser experts out there who are even more sure of themselves,
who've read a couple books on the subject and worked out some simple practice examples.

Another "factual error" was my prediction in the same article that
game theory based on hand-by-hand, two-player analysis would
never result in a program that could do well against a table of good
human players. "By definition," he writes, the game theory program
"cannot lose." The equations say it is so, so it must be true, even
though the equations describe a different situation than actual play. It
is not a question for evidence or experience, any more than you have
to test that triangles have three sides or that $2 + 2 = 4$. "And," he continues, "since humans are fallible and make mistakes, the human will
lose in the long run." But don't humans write the programs? And
wouldn't it take extraordinary nerve for a human to play anyway,
knowing his or her fallibility against a perfect machine?

DO NOT LIMP BEFORE THE LAME

The other type of consistent poker loser also doesn't care much about the game. This is the weak player. He plays a lot of hands, often staying in to showdown, but seldom raises. In poker argot he "limps" into hands. He thinks he is being bluffed more than any other type of player, but in fact is bluffed the least. He differs from the risker in when he shows even slight emotion. The risker is most engaged when she has a lot of money at stake and is about to see another player's hand. The weak player is instead motivated by curiosity. He pays the most attention after he has folded, to see whether he has been bluffed. His readings peak when looking at his own cards; physiologically he shows little interest in the other players' hands except for his obsession with being bluffed.

This pattern has an intriguing correlation to one of Colin's experiments. Cal Tech built him a brain scanner. Unlike conventional ones in hospitals and medical research sites, this one allows scanning of multiple people while they are engaged in normal behavior like playing games. He thinks this could lead to spectacular breakthroughs. He describes watching the scans while people play as like "watching a man walk on the moon." Physiological reactions are very revealing, but they're more like a telescope pointed at the moon. The brain scan is like holding the moon rock in your hand.

Anyway, one early finding is that there is a strong sex difference between men and women when playing games in which trust is an issue, such as wondering whether a poker bettor is bluffing (although Colin has not yet used poker in one of his brain scan studies). Men turn on the calculating part of their brain when making the decision; after the decision they turn off their whole brain. The bet is made, no point in worrying further. Women calculate less, but turn on the social part of their brain and leave it on until well after they find out the result. While it's dangerous to speculate too much on a single observation, this seems to say that men calculate whether to trust, then take whatever consequences ensue. Women make a less considered decision about whether to trust, but reason out the consequences closely. As Colin put it, "This is why I want to watch the football game when we come home from a party; my brain is turned off. My wife wants to discuss who felt what about whom; her brain is still fully engaged." A man is concerned about trust because it affects winning or losing. A woman is willing to risk loss in order to find out whether she can trust. Of course, future observations may lead to revised guesses, and this tells us nothing about whether such differences are genetic or social. But on the surface, this finding corresponds well to an old poker prejudice that most women are too curious to be good poker players. Today some of the top professional players are women; it would be interesting to know whether they learned typical masculine trust patterns or found a way to exploit typical feminine ones successfully. Idle curiosity is fatal in poker, but in a long session it can make sense to test other players early, even at the cost of some negative expectation.

In modern poker strategy terms, the weak player is loose/passive. Loose players play a lot of hands and put a lot of money in the pot; tight players are the opposite. Passive players check and call a lot; aggressive players bet, raise, or fold instead. When passive players do raise, it's with their best hands, and when they fold, it's with their worst. They do not practice deception (although they suspect it in everyone else), and their play is based entirely on their cards, not their cards relative to what the other players probably hold. Everyone agrees that loose/passive is the worst combination. Riskers are also loose/passive, although they raise a lot, because their raises are predictable. In a sense, riskers raise the way weak players call. The point isn't to force other players to make hard choices or to misrepresent their own hands—riskers raise to make the stakes larger. Riskers' raises don't make them more aggressive than weak players; the raises make them looser.

Weak players are weak for the session and play the same against all other players. But unlike riskers, the same player might play tight/passive or loose/aggressive tomorrow and make some money. Conventional wisdom in poker is that losing tends to push players to loose/passive (while winning encourages tight/passive), but Ethel Riddle found no evidence of this, nor of any other systematic strategy changes due to winning or losing. Aggressive players often claim that their tactics push other players to be passive against them, but this was also not supported by the study. The weak players walked in the door weak, played weak against everyone, and stayed that way all session.

FIERCE AS BLUFF KING HAL

All of this is mildly interesting, but it won't help you much at poker. Everyone knows how to play riskers and weak players, and they're easy to spot. Against riskers, you wait for good hands, then let the risker fill the pot for you. Against weak players, you raise when you've got them beat and fold when you don't. Their play is predictable enough that you generally have a pretty good idea which is the case. They always think they're being bluffed, so it never pays to bluff them, and you can raise with a good hand, secure that they will not fold. The only practical value of Ethel Riddle's work so far is to help you determine whether you are a risker or are playing weak at the moment. If you're feeling bored except when you're in the hand, and you feel real excitement only when another player turns over her cards, you could be a risker. If you're tormented about whether you were bluffed last hand, you're probably playing weak. While it's important to pay attention when you're not in the hand, you should forget about the cards you folded. You shouldn't notice if you would have won. Folded cards no longer exist.

Ethel identified three subtypes of aggressive players. Not having the dubious advantage of exposure to game theory, she used the word *bluff* to describe any kind of aggressive play. Her *bet bluffers* were tight/aggressive players. They played only strong hands, but when they did, they raised frequently. They were also willing to fold when they did not improve on the draw or in the face of another player's strong betting. From Ethel's point of view, their card play was normal; they played strong hands and folded when it looked as if they were beaten. But their betting was deceptive; they would check with a strong hand and raise with a relatively weak hand, considering the circumstances.

These players had the weakest physiological reactions of the aggressive players, but stronger than either riskers or weak players. Bet bluffers' reactions would occasionally spike and the players would get intensely involved in the game. When this happened, their emotion was directed at the entire table, not at specific other players. There was no obvious trigger for these episodes—they did not seem to happen more often when the player was winning versus losing, or after a winning versus a losing hand, or when the cards were running hot versus cold. For some reason, these players spent most of the time playing a mechanical tight game, giving little information away with their betting but not varying their hand strengths, then occasionally they would burst into intense play against the entire table. They did very well during these intense periods and lost slightly the rest of the time. There was no obvious superficial sign Ethel could detect between the intense and the normal play, but it stood out on the polygraph like night and day.

Hand value bluffers was Ethel's term for loose/aggressive play. These players bet more straightforwardly than the bet bluffers, but they often didn't have the hand the bet represented. They made game theory bluffs, playing weak hands as if they were very strong. Or they would play very strong hands as if they were marginal. Their emotional responses were the mirror image of bet bluffers—usually quite high, but punctuated with periods of low. Interestingly, they lost money during the high periods and made money during the low. Hand value bluffers appear to play slightly crazily most of the time, then revert to periods of cold calculation to collect on their reputations. If so, it's not an act. When they are raising on worthless hands or slowplaying the nuts, they're excited. When they switch to collection mode, they're as bored as a casino employee emptying the rake boxes.

One obvious implication of this is that you have to watch out for tight/aggressive players when they're excited and loose/aggressive players when they're bored. Don't expect any obvious external clues, at least from good players, but you can tell the difference without a polygraph. Pupil dilation and voice timbre are hard for most people to fake—Malcolm Gladwell's extraordinary book *Blink* will tell you all about this kind of thing. Most people don't try to fake their attitude in between hands or after they've folded, so be alert at these times. Moreover, you'll notice a difference in play, and this is impossible to fake.

When the tight/aggressive player loosens up for a spell, or the loose/aggressive player tightens, be on guard. The point is not to watch for what cards they have, as game theory encourages—you're watching for changes in strategy. These are easier to spot and more likely to give you advantage. When you do see the shift against type, the safest course is not to take them on at all. Fold most of your hands, and stay in against them only with very strong hands, which you can play straightforwardly. Also, this is a good time for you to mix up your own strategy, at least when you're in hands against them. You can win their money when they're back to their normal game. If you're so much better than they are that you can win even when they're at their peaks, you're going to get all their money, anyway.

The last combination is the tight/passive player. Ethel gave these players the curious name of *desire bluffers*—perhaps this was the phrase that meant something to David Spanier. Desire bluffers have an average overall level of excitement, but it spikes up and down according to who is in the pot with them. There are players they want to beat, and players they don't care about. However, most of the time, they don't play any differently as a result. Their emotions do not make them loosen up. The only time it matters is when they have a good hand against a player they want to beat—they will then turn aggressive. Against other players, they are passive with good hands and bad.

While tight/passive players are not dangerous, they can be frustrating. It's hard to win much money from them. They won't play except with a good hand. They cannot be bluffed; once they have a good hand, they will call to showdown. But they also can't be induced to lose large amounts when they have a good hand and you have better; they won't raise unless they have nuts (sometimes not even then). Overall, their play will lose money, like all passive play, but it doesn't lose very much. And sometimes they will tempt a frustrated player into mistakes.

The easiest strategy against tight/passive players is to ignore them.

Let them pay your blinds and rake, while you concentrate on winning from the loose or aggressive players. Take them on only when you have a stronger hand than their average hand, but when you do, raise at every opportunity. That won't happen often—a tight/passive player might play only 10 percent of his hands against raises, and only 5 percent of those times will you have a hand stronger than his average hand. That means 1 in 200 hands, or about once a session on average, you'll have this situation come up. It's actually a little more than that because you'll have some favorable drawing opportunities, especially in multiway pots, but it's still not enough to add much to your expected profit.

NEXT TIME STOP AT THE ETHYL PUMP

However, Ethel's research did reveal a way to attack desire bluffers. It's most effective if there are a lot of them at the table, because it works on all of them at once. That's also when there's the most point to it, because it's hard to win much money any other way. It actually works on all players—just most strongly on desire bluffers. However, in most games it's not a good idea, since it leads to losses, not profits.

The weak players are the least likely to be targets of aggressive play, although they are most apt to think they are the targets. The actual targets are players who

- ♦ Make large bets,
- ♦ Play aggressively,
- ♦ Win, and
- ♦ Have large stacks (this is not the same as winning, because you can buy in for larger or smaller amounts).

The more you do of these things, the more likely you are to turn other players, especially tight/passive players, aggressive against you. Normally, that's a bad idea—aggressive players win and passive players lose. But a lot of tight/passive players can change the situation. They are not good at playing aggressively, and you can exploit the fact that they play aggressively only against you. For example, you don't have to worry about an early position bluff—that player would be trying to bluff the whole table. But if a tight/passive raises after you call, and no one else has called also, that's likely to be a bluff.

The bluffs will not be thought out well. You can often catch inconsistencies. And you can raise to showdown—they're not going to give up on the bluff. Of course, sometimes it will be a strong hand, but you can pick your opportunities and should make money more often than not. Another advantage is that the looser players at the table will also be frustrated by the tight/passive players and may react by being too loose or too aggressive. If you can push them even further from optimal play and direct their aggressiveness against you, you should be able to win from them as well. So buy a large stack, and play aggressively. If it's spread limit, no limit, or pot limit, make large bets. If it's fixed limit, raise a lot. With luck and skill, you'll also win. If you want to really drive people crazy, act like you might quit the game (this works whenever you find yourself the target of aggressive tactics, and you want to ratchet it up). Then prepare for the onslaught of aggressiveness. Don't call me for money if it fails.

Another lesson from this work is to make sure your own aggressiveness is directed at the players it is most likely to work against, rather than at the players you want to beat the most. Generally the last person you want to play aggressively against is the big winner—the aggressive, big-betting, big-stack player. He looks like the most tempting target, but you win against this player by being tight/aggressive. Take him on rarely, but win big when you do. It's the passive, careful, low stackers—the ones who are losing or breaking even—that you can play with aggression every hand, so be loose/aggressive against these players.

These recommendations should only be considered suggestions to be tested against experience, since they were generated in one set of games played 84 years ago, not under typical poker conditions. They're valuable because they systematically recorded information that we normally don't get, but you can't base your whole game on them. I've picked and chosen among the results to find the ones that correspond to my poker judgment, so there's a layer of subjectivity here as well. The really important conclusion is that poker results depend on emotion over the whole table and the whole session, not the mathematics of one hand involving two opponents.

When I learned poker, this understanding was taken for granted. Everyone knew that a session of poker generally resulted in one big winner, a group of smaller winners, and a group of losers. Usually there wasn't much disparity within each group. If there was a big loser, which there sometimes was, it often meant there was only one significant loser. If there was a second big winner, often everyone else either lost or won only trivial amounts. In either case it meant that one of the groups contained only one player, not that there was an even spread of outcomes from big winner to big loser. Most poker strategy was directed to making sure you ended up in the winner group, rather than trying to maximize expected value while minimizing standard deviation, hand by hand. Being the big winner was considered mostly luck; if you had the skill to do it consistently, your success would break up your game. The steady long-term profit was to be in the winner's group almost every session, while rarely being the big winner. These techniques result in a higher percentage of winning sessions than random-walk play developed for tournaments and public card rooms.

They also resulted in different strategies than most modern books recommend. You don't compute pot odds or implied pot odds, nor do you decide in advance of the session which starting hands you would play. You base your play much more on the table situation and results of recent hands than on your cards. That doesn't mean you play garbage or throw away nuts, of course, but it does mean you're not making precise calculations of expected value per hand. When the table situation is right to go in, you go in with any playable hand, or even bluff with nothing. When the table situation is wrong, you go in only with unbeatable cards.

MY WAY IS MULTIWAY

For one specific difference, you like multiway pots. The standard modern advice is to try to force people out with a made hand (a hand that will probably win even if it doesn't improve), but keep them in with a drawing hand (a hand that is likely to win if it improves, but will almost certainly lose if it doesn't). If you follow that, you won't be in many true multiway pots. When you have a made hand, you will force it down to zero or one other bettor. When you have a drawing hand, you may have several other bettors in the pot, but you'll likely beat either all of them or none, depending on the cards that will be dealt. Moreover, if they read the same books, they'll all have drawing hands as well.

Another common piece of advice is that you should never try to bluff more than one player at a time (a great reason to like multiway pots is that a lot of book-smart players are certain not to be bluffing). That's foolish because multiway bluffs are more profitable and more effective. Of course, there's less chance the bluff will be successful, since if any of the players call, you lose. But there will be more money in the pot to win if it's successful. Usually that factor dominates. Moreover, even if the expected values are equal, you prefer winning a lot of money rarely to a little money more often, because you gain something when your bluff is called. Every time your bluff is exposed, you expect to make a little more profit on your next good hand. Most important, the biggest gain to bluffing is when it causes several players to call your best hands. If people know you never bluff more than one player at a time, that advantage is lost.

Two-way hands are the only ones game theory can handle, the only risks that can be calculated mathematically. Modern theory tends to assume that uncalculated risk is losing risk. The trouble is that other players can read books and calculate, too. If they're good, they'll eliminate any advantage from calculated risk. If the other players are weak, by all means stick to calculation. But to win against good players, in my experience, you have to dive into the risks that don't come with maps and compasses. Consistent winning poker comes in multiway pots, by taking uncalculated risks. That doesn't mean you should ignore calculation and play by feel; it means you should calculate what you can, but don't be afraid of everything else.

I don't mean to suggest that I'm right and other writers are wrong. My poker education was predicated on a private game, a single table of players who would play for a period and then stop. Modern theory is dominated by people who perfected their poker in the aforementioned California public card rooms or who made their names in tournaments—like Phil Helmuth, Doyle Brunson, and Erik Seidel. These are different environments. In private games, what you can win is limited by what the others are willing to lose, and in the long run by what they are willing to lose and play again next week (or recommend you to a bigger game). In a commercial establishment, you can win as long as you can keep playing; new players will replace the losers. The limit is instead enforced by other good players who will join your game if the profit per hour gets high enough, and also by the economic needs of the establishment.

In a tournament, losers are also replaced. If you want to have the highest expected money return in the tournament, you go for the consistent-small-winner tactic, but if you want to win the tournament, your best strategy is to go for being the big winner.

DO TRADERS CARE?

Wouldn't it be interesting to see whether these results apply to traders as well? That's what Michael Sung of the MIT media lab would like to do. Things have changed since 1921—Michael has developed a noninvasive, wireless fanny pack that can measure everything Ethel did and more. He doesn't need teams of young women watching the outputs and marking the sheets with pens; he has sophisticated computer algorithms to refine the data in real time. "People forget they're wearing it," he says, "and we can get completely natural readings." He has not yet talked a trader into wearing one. I asked around for him myself. Many traders would be perfectly happy to wear it and let Michael analyze their emotional states. Some were interested by the idea that they might find an edge that way. As a risk manager, my interest is in reducing stress-related problems that often crop up among traders. However, all of them balked at the idea of releasing trade information. You can peer into their hearts and minds, but trading logs are sacred. Still, it's only a matter of time before someone signs up, and we may learn quite a bit about how traders make and lose money.

Michael is an avid poker player and has tested his device at the table. He advertised for subjects willing to play heads-up (only two players), no-limit Texas Hold 'Em while wearing his pack. He played in a number of these games himself when one volunteer didn't show up. He measured heart rate, heat flux, palm sweat, voice timbre, and micromovements. Each of these correlated between 60 percent and 80 percent with hand outcome. For example, people normally make constant tiny movements in their muscles, possibly as a way of staying loose and comfortable. But in stressful situations, they freeze up. The movements stop. The guy showing more stress lost the hand between 60 percent and 80 percent of the time. When Michael combined all five measurements statistically, he could predict better than 80 percent of the outcomes, without knowing any of the cards.

"That's impressive," I told Michael. "If you could get the other players to wear these, you could clean up. I wonder if there's some way to use something like this in a casino." Michael's voice immediately dropped to a conspiratorial whisper. "You'd need to get it smaller, put it in a cell phone. Then you'd need a heads-up display in a pair of glasses, or maybe something audible or tactile." It hit me that Michael had made another technological leap with stunning social implications. The subject didn't have to wear the monitor— Michael can get the information he needs from a remote device. He could put something that looked exactly like a cell phone, or a pack of cigarettes, or a wallet, on the table, and know everyone's mental states. In case you're worried, he has no plans to cheat poker players. But if you work casino security, you might want to check his web site for a picture. (Sorry, Michael, I own stock in casinos.)

My guess is that Michael's casino scheme is just a pleasant fantasy, since he has too much going on to spend time on it. He's founded a company that markets the products he's developed, and he's thinking about branching into finance. He took his device to the psychiatric wards of Massachusetts General Hospital, where it gave staff continuous readouts of patient mental state. He's taken devices to speed-dating parties. Using only a microphone, he analyzed voice volume, in turn taking dynamics and the standard deviation of frequency changes, and correctly predicted over 80 percent of the outcomes.

Imagine a singles-bar watch—perhaps named "Lucky Time"—that could vibrate discreetly to say "you're in" or let off a sharp beep to tell you to "look elsewhere," and give you the excuse to do it at the same time. In search mode it could tell you which couples were not clicking and where you could cut in successfully. As an added feature, it could flash red to tell everyone else, "Take wearer to the psychiatric ward." Some—maybe most—people probably can do this unconsciously without the watch, but there are a lot of socially inept, or at least socially insecure, technophile geeks out there. I'll get mine when it gives poker readings.

LEARNING ABOUT LEARNING

Not all modern research in game theory is experimental. Drew Fundenberg and I share the same major and class year at Harvard. I took some graduate economics courses with Drew, but I couldn't think of any amusing or quirky anecdotes to describe him, as I had for Colin. I asked some friends, and none of them could, either. One said, "Drew's a mathematical economist. They aren't amusing or quirky." Another replied, "There are no amusing or quirky anecdotes about Drew." That's the best picture I can paint: Drew is serious and enormously intelligent; he expresses himself clearly and does brilliant original work. Perhaps he has a wacky side that people who know him better than I do see, but on casual acquaintance the words *calm* and *scholarly* come to mind. He writes about things like "self-confirmed Nash equilibria."

Drew is now an economics professor at Harvard and a leader in theoretical game theory. This has progressed far beyond the four-way payoff diagrams beloved of game theory textbooks. Drew's work tries to explain real-world observations—both the tests done by experimental researchers like Colin and important economic phenomena.

One big objection to classic game theory is that it has no role for learning. If you treat every poker hand as a game in itself, you leave no room for play on one hand to affect future hands. Real poker players bluff on this hand in order to encourage other players to call future strong hands. Game-theoretic poker players have a prespecified probability of bluffing so that other players who know that probability will optimally increase their probability of calling all raises. Real poker is based on learning. You win by learning about the other players—and by teaching them about yourself, then changing. Timing is everything. Done right, other players will fold to your bluffs, then call when you have a strong hand. You set the rhythm and keep the table off balance. Done wrong, with the exact same frequencies of bluffing and getting called, and you will be the big loser. You're trying to dance to other people's rhythm and tripping over your own feet.

Drew, working with UCLA economics professor David Levine, attacked the problem of learning starting from an ancient source, Hammurabi's Code. This is the oldest known written legal system. It codified legal practices in the Near East 4,000 to 5,000 years ago. The second law reads:

> If anyone bring an accusation against a man, the accused must leap into the river. If he sinks in the river his accuser shall take possession of his house. But if the river proves the accused not guilty, and he escape unhurt, then the accuser shall be put to death, while he who leaped into the river shall take possession of the house that had belonged to his accuser.

Here we have a straightforward game. If I accuse you of something, we bet our houses and lives on how well you swim. Actually, the details of the trial are not known. Leaping in from the shore would not be particularly dangerous. My guess is that the leap was from a cliff or a bridge selected for height and river turbulence to be roughly an even shot. In more severe cases, the accused was tied up first, and we know these people seldom survived.

If this seems a relic of impossibly primitive times to you, recall that as late as 200 years ago in England, the accused had the option of trial by combat. That's the same basic bet—life and property between accused and accuser—but it's less fair. Hammurabi's game is random. Trial by combat favored good fighters. Although today's law has no personal combat provision, large disputes are still settled by wars, and small ones by various kinds of personal confrontation; only a tiny minority in between are resolved in a courtroom. Statistical studies of the accuracy of courtroom decisions do not support significant improvement over Hammurabi's probable accuracy rate. The legal system works only because the vast majority of cases are settled before judgment is required. If guilty people didn't almost always plead guilty, and if false accusations were not reasonably rare, the courts could not possibly offer adjudications that were significantly better than random.

Drew and David point out that the code relies on superstition. If subjects believe the river reveals guilt, people will not commit crimes nor will they make false accusations. But if Hammurabi could rely on superstition, why take all this trouble? Why not just write "the guilty will be struck dead by lightning," and be done with it? Alleged criminals in the Near East of 4,000 years ago may seem remote from a poker game today, but bear with me.

The trouble with the "struck dead by lightning" rule is that people will notice it doesn't work. Someone will test it—perhaps the least superstitious or most desperate person, or maybe someone who's bought a countercharm of some sort. Once the rule is shown not to work, it will lose potency. A smarter version is "criminals will burn forever in Hell," which cannot be tested. That's still effective today— arguably, it prevents more crime than fear of legal sanction. But it's not enough for everyone.

Another possibility that seems more rational is for the state to execute criminals. But this creates an incentive for false accusations. Someone steal your girl or buy a bigger chariot or make fun of your temple offering? Just pick one of those other laws at random and accuse the person of breaking it.

The genius of the second law of Hammurabi is that it creates a game no one wants to play. Someone, accuser or accused, always dies. Even if I have no superstition, I know that committing a crime involves a 50 percent chance of dying. That's enough of a sanction to discourage most people.

It might seem as if people also won't make accusations, true or false, because that exposes them to a 50 percent chance of dying as well. If that were true, criminals could plunder at will, knowing there would be no accusations. But it takes only one superstitious person to ruin that pleasant state of affairs. Hammurabi's Code works as long as there are some superstitious people who will make true accusations, secure in divine protection and in anticipation of winning a house. "Struck dead by lightning" and "burn forever in Hell" require everyone to be superstitious, but the river game requires only that some people be superstitious. As long as that is true, the game will be played seldom, and there will be no convincing proof that the outcomes are random.

Drew and David's paper on the subject is much more sophisticated and considers the impact of overlapping generations of people learning the game. "Patient rational Bayesians"—and aren't we all PRBs?—will quickly see through the lightning rule, but under the river rule will become law-abiding citizens who report crimes without making up accusations.

HAMMURABI'S RULES OF POKER

So far, so good, if this were a book on how to get away with murder or win a house in ancient Babylon, but what does Drew's work have to do with poker? The key observation is that when people learn, you have to design your ploys so that they seldom get tested. In classic game theory, you select an optimal bluffing frequency, then bluff completely at random. For example, you could look at your digital watch before every deal and if the seconds read exactly 33, you could bluff. A pocket random-number generator would be even better. Any deviation from pure randomness violates the strictures of simple game theory.

That's fine for heads-up (one-on-one) play, although even there you can do better by timing your bluffs, exploiting the fact that the other guy doesn't actually know your bluffing frequency and can't calculate the optimal response, anyway. But it's different at a table full of players. Some of those players will be the "keep you honest" types, willing to lose money to be sure no one gets away with a bluff. Others will be "better safe than sorry" players who fold at any show of strength unless they hold the nuts.

The first type of player performs a service for the table, at the expense of his own stack, by providing a public measurement of your bluffing frequency. You can run bluffs against the second type of player and play honestly against the first. There's value to that, but by itself it's too predictable to be good poker. You'll force equalization: The first kind of player will start folding when he figures out you never bluff him; the second kind of player will find the courage to call eventually. Moreover, convincing bluffs have to be planned before you know who will be in the pot against you.

Hammurabi's second law works because it involves a second person in the game. It's not just criminal versus lightning, it's criminal versus accuser versus the river. It's structured to prevent people from playing it, which means no one learns to beat it. You need to think in terms of multiple players and structure your bluffs so no one wants to try to outguess you. You want a bluff that works if anyone at the table is afraid to lose, not one that requires everyone at the table to be afraid, just as the river game works as long as anyone is superstitious.

You don't think just about whether your bluff will win or lose, but about whether the person who calls it will be punished or rewarded. He can be punished only if there's a third person in the hand, who doesn't call your bluff, either, because he acts after you've folded or because he had the nuts and didn't care whether you were bluffing. It's not that you want to lose bluffs; it's that you want to make them productive losses when they do occur. That means embracing multiway bluffs that are too complicated to calculate. Let the game theorists and calculated risk takers run for cover, or close their eyes and leap blindly; you have the edge in either case.

Looking at things another way, you will have the strongest hand only one time in N, where N is the number of players. To be a winner, you need either people with weaker hands than you to bet or people with stronger hands than you to fold. In the first case, you win big pots when you win; in the second, you can win more than your share of pots. The trouble is that play to encourage one of those things discourages the other. The game theory strategy is to find an optimum middle ground and hope the other players are fallible (although it doesn't matter much if they are—since if you play in the middle, it doesn't hurt them much to be too loose or too tight).

What this two-player view misses is that what matters is not how often people call or fold, but whether they do it on the same or on different hands. You win only if *all* the stronger hands than yours fold, and you win biggest when weaker hands bet on that same hand. It doesn't help you if all but one of the stronger hands fold and all the weaker hands stay in. The other players care only about their individual results. It's hard to persuade good players to call or fold too much against you, and harder to get them to guess wrong about when to do each consistently. It's much easier to distribute those calls and folds to your liking, so everybody calls on one hand and nobody calls on another.

How you do this depends on the specific poker game and players. But the key is to try to be the primary uncertainty in the hand. That means bluffing a lot, and also throwing away a lot of pretty good hands. If you either have nothing or the nuts, you're apt to get everyone or no one calling. It means entering a lot of hands with unusual cards, so no one can be sure of anything, and so you make the most of good situations that develop. Of course, you play like this only if the other players are too good for simpler tactics to work. If, instead, you always have a pretty good hand, the strongest hands will call and the rest will fold. If you're unpredictable, no one wants to call your possible bluff one on one—there's not enough payoff if it's right. It would be to the advantage of the table to designate one caller, but the other players are each trying to maximize their own advantage. There's no way to capture this in two-person game theory analyses.

I asked Colin and Drew the same, simple question. Both of them study games to understand economics. Does that mean they think people really play games all the time? Or does game theory just provide a good model for predicting decisions and outcomes? Does a person thinking about going to law school, or a business considering a research project, or a home owner putting her house on the market, think of it as a game, with opponents and strategies?

Surprisingly, Colin, the guy who sets up actual games, thinks the answer is no, while Drew, whose interests are more abstract, thinks yes. Colin told me:

> The ultimate scarce resource in cognitive processing is attention. Things are going on right now that we're not paying attention to. Information is flowing all around us, ignored. The trade-off is between attention and memory. A court stenographer can record every word everyone says in court, while reading a novel, but ask her what happened ten seconds ago and you get a blank stare. Attention is the tool you need to get information. People are using unconscious strategies because they don't have the attention to solve everything optimally. We can predict their actions using simple game models because they're not paying attention, not because they are.

Drew, conversely, thinks games are in our genes. Biology has shaped us, and all living things, to strategize and win. The point of game theory is not to make simple predictions about how people actually act, but to understand how to act smarter. Figure out what game is being played, then figure out the optimal strategy.

This seems to contradict simple textbook examples of game theory in which you figure out the equilibrium solution such that everyone knows everyone's strategy and adopts the optimum counter. Drew agrees that's "not the best advice," which is strong criticism from him. It confuses equilibrium analysis, often a weak tool, with game theory. Drew wants to beat the game, not find and play the part that makes it stable if everyone else does the same thing.

Both Drew and Colin agree that playing poker is very helpful. So from the extremes of theory to experiment, liberal arts to rocket scientists, Boston to Los Angeles, experts agree that poker is good for you. Colin thinks it's the best game for training attention; Drew thinks it teaches you to find and exploit strategic advantages. Colin, the brain scientist, thinks it's good for your brain. Drew, the theoretical economist, thinks it's good for your practical economy. I agree with both of them.

CHAPTER 10

Utility Belt

*How Gamblers Think, and How Other
People Think They Think, and Why
We All Think Like Gamblers*

Why do people gamble? No one seems to have thought much about that until about 100 years ago. It seemed obvious that people gambled because it was fun, or because they were trying to make money, or both. A lot of people disapproved: Some thought it was immoral or impious; others that it was dissipated and led to other forms of vice; still others that it created social problems. But most criticism was simpler: Gambling was a waste of time and money—useless, but not bad. However, then as now, most people gambled.

I PONDER THE PSYCHOLOGY THAT ROOTS THEM IN THEIR PLACE

It took psychology to really gang up on gamblers. In 1914, H. Von Hattingberg decided that gamblers eroticize the tension involved in gambling, due, of course, to a fixation in the anal stage of development. Fourteen years later, in "Dostoyevski and Parricide," Freud claimed that gambling is a substitute for masturbation. That's not very flattering, but at least it makes some sense. Gambling gives you the excitement of risk taking, without your actually attempting anything useful like rescuing children from a fire. On that basis, a lot of things are like masturbation. Drinking diet soda, for example, gives you the fizz and taste of soda, without your actually ingesting calories.

Watching baseball on television gives you some of the thrill of the game, without your actually being at the ballpark.

In 1957, Edmund Bergler turned up the heat. Gamblers want to have sex with their mothers, so they wish that their fathers would die, he contended. When their fathers do die, gamblers are consumed with guilt. The only way to alleviate that guilt is to prove that their desires are ineffectual, because that means they weren't responsible for their fathers' deaths. They prove how ineffectual desires are by wishing to win at gambling, then losing. Of course, winning would be unbearable, so gamblers adopt strategies that guarantee failure.

Wait—it gets worse. That was only the male psychologists. In 1963, Charlotte Olmsted proposed that gamblers are impotent. They meet women who want impotent men, because the women are afraid of sex. But the women also hate and therefore humiliate the men who turn to gambling in order to hide their inadequacies (with a wife like that, getting out of the house isn't reason enough?), and their women like it because it gives them something besides their frigidity to blame for their marriage problems. In Charlotte's world, the men want to lose, and their women want them to keep losing. Suddenly a little harmless fun, like eroticization and masturbation, seems something to be proud of.

None of this is actually based on studying more than a few real people. See, most gamblers don't think they have problems. The ones who do think they have problems generally don't think much of these kinds of theories. Once people started doing actual research, it became pretty clear that gamblers as a group enjoy better mental health than nongamblers. They're happier, have more friends, are more involved in their communities, and experience fewer other psychological problems.

Still, there is a subset of gamblers who appear to have severe problems. The modern approach is not to call them compulsive, pathological, or addicted; the syndrome is not similar to any of these. Instead they are "problem gamblers." Most of those problems are for other people.

I don't know anything about psychology, and I've never worked with problem gamblers. But I like to explain behavior by the result it achieves. That's just a bias, but it's common among people in finance. If someone does something with predictable results, it seems reasonable to assume that they like those results.

From this viewpoint, it seems that problem gambling is a ticket out of the middle class. You win; you're rich. You lose; you escape all middle-class ties. You lose your job, your assets, and your family. You really lose them. One thing that's clear from reading accounts of people who work with problem gamblers is how unlikable the gamblers are after the surface charm wears off. After a year or two with the problem gamblers, most doctors quit to work with nice people like drug addicts and paranoid schizophrenics. Wives and mothers forgive alcoholics and murderers far more often than they forgive gamblers. After a few years of being lied to, stolen from, and neglected so some moron can get more excitement throwing his money away with smelly lowlifes than he ever had with you, you don't forgive and forget. Did you ever see a more painless breakup than when Matt Damon rids himself of cheerless millstone Gretchen Mol in the movie *Rounders*? She sees a roll of money, knows he's played poker, packs up her stuff, and leaves—not even a sharp word—then looks at him wistfully for the rest of the movie.

SAFER THAN SUICIDE

I'm not making light of the genuine misery that problem gamblers face. But if the goal is to sever all middle-class ties, gambling is safer than suicide, cheaper than drugs, and surer than alcoholism. It's miserable, but so are the alternatives. Most of the pain is inflicted on friends and family. A couple months after hitting bottom and leaving town, the problem gambler is out somewhere drinking and playing poker with new buddies, while the wife is struggling with being a single mother loaded with overwhelming debts, the mother is left without her retirement assets, and the employer is struggling to avoid bankruptcy after covering embezzlements.

Let me tell you a story that might shed some additional light on this subject. In Andy Bellin's incisive and hilarious *Poker Nation*, he describes making book in his poker club about whether a player just released from prison will first visit his wife, a brothel, or the poker game. I won't give away the surprise ending, but I'll tell you about Slick. I don't like him, but he is friends with some of my friends. We need a word for that; I'll settle for *acquaintance*.

Slick took expensive trips to Las Vegas, Atlantic City, and other gambling venues frequently. People said he paid for them, and turned a profit, counting cards at blackjack. Anyone who had ever counted cards at blackjack would know upon meeting Slick that he wasn't a counter. Plus I never saw him playing blackjack. He was throwing large sums away at craps and roulette. He was far too popular in the casinos to be winning money.

It turned out that Slick was committing a long list of crimes— mostly embezzlement and money laundering. When his house of cards came tumbling down, Slick talked some softie of a federal prosecutor into believing that about 200 felony counts committed over seven years were really one big crime, and it wasn't so bad. He'd helped drug dealers and murderers, but never physically touched cocaine or guns (or no one could prove it, anyway); he'd ruined at least a dozen friends, relatives, and associates who had trusted him, but none were sending impassioned pleas to the judge for harsher treatment. He ended up serving slightly over two years. I think there are people getting lethal injections in Texas every day who are bigger losses to society than Slick would be, but I don't set the sentencing rules.

A friend of mine picked Slick up when he got out of prison. I don't understand her judgment, but I never criticize friends for having too much loyalty (I may need it myself someday). Even a cheerful optimist with a rhinoceros skin like Slick had to be dreading going back to life as a parolee among the people he had lorded it over during the good times, and cheated in the bargain. Did he first visit his wife? No, he had my friend drive him to a casino (crossing a state line and entering a gambling establishment, both parole violations).

Did the casino manager say, "Slick, you're a crook and all that money you lost was stolen from good people," or "Slick, you're broke and have zero prospects, get out," or even "Who are you?" No, he said, "Welcome back, Slick, we have a party for you, and your credit is good." See, Slick wasn't just blowing his stolen money all those years; he was depositing it in the casino bank. He got high-roller treatment and lots of credit, although he was broke and legally prohibited from gambling.

Why would the casino advance the credit? One reason is that Slick was a gambler. Gamblers never give up gambling. Although they lose in the end, along the way they win. As long as the casino is there to collect when Slick did win, its money was safe. Also, Slick had always brought along acquaintances and encouraged them to bet big and stupidly. Now Slick was an extreme case, and might have been a bad risk (although I have heard that he has money again—I don't know how, but would bet not honestly—and is losing at the casinos). However, going to prison actually helped him. The other high rollers were watching; some of them had long odds against avoiding prison forever. If the casino cut people off after a prison stay, some of those high rollers might look for another place to deposit funds.

The beauty of the casino bank is that no one can seize your assets. Several tough investigators had tried to collect every penny Slick hid away, but there was no way to touch his casino deposit. A more common case than Slick's is a guy who loses every penny he can earn, beg, borrow, or steal in casinos for a few years; then he gets fired and divorced. Any cash or savings account or retirement fund would have been forfeited. But by now he's a good customer who will be given credit and comps at casinos. If he's a poker player, he can get staked as a shill or house player. It's not a great life, but it's not the middle class, either.

FIVE OUT OF TEN TO PASS

The American Psychiatric Association has 10 criteria for problem gambling; if you meet five or more, the APA says you're sick. Three of them just say that you like gambling a lot. They are preoccupation, withdrawal, and chasing. You think about gambling a lot, you get unhappy when you can't gamble, and if you lose you come back tomorrow instead of quitting forever. Two of them say that you've done other bad things that you blame on your gambling: illegal acts (embezzlement or fraud, for example, but not just violating gambling laws) and bailout (getting someone else to pay your gambling debts). Two more mean that someone else doesn't like your gambling: lying and risked significant relationship. If your girlfriend says she'll leave you if you gamble, and you lie and say you'll stop, and don't, then you've got two points. The last three are in your head: tolerance, escape, and loss of control. Tolerance means you need to keep increasing the stakes, escape means you gamble to avoid other problems or bad moods, and loss of control means you've tried to stop and you can't.

Let's start by assuming you like to gamble, so you've got three points. You are a certifiable problem gambler if either (a) you do other bad things and blame gambling for them, (b) someone else really doesn't like your gambling, or (c) you don't like your gambling. That's a pretty good definition of a problem: You enjoy doing something and it either causes you to do bad things, or someone else doesn't like it, or you don't like it. But it doesn't sound much like a mental disease.

A lot of problem gambling comes down to the implicit assumption that gambling is bad in the first place, so any difficulties it causes are evidence of a weak or troubled mind. If something is important, we admire someone who surmounts problems to achieve it, even if it means hurting people's feelings and breaking the law. Think about eating, for example. You probably think about it—that's preoccupation. You get hungry if you don't eat (withdrawal) and eat more at dinner if you skip lunch (chasing). You may not have committed a crime to eat, but you would if you had to. If you've ever let someone pay a restaurant check or serve you a meal, that's bailout. Ever lied about eating ("No, Mom, I didn't take that cookie")? Or broken up with someone over a food disagreement ("SWF wants nonsmoking vegetarian")? You develop tolerance for spicy food, a lot of people eat to escape and eat more than they want to every Thanksgiving (they even have a holiday to celebrate their disease!). I think most people could get at least a 7 on this test for "problem eating," and 10 is not hard to achieve.

APLOMB IN THE MIDST OF IRRATIONAL THINGS

Although gambling is ancient, and criticism of it almost as old, the idea that it is irrational dates only to 1738, when Daniel Bernoulli tackled the issue. To see how he worked himself into this novel and absurd conclusion, we have to go back to 1654 and pick up the story of Antoine Gombaud.

Antoine Gombaud appears in every statistics book, but under the name Chevalier de Méré. Depending on the author, he is described as a nobleman, a self-styled nobleman, a gambler, or a con man. He was none of the above. He was the first and most important Salon theorist, whose ideas were important in Europe until the French Revolution. He believed the key social institution was the salon, filled with witty, fashionable, intelligent thinkers. As it happened, the world preferred democratic institutions run by dour middle-class Protestants to aristocratic institutions run by brilliant upper-class Catholics, but there's a lot of closet Gombaudists around. Anyway, Gombaud was not a nobleman and didn't claim to be, he just used Chevalier (Knight) de Méré as the character in his dialogues that represented his own thoughts. This was a common literary device of the time. He was not a particularly avid gambler; he was just interested in the mathematics of the games.

Antoine asked his friend Blaise Pascal to tackle an old problem in gambling, called the problem of the points. Blaise wrote to his friend Pierre de Fermat. Getting two of the greatest mathematicians in history to solve his dice problem is a pretty good illustration of the strength of Salon methods. The two solved the problem in totally different ways. Pascal applied his famous triangle (which he did not invent), and the science of probability was born.

One immediate consequence was the idea of expected value. To find the expected value of a gamble, you take all possible outcomes, multiply the probability times the outcome, and add them up. For example, if you bet \$38 on the number 7 (or any other number) in American roulette, you have 1/38 chance of winning \$1,330 and 37/38 chance of losing \$38. Your expected value is $\$1{,}330 \times (1/38) - \$38 \times (37/38) =$

$35 − $37 = −$2. If, instead, you bet on red or black, you have 18/38 chance of winning $38 and 20/38 chance of losing $38, so your expected value is $38 × (18/38) − $38 × (20/38) = $18 − $20 = −$2. So although these two bets are quite different, they have the same expected value.

Philosophers of the day immediately jumped on the idea that all gambles should be evaluated by expected value. For 84 years until Daniel Bernoulli, experts insisted it was irrational to turn down any gamble with positive expected value, just as smugly as experts today insist that it's irrational to accept risky gambles with zero or negative expected value. But a few people questioned whether it really made sense to flip a coin to double your wealth or become impoverished. Daniel finally convinced people that more theory was needed by solving a problem posed by his cousin Nicholas 25 years earlier (another Swiss mathematician, Gabriel Cramer, had offered the same solution a decade before Bernoulli, but contented himself with the mathematics without calling anyone irrational).

The St. Petersburg gamble (named because Daniel's paper was published by the St. Petersburg Academy, not because it concerns Russians particularly) begins with a pot of $2. A coin is flipped; if it comes up heads you win the pot, and if it comes up tails the pot is doubled. This continues until the coin comes up heads. How much would you pay to play this game?

The expected value is easy to compute. There is a 0.5 probability that the first flip will be heads, in which case you collect $2. $0.5 × $2 = 1. There is 0.25 probability that the first flip will be tails, doubling the pot to $4, and the second flip will be heads, in which case you get $4. $0.25 × $4 = 1. If you keep computing the expected values for the third, fourth, and subsequent flips, you will find they all equal $1. Since there is an infinite number of possible flips, the expected value of this gamble is infinity. So you should (according to standard theory between 1654 and 1738) pay any amount of money to play this game. Moreover, it doesn't matter if we start the pot with a penny instead of $2, or 0.000001¢ or 100^{-100}, or if we say you need a million or 100^{100} tails before we start the doubling. Not only would you still pay any amount of money for the gamble, you would say you don't care about the changes. In fact, most people would pay $5 for the original gamble (and nothing at all for the variations), which corresponds to the expected payout if you think the other player won't actually give you more than $32.

Daniel resolved this paradox with an advance called *utility theory.* It said that you had to apply a function to outcomes before computing the expected value. For example, a person's happiness might depend on the square root of wealth rather than on wealth directly. That means $16 is twice as good as $4, not four times as good, because the square root of $16 (4) is only twice the square root of $4 (2). If I offer to flip you a coin—heads you get $16, tails you get $0—the expected value of the gamble is $16 \times (1/2) + \$0 \times (1/2) = \$8$. But the utility of the gamble is $4 \times (1/2) + 0 \times (1/2) = 2$, which is the same utility as having $4 for sure. The expected-value gambler will pay $8 for a coin flip that might win $16—in modern language we call her *risk neutral.* She doesn't care about risk; she evaluates gambles by their expected value. The square-root utility gambler will risk only $4 for the same coin flip—we say he is *risk averse.* He requires increased expected value in order to assume risk.

How does this resolve the St. Petersburg paradox? For a person with square-root utility, the expected utility of the gamble is not infinite, it is 2.41, which is equivalent to getting $5.83 for sure (because 2.41 is the square root of 5.83). This corresponds reasonably well to intuition. Actually, you can modify the paradox to defeat square-root utility as well, but there are other functions that work better. John von Neumann and Oskar Morgenstern came up with a much more rigorous and complete version of utility theory in 1947, in the same book that introduced game theory.

LET'S MAKE A DEAL

This is a fine theory, but it seems to have no relation to how people actually make decisions about gambles and everything else. One simple example is Allais's paradox. Suppose you're at the final table of a poker tournament with two other entrants left. There is a $2.5 million first prize, $500,000 second prize, but no third prize. You have the middle stack, the woman on your right has 10 times your stack, and the guy on your left is down to a chip and a chair. You think there is a 10 percent chance you will win, an 89 percent chance you will take second, and a 1 percent chance you will take third. The other players offer a split. You get $500,000. The chip leader gets $2.5 million and will compensate the short stack out of that. Do you take the split?

No split	Probability	1%	89%	10%
	Outcome	$0	$500,000	$2.5 million
Split	Probability	100%		
	Outcome	$500,000		

Almost everyone says yes to this split. But now consider this situation. Same tournament and prizes, but you now have a short stack. You figure you have no chance at all to win, an 11 percent chance of picking up the $500,000, and an 89 percent chance of getting nothing. The chip leader offers to settle for second place, taking $500,000 and her chips off the table. The middle stack agrees eagerly. The only downside to you is that you think you have slightly less chance to beat the middle stack without the possibility of the chip leader taking care of him for you. With this deal, you figure to have a 90 percent chance of ending up with nothing and a 10 percent chance of winning $2.5 million. Again, everyone jumps at this split.

No split	Probability	89%	11%
	Outcome	$0	$500,000
Split	Probability	90%	10%
	Outcome	$0	$2.5 million

We've just violated the axioms of utility theory. In the first choice, we eagerly gave up a 10 percent chance to win $2.5 million to avoid a 1 percent chance of getting nothing. In the second choice, we were just as eager to get a 10 percent chance to win $2.5 million by also accepting an additional 1 percent chance of getting nothing.

The most thoughtful analysis of this paradox is in one of the great books of all time, Leonard Savage's *The Foundation of Statistics*. He makes a pretty good case that although everyone makes these choices, everyone is wrong, and utility theory is right. Recast the decision as a lottery with 100 tickets and the following payouts:

		Ticket 1 to 89	Tickets 90 to 99	Ticket 100
Situation 1	No split	$500,000	$2.5 million	$0
	Split	$500,000	$500,000	$500,000
Situation 2	No split	$0	$500,000	$500,000
	Split	$0	$2.5 million	$0

Note that this is the same as the preceding deals. In the first case, if we don't split we have an 89 percent chance to get $500,000, a 10 percent chance to get $2.5 million, and a 1 percent chance to get $0. If we split we get $500,000 in all cases. In the second situation, without a deal we get nothing 89 percent of the time and $500,000 the other 11 percent. If we split, we get nothing 90 percent of the time and $2.5 million the other 10 percent.

Savage pointed out that the decision makes no difference for tickets 1 to 89, so we should not bother considering these. For the remaining tickets, the two situations are identical, so we should make the same choice in both situations.

A curious fact about this paradox is that we are richer in situation 1. It is usually assumed that rich people have greater risk tolerance. But in Allais's paradox, the richer person turns down the gamble with the big positive expectation, while the poorer person always takes it.

So we're left with two lessons. First, people don't behave according to utility theory. Second, sometimes the theory is right. Thinking about utility theory can improve your decision making. In fact, I believe in von Neumann–Morgenstern utility theory. It's simple and elegant and gives useful predictions. When it seems to be wrong, it's usually not.

There's nothing in the theory that says gambling is irrational. That conclusion comes from restrictions people put on the theory, to make it easier to handle mathematically. A lot of people took models developed under Bernoulli's utility theory and transferred them to von Neumann–Morgenstern utility, without making use of any of the additional power and subtlety.

The key problem is that people have to make utility "time separable" to get equations that are easy to solve. Fischer Black highlighted the problem with this in his *Exploring General Equilibrium*. Suppose I ask you whether you would rather have $10,000 now and $100,000 in a year, or $20,000 both times. Suppose, instead, I ask if you'd rather have a coin flip—heads you get $10,000 and tails you get $100,000, or $20,000 for sure. These are entirely different questions, but time separability forces you to assume that people always give the same answer to both. Looking at things another way, the simplified theory assumes that having a 50 percent chance of something is the same as having it for half as long. For some things and some people that can be a reasonable approximation, but it is often wildly incorrect.

MORE PATIENT THAN CRAGS, TIDES, AND STARS; INNUMERABLE, PATIENT AS THE DARKNESS OF NIGHT

There has been quite a bit of research about people who spend a significant fraction of their income buying lottery tickets. There are three main groups. The first is very poor and buys tickets erratically. When these people get some extra money, they buy tickets in games with relatively low payouts, such as instant-win games. When asked why, they point to the lack of alternatives. No financial institution wants the odd $5 or $10 these people come across. They often live in neighborhoods or social situations where spare cash is likely to be stolen or borrowed and not repaid. A $500 lottery win is enough money to possibly protect and take advantage of in some way. Before state lotteries, these people would play either bingo or illegal numbers.

The next group is made up of older working members of the lower middle class, who report feeling trapped and frustrated. These people typically spend regular amounts—say, $10 per day—on the highest-payout games they can find. Any intermediate prizes are used to buy more tickets. While the odds of winning a million dollars or more are very low, if you do this consistently for a long period of time, the odds are not astronomical. You must have far more patience than most economists—in Carl Sandburg's words, you must be "more patient than crags, tides, and stars; innumerable, patient as the darkness of night." You must even have more patience than the life insurance beneficiary waiting for a changed life, freed from social, marital, and financial burdens; at least she knows she will probably collect on her ticket. These people emphasize that they feel they have no other hope of achieving basic middle-class goals like sending children to college or enjoying a financially secure retirement. They feel that lesser amounts saved for these goals will be eroded away or taken.

The final group is younger people who have suffered significant financial reverses due to job loss, illness, divorce, or lawsuit. These people are often deeply in debt. They play regularly and look for intermediate payouts. They are hoping to win $25,000 or $50,000 to regain their former status. If they fail, it appears they will sink down into bankruptcy.

All three of these cases make perfect sense to me. The people may not be correct in their perceptions, but they are not irrational. The lottery gives hope, which is valuable in itself, and appears to be more than competitive with the financial services they are offered. A kinder world would help people pull themselves out of poverty, attain basic middle-class goals, and regain their former positions in life after bad luck. Instead, we live in a world that criticizes the lottery players, while taking over half their ticket money for the state government and 28 percent of any winnings on top of that for the federal government (plus additional state and local taxes).

How about the casino gambler? The lottery player may have only one chance in a million of winning, but she wins big if she wins. After 5,000 spins of the roulette wheel, the chance of being ahead even by $1 is much less than one in a million million. To understand the casino gambler, you have to recall that a casino in a competitive market will repay about 75 percent of the gambler's losses. Small-time slots players take this in the form of casino overhead and coupons; some high rollers take it in luxury comps; others take it in credit (there's a casino management saying that you have to win the money twice, once at the table, then again by collecting the debt). I know economists who think the 33 percent markup on the entertainment ($100 of losses buys $75 of comps or other services) is irrational, which they'll tell you while spending $5 in a bar to buy a bottle of beer that costs $1 in the supermarket and $0.05 to make. For some reason, the house edge in a casino, 75 percent of which is returned to the player, makes gambling irrational—while every other business with a markup is just normal economics.

For the small-time players, the casino seems to serve for entertainment and social gathering. For the high rollers who like lavish entertainment, a casino weekend is a splurge. They could get the same rooms, food, drink, and entertainment cheaper, but the casino also offers the entertainment of the gambling and better service than most resorts. Plus it's more fun to live it up when the cost is indirect. Many people could not enjoy a $200 dinner, $500 show ticket, $1,000 bottle of wine, or $3,000 hotel room, because they would think about the cost and kill the pleasure. But the same things offered as comps in reward for losses suffered months before give enjoyment without regret, and the open-handed friendliness of the casino staff contrasts with the intimidating snobby rudeness affected by some sellers of luxury goods.

For the credit high rollers, the casino offers a form of investment. They'll lose over their lifetimes, but whatever bad luck comes their way, they might be able to find a welcoming casino offering them credit, as Slick did. Casino losses are by no means a secure investment, but for some people they're more secure than a bank account or a safe deposit box.

In all these cases, I think people turn to gambling because other businesses, particularly financial services businesses, have failed to meet their needs. I don't think they have compulsions to gamble; I think they find gambling a rational choice in their circumstances. I don't say it's always, or even often, a wise choice. But there are straightforward reasons for it—it's not a form of mental illness.

This book is not about that type of gambling—trying to squeeze a small amount of hope out of a basically hopeless situation or gambling for entertainment. I'm interested in solid economic reasons for taking risk—the reasons people play poker as opposed to the reasons people buy lottery tickets or play casino games.

Why would someone take risk without getting compensated by increased expected value? One such occasion is when that risk operates in the opposite direction of your larger risks. If your country's government is unstable, for example, holding gold coins could be a good idea. The price of gold goes up and down, but if the country collapses into anarchy you may find that all your other assets are worthless, at which time the gold coins will skyrocket in value.

Another reason familiar to sports fans is that you take risk when you're behind. The team that's ahead in a football game is content to call low-risk running plays, but the team that's behind will fling long passes down the field. In business, well-run companies act as if they are always behind. There's somebody out there—maybe a competitor, maybe two gals in a garage, maybe a shop with one-tenth your costs in another country, or maybe someone you cannot imagine who has an edge on you. Low-risk business strategies fail routinely.

Risk also attracts, motivates, and creates opportunities for the best people. Suppose you just landed in a strange country where you did not know the language or have maps. You do have 550 men, but they're not really under your command. You sort of hijacked the expedition, and the guy who organized it has sent an army of 1,400 men after you. Meanwhile, you're facing one of the greatest empires on earth, with 240,000 fighting men. You'd like to conquer them.

In this situation, of course, you keep maximum strategic flexibility and look for ways to reduce your risk. Unless your name is Hernando Cortés. In that case, you burn your boats. Why? Because things seemed too easy with all your resources? Because you were cold? No, because it eliminates dissension and focuses everyone on the main goal. No doubt hundreds of conquistador wannabes ordered boats burned and were laughed at or killed by their men. Others probably were pushed back to the beach and regretted bitterly the loss of the option to retreat. But the assumption of extra risk worked for Cortés, and in less dramatic ways for many others.

Another person who loves risk is an option owner. The value of an option increases with the volatility of the underlying security. Modern finance teaches that most of the valuable assets of a business are options. Not the paper securities that trade on exchanges and over the counter, but real options. When a business tries a new idea, most of the value comes from the option to expand if it is successful. The riskier the idea, for the same expected value of first-order success, the more valuable the option to expand.

For example, suppose a movie studio is faced with two proposed movies; each will cost $100 million to make. The first one is a standard genre picture that will make between $100 and $140 million, with an expected value of $120 million. The other is an offbeat new idea that could make between $0 and $240 million, with the same $120 million expected value. Both have the same 20 percent expected return, but the standard movie has less risk. However, the new idea has lots of follow-on benefits. It will appeal to people who don't go to other movies, who may form a valuable new core audience. It will attract energetic and talented people to the studio. It can generate new good ideas and valuable information about how to manage them. All of those happen even if the movie fails financially. If it succeeds, it could create a new genre and other opportunities. A related concept is the option to abandon. Let's say that 20 percent of the way through the filming you will learn how much the movie will make. That's useless with the standard picture—it always makes at least its cost, so you wouldn't abandon it regardless of the information you got. But with the new idea, you can increase your expected return from 20 percent to 32.5 percent by abandoning failures early.

When people are faced with a lot of options, as in the nineteenth-century United States, taking risk just makes sense. If there is literal gold in them thar hills, or figurative gold in new technology, the more risk, the better. If you win, great. If you lose, you pick up the next option. That's gambling, and it's not a problem.

Annotated Bibliography

HISTORY AND MEANING OF POKER

The earliest published references to poker date to 1829 (the published diary of English actor Joseph Cowell), 1837 (*Dragoon Campaigns to the Rocky Mountains* by James Hildreth), and 1842 (*Gambling Unmasked* by Jonathan Green). Standards of nonfiction reliability were quite different than they are today. Few people were literate enough to write a book, so publishers relied on professional hacks to supply popular literature. These people mostly lived in cities near publishers and were unlikely to have any firsthand experience with poker.

Green is the least reliable of the three—he clearly had no idea how poker was played and his accounts of life on the Mississippi are so unconvincing that I don't think he ever left Philadelphia. Hildreth didn't write the book attributed to him; he left the regiment long before the events described and may well have been illiterate. Several candidates have been put forward, all of whom imply that the author would not have been present at the poker scenes described. In any event, the game in question is so sketchily described, it could have been anything. Read Hildreth's book for geography and military tactics, not for poker.

Cowell is the only one of the three who is a real person and who was definitely present at the events he describes. However, the stories he tells are standard gambling anecdotes, clumsily re-created for a Mississippi riverboat setting. He probably did see poker played, unlike Green and Hildreth, but he probably didn't describe it.

What is interesting about all three accounts is what they don't say. All three authors are writing about strange and barbarous places (from the standpoint of their probable readers) and often introduce new words with comments about pronunciation. All of them use the word *poker* as if it would be familiar to their readers, and none suggest that it had a foreign or unusual pronunciation. That seems to contradict silly accounts of the origin of the name as being French or Persian words. None confuse it with other, similar games. All mention that the game was played throughout a large region. All assume their readers know general principles such as that players put money into a pot that one player wins, that players can fold and thereby lose any interest in the pot, and that hands with aces beat hands with kings. So even by the 1830s, poker was a well-known regional game, and people on the East Coast of the United States and in Europe knew the type of game but not the specific rules. It has its own identity; it was not considered a variant of poque or bragg.

All of this places the origin of poker much earlier than most histories state, given the slow spread of games without written rules. Not only was it established throughout the American Southwest, but it was known (if not played) more broadly by 1830. There was no hint of any ancestral relationship to any other game, meaning either that it had separated long ago and completely from its roots or that it was a new invention (of course, it borrowed from other card games, but that's not the same as being descended from them). This is typical of the way card games evolve—not through gradual rule changes.

There are much better sources about the development of poker. I start with the wonderful stories collected in G. Frank Lydston's 1906 *Poker Jim*. Lydston was a new medical school graduate who joined the California gold rush and chronicled the life of miners, with an emphasis on poker, from the 1850s to the 1890s. This is real life, real poker. The other good source for this period is *Hutchings' California Magazine*. *The Complete Poker Player* by John Blackbridge (1880) gives a lot of color about the East Coast version of the game at that time, as well as theoretical thinking. Among modern books, *Seeking Pleasure in the Old West* by David Dary (University Press of Kansas, 1995) has a lot of useful and entertaining information.

Foster on Poker by R.F. Foster (1904) is similarly useful. Its other virtue is that it draws on both an extensive library of poker texts and the results of efforts to find old poker players and learn about the early days of the game. A more recent book, *The Oxford Guide to Card Games* by David Parlett (Oxford University Press, 1990) is the most professional history of poker available—and a wonderful book to read.

Seattle newspaperman Kenneth Gilbert picks up where *Poker Jim* left off. I read his stories as a kid in reprinted newspaper columns; they were collected as *Alaskan Poker Stories* in 1958. He covers poker in the Alaska gold rush from 1898 to 1916.

Herbert Yardley is a crucial transitional figure. He learned poker around 1900 from an authentic Old West gambler, but went on to a career in cryptography and international espionage. So he links the roots of poker to modern mathematics and political thinking. His 1956 work, *The Education of a Poker Player* (reprinted by Orloff Press in 1998), is a classic.

Allen Dowling handled public relations for Louisiana political boss Huey Long in the 1930s. As a newspaperman and publicist in New Orleans from the 1920s to the 1960s, he provides invaluable accounts of that time and place in *Confessions of a Poker Player* (1940), *Under the Round Table* (1960), and *The Great American Pastime* (A.S. Barnes, 1970). The first two were written under the pseudonym Jack King, and are now out of print. A different view of the period is presented in Alfred Lewis's great biography, *Man of the World: Herbert Bayard Swopes: A Charmed Life of Pulitzer Prizes, Poker and Politics* (Bobbs-Merrill, 1978). *The Complete Card Player* by Albert Ostrow (McGraw-Hill, 1945) and *Common Sense in Poker* by Irwin Steig (Galahad, 1963) cover poker from the 1930s to the 1950s.

A couple of wonderfully literate English authors next picked up the poker nonfiction mantle. Anthony Alvarez's *The Biggest Game in Town* (1982; new paperback edition from Chronicle, 2002) and David Spanier's *Total Poker* (High Stakes, 1977) and *Easy Money* (Trafalgar,

1987) should not be missed. Anthony Holden wrote *Big Deal* in 1990. More recently, *Poker Nation* by Andy Bellin (HarperCollins, 2002) and *Positively Fifth Street* by James McManus (Farrar, Straus and Giroux, 2003) are the most recent proud additions to the line of great poker nonfiction.

John Stravinsky has collected lots of great excerpts in *Read 'Em and Weep* (HarperCollins, 2004). Another fun collection is *Aces and Kings* by Michael Kaplan and Brad Reagan (Wenner Books, 2005).

HISTORY AND MEANING OF GAMBLING

We have to start with Gerolamo Cardano's 1520 classic, *The Book on Games of Chance* (translated by Sydney Gould, Princeton University Press, 1953), followed 154 years later by *The Compleat Gamester* by Charles Cotton (1674) and then *Lives of the Gamesters* by Theophilus Lucas (1714). All of these describe early modern gambling in theory and practice.

Getting a little closer to the present, there are important surveys: *The Gambling World,* by Rouge et Noir (1898); *Suckers Progress: An Informal History of Gambling in America from the Colonies to Canfield,* by Herbert Asbury (Dodd, Mead, 1938); and *Play the Devil: A History of Gambling in the United States from 1492–1955* by Henry Chafetz (Bonanza Books, 1961). Oscar Lewis's 1953 book *Sagebrush Casinos* (Doubleday) is essential for information about early Nevada (Reno more than Las Vegas).

On the meaning of gambling and attitudes toward it, *Something for Nothing* by Clyde Davis (Lippincott, 1956) is an excellent early work. Charlotte Olmsted's 1962 book *Heads I Win, Tails You Lose* (Macmillan) appears unfavorably in my book, but it has lots of great parts.

The explosion of gambling in America from 1970 to 2000 has stimulated work. *Gambling and Speculation* by Reuven Brenner and Gabrielle Brenner (Cambridge University Press, 1990), the best-selling *Against the Gods* by Peter Bernstein (Wiley, 1996), *Gambling in America* by William Thompson (ABC-CLIO, 2001), *Wheels of Fortune* by Charles Geisst (Wiley, 2002) and *Something for Nothing* by Jackson Lears (Viking, 2003) are redefining the way people think about gambling.

FINANCE AND GAMBLING

There is some literature combining finance and gambling, beginning with Dickson Watts's 1878 work *Speculation as a Fine Art* (available in reprint from Fraser Publishing, 1965). John McDonald did a lot to popularize game theory with *Strategy in Poker, Business and War* (Norton, 1950). Ed Thorp and Sheen Kassouf (who died on August 10, as this book was going to press) wrote *Beat the Market* (Random House) in 1967. Ed's 1962 *Beat the Dealer* (Vintage) fits squarely into this intellectual tradition. An interesting recent entry is *The Poker MBA* by Greg Dinkin and Jeffrey Gitomer (Crown, 2002). I'd also put Marty O'Connell's wonderful *The Business of Options* (Wiley, 2001) and the masterpiece *Paul Wilmott on Quantitative Finance* (Wiley, 2000) in this category, but do not think on that account that they are less than superlative financial texts.

For pure poker, you cannot miss books by Mason Malmuth and David Sklansky. I list only one from each, *Gambling Theory and Other Topics* by Mason Malmuth (Two Plus Two, 2004) and *The Theory of Poker* by David Sklansky (third edition, Two Plus Two, 1994), but both authors are prolific. *Poker for Dummies* by Richard D. Harroch and Lou Krieger (For Dummies, 2000) covers the basics for absolute beginners and has good intermediate material as well.

Some important pure finance works for understanding the ideas in this book are *Money and Trade Considered* by John Law (1705), *The Economic Function of Futures Markets* by Jeffrey Williams (Cambridge University Press, 1986), *Futures Trading* by Robert Fink and Robert Feduniak (New York Institute of Finance, 1988), *Exploring General Equilibrium* by Fischer Black (MIT, 1995), *Dynamic Hedging* by Nassim Taleb (Wiley, 1996), *Iceberg Risk* by Kent Osband (Texere, 2002), and *Trading and Exchanges* by Larry Harris (Oxford University Press, 2003).

My Life as a Quant (Wiley, 2004) is the autobiography of Emanuel Derman, physicist and financial quant. It's a tremendous book that gets inside the quant part of Wall Street. William Falloon's biography of supertrader Charles DiFrancesca, *Charlie D.* (Wiley, 1997), *Fortune's Formula* by William Poundstone (Hill & Wang, 2005), Timothy Middleton's biography of superinvestor Bill Gross, *Bond King* (Wiley, 2004), and Perry Mehrling's biography of superthinker Fischer Black, *Fischer Black and the Revolutionary Idea of Finance* (Wiley, 2005) also offer important behind-the-scenes views of these principles in action.

Three wonderful books that are hard to categorize but deal with many of the ideas in this book in different ways are Nassim Taleb's *Fooled by Randomness* (Norton, 2001), James Surowiecki's *The Wisdom of Crowds* (Doubleday, 2004), and Malcolm Gladwell's *Blink* (Little, Brown, 2005).

There are some excellent books on the history of futures trading including *A Deal in Wheat* by Frank Norris (1903), *The Plunger: A Tale of the Wheat Pit* by Edward Dies (1929—both of these are fiction, but reliable nonetheless), *The Chicago Board of Trade* by Jonathan Lurie (University of Illinois, 1979), *Brokers, Bagmen and Moles* by David Greising and Laurie Morse (Wiley, 1991), *The Merc,* by Bob Tamarkin (HarperCollins, 1993), *Pride in the Past, Faith in the Future: A History of the Michigan Livestock Exchange* by Carl Kramer (Michigan Livestock Exchange, 1997), and *Market Maker: A Sesquicentennial Look at the Chicago Board of Trade* edited by Patrick Catania (Chicago Board of Trade, 1998). I'm going to toss in a great book on Chicago, *City of the Century* by Donald Miller (Simon & Schuster, 1996), because it covers much of the same material, and other aspects as well.

SPECIFIC SOURCES

Leonard Savage's *The Foundation of Statistics* (Wiley, 1950) is the best account of both utility theory and the philosophy behind probability. *Savage Money* by Chris Gregory (Harwood, 1997) will change the way you think about change. Daniel Usner's 1992 classic, *Indians, Settlers and Slaves in a Frontier Exchange Economy: The Lower*

Mississippi Valley Before 1783 (University of North Carolina), is a fascinating, pathbreaking look at a fascinating, pathbreaking period.

Janet Gleeson's *Millionaire* (Simon & Schuster, 1999) is an entertaining popular biography of John Law.

Two useful books about the economics of poker are *Games, Sport and Power* edited by Gregory Stone (Transaction, 1972) and *Poker Faces* by David Hayano (University of California, 1982).

Two of the best books on social networks are Harrison White's *Markets from Networks* (Princeton University, 2002) and his student Duncan Watt's *Six Degrees* (Norton, 2003).

Index